THE ECONOMICS
OF NEIGHBORHOOD

STUDIES IN URBAN ECONOMICS

Under the Editorship of

Edwin S. Mills
Princeton University

THE ECONOMICS
OF NEIGHBORHOOD

Edited by

DAVID SEGAL

Department of City and Regional Planning
Harvard University
and
Department of Economics
Oberlin College

ACADEMIC PRESS   New York   San Francisco   London   1979
A Subsidiary of Harcourt Brace Jovanovich, Publishers

ACADEMIC PRESS, INC.
111 Fifth Avenue, New York, New York 10003

United Kingdom Edition published by
ACADEMIC PRESS, INC. (LONDON) LTD.
24/28 Oval Road, London NW1   7DX

Library of Congress Cataloging in Publication Data

Main entry under title:

The Economics of neighborhood.

    Includes bibliographies.
    1. Urban economics--Addresses, essays, lectures.
2. Neighborhood--Mathematical models--Addresses,
essays, lectures. 3. Neighborhood--Economic aspects--
United States--Addresses, essays, lectures. 4. Land
use, Urban--United States--Addresses, essays, lectures.
5. Residential mobility--United States--Addresses,
essays, lectures. I. Segal, David.
HT123.E3   330.9'173'2   78-22534
ISBN 0-12-636250-5

PRINTED IN THE UNITED STATES OF AMERICA

79 80 81 82   9 8 7 6 5 4 3 2 1

Contents

11   A Computational Approach to the Study of Neighborhood Effects in General Equilibrium Urban Land Use Models
DONALD K. RICHTER

12   Local Public Goods and the Market for Neighborhoods
BRYAN ELLICKSON

List of Contributors

Numbers in parentheses indicate the pages on which the authors' contributions begin.

WILLIAM C. APGAR, JR. (161), Department of City and Regional Planning, Harvard University, Cambridge, Massachusetts 02138

ROBERT S. BEDNARZ (219), Department of Geography, Texas A & M University, College Station, Texas 77843

BRIAN J. L. BERRY (219), Department of City and Regional Planning, Harvard University, Cambridge, Massachusetts 02138

THOMAS P. BOEHM (43), Department of Economics, Washington University, St. Louis, Missouri 63130

LESLEY DANIELS (147), Department of Economics, Washington University, St. Louis, Missouri 63130

BRYAN ELLICKSON (263), Department of Economics, University of California, Los Angeles, Los Angeles, California 90024

A. MYRICK FREEMAN, III (191), Department of Economics, Bowdoin College, Brunswick, Maine 04011

JOHN F. KAIN (161), Department of City and Regional Planning and Department of Economics, Harvard University, Cambridge, Massachusetts 02138

CLIFFORD R. KERN (121), Department of Economics, SUNY at Binghamton, Binghamton, New York 13901

STEVEN R. LERMAN (83), Center for Transportation Studies, Department of Civil Engineering, Massachusetts Institute of Technology, Cambridge, Massachusetts 02139

CHARLES L. LEVEN (43), Department of Economics, Washington University, St. Louis, Missouri 63130

JONATHAN H. MARK (43), Faculty of Commerce and Business Administration, The University of British Columbia, Vancouver, B.C., Canada V6T 1W5

DONALD K. RICHTER (247), Department of Economics, Boston College, Chestnut Hill, Massachusetts 02167

DAVID SEGAL (3, 57), Department of City and Regional Planning, Harvard University, Cambridge, Massachusetts 02138, and Department of Economics, Oberlin College, Oberlin, Ohio 44074

ROBERTON C. WILLIAMS, JR. (17), Department of Economics, Williams College, Williamstown, Massachusetts 01267

Foreword

The concept of a neighborhood has been something of a tar baby to social scientists. Motivated by their feelings, by feelings reported by friends, and by feelings expressed in opinion polls, sociologists and urban planners have long assigned an important role to the notion. Economists, being more concerned with physical than with verbal behavior, have held off making neighborhood a focus of analysis, presumably doubting whether neighborhood characteristics affected market and other physical behavior.

Interest in public goods was the catalyst that focused economists' attention on the concept. If neighborhood affects economic behavior, it must do so as public goods do: Consumption requires only that one be in the right place at the right time and results only indirectly from market transactions. The first serious economic measurement was of effects of neighborhood characteristics on housing demand, using hedonic pricing models. Evidence rapidly accumulated that people are willing to pay substantial amounts for desirable neighborhood characteristics.

Demand measurement has been important and has generated high quality research. More recently, attention has turned to the much more difficult issues on the supply side. Of course, Tiebout was the first economist to produce a careful analysis of interaction between private market decisions and the public sector in controlling the supply of public goods. Starting in the mid 1970s, several basic theoretical papers appeared on market provision of public goods. And three papers in this volume discuss the supply side of neighborhood characteristics.

Beyond doubt, the most difficult questions about neighborhoods concern the interaction between supply and demand and the proper role of public sectors. The papers in this volume show clearly that neighborhood is a concept that can be analyzed by economists' tools. The volume brings together a set of valuable contributions and should stimulate additional research.

EDWIN S. MILLS
Princeton University
April 1979

Acknowledgments

This set of original essays attempts to integrate neighborhood into contemporary notions of the urban economy. Neighborhood is seen here the way an economist might be inclined to view it, as a good having demand, supply, and equilibrium aspects.

The book is a product of many hands. The authors owe appreciation for critical review and helpful comments from Ed Mills, John Meyer, George Peterson, Martin McGuire, Bill Wheaton, and Frank Westhoff. Special thanks are owed to colleagues in the Department of City and Regional Planning for inspiration along the way, including Brian Berry, Dave Harrison, and John Yinger.

A debt is also owed to Donna Shalala, Assistant Secretary for Policy Development and Research at the U.S. Department of Housing and Urban Development, for providing resources to convene the authors for a public reading of their papers and to defray editorial costs. The biggest debt on the ledger is to Friederike Snyder for continuing and enthusiastic support throughout the project: To her this volume is dedicated.

THE ECONOMICS
OF NEIGHBORHOOD

I

INTRODUCTION

1

Introduction

DAVID SEGAL

1. NEW CONCERN FOR NEIGHBORHOODS

Always a household word, "neighborhood" has now become a policymaker's word as well. Neighborhood preservation and revitalization have become twin themes of the president's national urban policy, as well as the central focus of the first lady's public-service efforts. A National Commission on Neighborhoods was formed in 1977, and preserving historic buildings and neighborhoods has become a new national obsession.

Why all this now? Certainly neighborhood quality has always been close to the heart of urban settlers. Neighborhood, after all, is an extension of one's own house. While most workers travel beyond their neighborhood on work trips, school, church, shopping, and recreational trips are frequently intraneighborhood.

Part of the reason is that a national awareness has been mounting that our policies of local finance, home subsidy, and road building have, until recently, tilted urban development in favor of new suburban communities, to the neglect of the inner suburbs and central city neighborhoods. A system of subsidies, some explicit and some hidden, has

3

THE ECONOMICS OF NEIGHBORHOOD

promoted new construction over the rehabilitation of existing structures and, because of this, government intervention in urban markets
has shown a distinct locational bias: Government policies have pushed
the rate of return on investment in older neighborhoods below its
preintervention equilibrium level, with the predictable private-sector
response (Peterson, 1977). Other urban policies, primarily urban
renewal, have destroyed neighborhoods more often than they have
developed them.

Whether such an area bias was the intention of policymakers over-
seeing urban development is, of course, a moot point. The postwar
baby boom and growth in household incomes had shaped a willing clientele. National elections were no longer determined by an electorate
that was largely city: By 1968 the Dayton housewife had moved with her
family to the suburbs.

Because neighborhoods are viewed as rungs on a socioeconomic
ladder, public funds for improvements having high visibility in low-
income enclaves have often appealed to taxpapers. Community Action
programs and the Model Cities program were efforts at redistribution
toward target neighborhoods, programs that Mayor Kenneth Gibson of
Newark has disparagingly referred to as providing "cool it" money.
Whatever the success of these programs, a half-dozen presidential commissions on urban problems since the late 1960s have advocated some
kind of neighborhood dimension in urban policy. The latest national
commission will likely support the same goal. [1]

Some of the current national concern to revive older urban neighborhoods may have sprung from a variety of sources other than altru-
ism. Alonso (1977) and others have suggested that neighborhood and
locational preferences may be shifting because of the emergence of a
new demography. Urban households, according to this view, are now
increasingly smaller in size, have fewer children, better education,
higher income, and more frequent labor-force participation by adult
females. He speculates that such households may have a relatively
stronger preference for city-based public goods and amenities. (Evidence supporting the in-city locational preferences of upper-income
households in New York City is cited by Kern, Chapter 6 of this volume.)

Others have suggested that a series of price shifts has increased
households' interest in older neighborhoods. A big jump in the relative
price of new residential construction in the early 1970s may have played
a role. The sharp rise in public service costs and property taxes that are

---

[1] An inventory of the "neighborhood" proposals of previous commissions may be
found in Yin (1977).

borne by homeowners (ownership has a suburban bias too) may have tempted some households to consider tenure forms more readily available in the city. Also, higher energy prices may have had a slight tendency to make households favor higher density living. And a greater taste for open space and recreational amenities outside urban areas may have caused some nearby land to be placed off limits for residential growth.[2]

All of these explanations are economic, as is the notion that the housing recession of 1973–1975 put the suburbs temporarily beyond reach for many households desiring to locate in them. These price and income shifts, and their impact on urban form, simply remind us of the locational and neighborhood dimensions of housing demand. In a possible break with historic trends (whether this break is merely an interruption is still unclear) some of these shifts, coupled with the new demography, may favor the revival of *some* in-city neighborhoods in *some* cities, particularly of areas that have inherited intact large numbers of high-quality residential units. Such cities tend to be concentrated in the east and midwest, so it would be premature to speak of a national trend.

Many of the shifts in housing market parameters cited have had implications for specific neighborhoods. Some shifts, as was just noted, have been mutually reinforcing. Further contributing to the impact of changing market parameters is the fact that many households tend to make neighborhood decisions, as well as those regarding general location and tenure, before selecting a specific unit. Sometimes, of course, these prior choices are intertwined so that the notion of a hierarchy of decisions may be artificial.

Welfare economists have long recognized the importance of neighborhood effects, which are said to arise whenever the utility function (production function) of one economic agent depends upon the consumption (production) of another agent. In the literature of local public economics, Davis and Whinston (1961) were early to recognize that neighborhood effects causing slums to persist could be internalized by government action. Still earlier Tiebout had laid the foundation for a theory of optimal provision of local public goods across communities and the assignment of households among them. What is noteworthy is that urban economics, the branch of applied economics we might expect to deal most thoroughly with the subject of neighborhood, has in fact paid so little attention to it.

The allegation that urban economists have neglected all aspects of neighborhood would not be entirely fair. Since the early 1970s a litera-

---

[2] A recent discussion of the consequences of some price effects for older neighborhoods may be found in James (1977).

ture has developed applying hedonic price theory to the measurement of demand for specific neighborhood and environmental characteristics.[3] Also there is a set of general equilibrium models integrating prejudice with urban structure, with functions expressing supply and demand for racial composition (see Rose-Ackerman, 1975; Yinger, 1976; Courant and Yinger, 1977). One particular type of neighborhood externality and its implication for urban form—congestion on urban highways—has been studied by the "new urban economists."[4]

Aside from these examples, there has been little effort to integrate neighborhood externality into models of urban spatial structure. The reason is not hard to imagine. While the demand for neighborhood attributes may be relatively easy to analyze, neighborhood supply is quite another matter. If we take as our idea of neighborhood *some physical clustering that provides collective externality to a well-defined group of people living inside or nearby the cluster*, the supply question requires that we explain why neighborhoods so defined come into existence, how much of them is provided, and what sustains them.

These "clusterings" may refer to the attributes either of structures, of people occupying them, or of other publicly or privately provided aspects of the microenvironment. While the provision of residential structure services is largely a question of housing supply, the assignment, or self-assignment, of households to these structures is part of the demand for housing. How the two relate tu one another over time—structures and occupants—is very complicated and requires nothing less than a complete general equilibrium model of a local economy. For some publicly provided neighborhood goods, such as roads and their improvements, we have as yet no empirically based theory of supply.

Even if we confined our analysis to the relatively easy matter of structures (and ignored occupants and collectively provided goods) the analysis could easily become complicated. Consider producers of residential structures inside a contiguous urban land area. Just how such areas should be delimited—what the extent of the structures externality is—is in itself a tricky question. Our interest would focus on investment behavior—"reinvestment" in the case of older neighborhoods—and this in turn would have to reflect not only (*a*) builder and buyer expectations; but also (*b*) the various externalities flowing from both the services and occupants of structures in the area; as well as (*c*) the rate at which structures age and reinvestment is required.

---

[3] A review of this literature is provided by Freeman in Chapter 9 of this volume. Examples are Harrison and Rubinfeld (1978), Polinsky and Shavell (1976), Freeman (1974).

[4] For a definition of the "new urban economics" and a set of articles venturing into the subject, see Symposium on the New Urban Economics (1973).

Specification of these expectations, externalities, and aging phenomena—their relation to one another and to supply behavior—is no easy matter.

In the balance of the introduction we look at some of the efforts to measure neighborhood effects; we then turn to a brief description of approaches used by the authors in analyzing the role of neighborhood in the urban economy.

2. CAN NEIGHBORHOOD BE MEASURED?

Economists are by no means the first to show an interest in measuring the extent of neighborhood effects and the neighborhood boundaries they give rise to. Sociologists have historically been interested in one of the three sources of externality cited earlier, neighborhood effects flowing from *occupants.* Accordingly, an approach was devised during the early 1950s, called *social area analysis,* for identifying geographic clusters of households within a city with like occupants. In their studies of Los Angeles and San Francisco, Shevky and Williams (1949) and Bell (1953) employed three basic constructs for differentiating urban households: social rank (economic status), urbanization (family status), and segregation (ethnic status). For each construct they devised an index, using from one to three census variables; these indexes revealed the positions of census-tract populations on scales of economic, family, and ethnic status. The analysis allowed the classification of census tracts into social areas based upon index scores.

By using factor analysis sociologists and urban geographers since the 1950s have obtained a greater degree of precision in isolating the factors differentiating neighborhoods than social area analysis allowed. *Factorial ecology* (see Berry and Kasarda, 1977, pp. 123ff) is the term now used to describe studies applying factor analysis to urban ecology. A data matrix is formed arraying measurement on m variables for each of n units of observation (census tracts, wards, etc.) with the objective of (a) revealing common patterns of variability among the m variables in $r < m$ dimensions that additively reproduce the common variance; and (b) studying the patterns of scores of each of the n observed geographical units on each of the r dimensions. According to its practitioners, factorial ecology brings out dimensions that are an objective output of the analysis.

While social area analysis or its successors may be useful as descriptors of the *types* and *placement* of neighborhoods in a city, they are of limited use in economic analysis. Questions about the determinants of neighborhood change and about economic welfare and the role of public policy cannot be adequately addressed with these tools.

Empirical studies of neighborhood effects by economists can be grouped according to the three sources of externality alluded to in the previous section: the *occupants* of structures (according to race, income, and stage of family cycle),[5] *privately provided goods* of households (such as housing structures, noise or air pollution from cars) or of firms (factories or shopping centers), and *publicly provided goods* (schools, parks, or highways).

An extensive yet inconclusive literature exists on the extent to which the race or income of housing occupants impact the prices or demographic composition of the occupants of nearby houses. Early work on the extent of externality from race differences is associated with Martin Bailey, who assumed that boundary externalities between black neighborhoods in Chicago and adjacent white neighborhoods were felt for one block only (Bailey, 1966). In the past decade, articles, probably numbering several hundred, have developed empirical models of border effects, tipping, and discrimination. (A good survey of this literature can be found in Yinger, 1979; see also Segal, 1977, Ch. 10.) Like some sociologists before them, economists have found household income and race (and after them, life cycle characteristics) to be the variables that best define neighborhoods or changes in them. What differentiates the work of economists studying neighborhood from that of sociologists is the explicit role they assign to market processes in transmitting and distributing the consequences of demographic forces and changes in them.

If after measuring the externality of occupants we turn to that conveyed by privately or publicly provided local public goods, we once again find a growing literature, for the most part of recent vintage. Much of the empirical work here has been done applying hedonic price theory. While the hedonic approach was introduced as far back as the early 1960s to evaluate quality changes in automobiles, it has only recently been applied to evaluating the benefits of environmental or neighborhood improvement (or the costs of deterioration).

Hedonic estimating procedure involves two stages. (For a complete description of the technique, see this volume, Chapter 10 by Freeman.) First the impact on property values of prevailing levels of a local public good, such as air quality, public safety, school quality, or fire protection, is determined by regressing property value on a set of explanatory

---

[5] Schnare's (1976, p. 107) term is *demographic externality*, "the influence of the demographic mix of an area on a household's evaluation of neighborhood quality."

characteristics including the public good under study. Observations may be on housing or lot prices, on individual units or census tract means. Once the import of the good has been established, a second stage involves the estimation of demand or "willingness to pay" functions by looking at how different demographic groups evaluate small changes in the level of the good.[6]

The willingness-to-pay function for a given income class tells us how its members are affected by, or what they would be willing to pay to have (or to avoid), one more unit of a public good (or bad). The function thus puts a price on varying amounts of the externality.

While the literature measuring externality from occupants or publicly and privately produced environmental goods has recently been burgeoning, surprisingly little has been said about the extent of neighborhood effect, measured in price or distance, of nonconforming structure uses, such as commercial or industrial buildings, on housing. The paucity of evidence on this is surprising because the presumed presence of this externality has often been used as one of the pretexts for zoning regulations.

Existing studies are inconclusive on the extent of externality. Crecine et al. (1967) in a study of the Pittsburgh area, found no systematic evidence that the presence of nonresidential land uses adversely affected the values of single-family homes in the immediate vicinity. Their results were generally replicated by Reuter (1973), who used a somewhat better data base. A finding that nonconforming commercial and industrial uses do have a significant negative impact on apartment rents and on the value of single-family houses was reported by Kain and Quigley (1970) in their well-known study of St. Louis. Stull (1975) found similar results in his study of 40 suburban communities in the Boston area: The value of single-family homes tends to fall as the proportion of commercial land in a community exceeds 5%. And Grether and Mieszkowski (1978) found in their study of the New Haven area an impact that was slight (a discount of 2% within 200 yards) when the nonconformities were low-density apartment developments or minor commercial centers, and substantial when the nearby activity was heavy industry or public housing.

An interesting finding emerges from a new study by Li and Brown (1978) of 1971 housing sales data in the southern suburbs of Boston. Commercial centers have a twofold impact on nearby property values. Accessibility to them is valued by neighboring households and affects property values positively; the traffic congestion and unsightliness of

---

[6] This may be done by taking the first derivative of the regression equation of stage one with respect to the public-good variable, for different socioeconomic strata.

such centers have a negative effect, although this externality tapers off relatively quickly. The combined force of these two factors affecting price is nonlinear: Housing values, ceteris paribus, peak at distances of one-fifth mile from commercial establishments.[7]

A difficulty posed by many of the hedonic pricing studies of the different types of externality is that they make inappropriate assumptions about the supply side of the externality. Why offending uses locate where they do must be known before price effects can be correctly assessed. Similarly, many of the moels assume continuous price–distance functions; discontinuities at neighborhood borders are not easily incorporated into their analysis. Interactions among types of externality that may provide a source of discontinuity are also excluded, even though there is reason to believe they are important. In the chapters that follow different authors have tried to address some of these problems.

3. ABOUT THE BOOK

The authors believe that neighborhood can be analyzed like a good, and accordingly that it has demand, supply, and equilibrium outcomes that can be studied like those of other goods. The volume is thus divided into three parts: the demand for neighborhood, the supply of neighborhood, and equilibrium aspects of neighborhood.

3.1. Demand

This section of the book includes four chapters, all dealing with the determinants of neighborhood demand in different eastern and midwestern cities in the mid- to late 1960s.

Roberton Williams broadens John Quigley's earlier work (1976) analyzing the location choice of a sample of Pittsburgh households by including neighborhood variables as a choice determinant. The neighborhood variable that Williams finds best for this purpose, and most significant, is mean neighborhood income. Williams focuses just on households that changed location during the study period, 1962–1967.

Mark, Boehm, and Leven look not only at households that changed neighborhoods in St. Louis during the 1967–1972 period, but at those that stayed put as well. Their primary interest is to study the role that

[7] Li and Brown (1978) made similar calculations for the impact of industrial areas and major throughways on residential areas, finding that households prefer to locate at a greater distance from them than from commercial centers.

neighborhood transition at the origin played in governing the move—stay-put decision. They find that household demography heavily influences this decision for households in transition neighborhoods.

Segal looks mainly at households moving into Wilmington, Delaware from elsewhere during 1965–1970. He assumes that, despite imperfect information, their neighborhood preferences are revealed better than those of households already in place. This is because households in place have sunk moving costs in the decision to come to Wilmington, and by definition they are in disequilibrium. Segal looks at the preferences for a variety of neighborhood characteristics revealed by these households and how the preferences vary across household types.

Lerman looks at the neighborhood choice of households already living in Washington, D.C., in 1968 as a joint prior choice of residential location, housing type, automobile ownership, and mode of travel to work. He thus expands the analysis of authors like Williams and Quigley to include two transportation variables.

3.2. Supply

Definitive work modeling the supply side of neighborhood, as defined in the opening part of the introduction, has yet to be written. What is offered by the three chapters in the supply section here are sketches reporting special aspects of how neighborhood is supplied.

Kern examines how the supply of certain kinds of neighborhoods—how such neighborhoods form, persist, and evolve—can be determined by the interaction of residential demand and housing supply in the private sector. Using the example of the recent growth in upper-income demand for those inner-city locations in New York City having an abundance of entertainment, cultural, and other "nonwork" activities, he shows how the locational decisions of households and housing suppliers are patterned by the supply of existing neighborhoods, and how these decisions in turn determine the supply of neighborhoods later on. The implications of this process for welfare and for public policy are also assessed.

Daniels develops a theoretical model of optimum neighborhood supply by local governments. With the model she explains a tendency for there to be an array of neighborhood types in a city which, depending upon taxing arrangements, will be lesser than envisioned by Tiebout. Significantly, Daniels demonstrates circumstances under which larger cities will exhibit greater neighborhood variety. A welfare gain can be associated with this greater range of choice.

The chapter by Kain and Apgar describes how the National Bureau

of Economic Research (NBER) Urban Simulation model can be used to
represent how neighborhood characteristics influence the behavior of
housing consumers and suppliers, and how their decisions, in turn, affect neighborhood quality. They explain how housing suppliers (rein-
vestors in the case of existing neighborhoods) respond to existing
neighborhood conditions and expectations about future demand in
fashioning their investment behavior. They find that the NBER model
simulates a pattern of neighborhood change that conforms broadly to
what in fact occurred in Pittsburgh and Chicago from 1960 to 1970.

3.3. Equilibrium

The four chapters in the concluding section of the book analyze
neighborhood in an equilibrium setting. The first two chapters stress
price outcomes, the latter two quantity aspects of neighborhood.

Freeman offers a concise statement of hedonic estimating procedure and the nature of the assumptions required in order to use it successfully. He summarizes 15 studies that have employed the approach
to evaluate environmental quality in urban neighborhoods and concludes with a plea that the technique be used to measure the value of
other neighborhood attributes as well.

Berry and Bednarz apply the hedonic pricing approach to 1971 sales
prices of single-family homes in Chicago, controlling for property characteristics and improvements, neighborhood attributes, the effects of
race and ethnicity, environmental pollution, and distance from Chicago's central business district (CBD). While most of their findings ac-
cord with previous work, two do not: There is a negative sign for
minority groups (blacks pay *less* for equivalent housing) and a positive
sign for distance (property values *increase* with distance). The authors
explain the first deviation by citing accelerated white-to-black filtering
during the study period, and the second by omitted suburban amenity
variables that are highly correlated with distance.

The chapter by Richter suggests one way to avoid some of the
problems with continuous price–distance functions which were alluded to in the previous section. His approach, extending earlier work
by MacKinnon (1974) and King (1977), is to use a general equilibrium
computational technique that mathematical economists call "simplicial
search" or "fixed point" algorithms to allocate land use among different
groups of users. The technique's primary advantage is its flexibility,
which allows the study of a wide range of neighborhood effects from a
spatial general equilibrium point of view, within a single unifying
computational framework.

Ellickson is concerned to establish the conditions under which a competitive market for neighborhoods—one which because of this would avoid the need for government intervention for reasons other than income distribution—could exist. His approach is to apply a theory of local public goods (one he developed earlier) in which such goods are seen as indivisible private goods to the market for neighborhoods. Ellickson presents several models in order to illustrate his point that externalities, collusion, and neighborhood deterioration may all be consistent with efficiency criteria.

Our volume represents a concentrated effort to integrate notions of neighborhood into prevailing models of the urban economy. The authors hope their initiative will stimulate further work in this important area.

REFERENCES

Alonso, W. (1977). The population factor and urban structure. Center for Population Study Working Paper 102. Harvard University, Cambridge, Massachusetts.

Bailey, M. J. (1966). Effects of race and other demographic factors on the value of single-family homes. *Land Economics* **42.**

Bell, W. (1953). The social areas of the San Francisco Bay Region. *American Sociological Review* **18,** 29–47.

Berry, B. J. L., and Kasarda, J. B. (1977). *Contemporary urban ecology.* Macmillan, New York.

Courant, P. M., and Yinger, J. (1977). On models of racial prejudice and urban residential structure. *Journal of Urban Economics* **4,** 272–291.

Crecine, J. P., Davis, O. A., and Jackson, J. E. (1967). Urban property markets: Some empirical results and their implication for municipal zoning. *Journal of Law and Economics* **10.**

Davis, O., and Whinston, A. B. (1961). The economics of urban renewal. *Law and Contemporary Problems* **26,** 105–112.

Freeman, A. M. (1974). On estimating air pollution control benefits from land-value studies. *Journal of Environmental Economics and Management* **1,** 74–83.

Grether, D. M., and Mieszkowski, P. (1978). The effects of nonresidential land use on the prices of adjacent housing: Some estimates of proximity effects. *Journal of Urban Economics* (forthcoming).

Harrison, D., and Rubinfeld, D. L. (1978). Hedonic housing prices and the demand for clear air. *Journal of Environmental Economics and Management* **5,** 81–102.

James, F. J. (1977). Private reinvestment in older houses and older neighborhoods. Recent trends and focuses. Statement before the Committee on Banking, Housing, and Urban Affairs of the U.S. Senate, July 10.

Kain, J. F., and Quigley, J. M. (1970). Measuring the value of housing quality. *Journal of the American Statistical Association* **65.**

King, T. (1977). Computing general equilibrium prices for spatial economics. *Review of Economics and Statistics* **59,** 340–350.

Li, M. M., and Brown, J. H. (1978). Micro-neighborhood externalities and hedonic housing prices. City and Regional Planning Discussion Paper D78-3. Harvard University, Cambridge, Massachusetts.

MacKinnon, J. (1974). Urban general equilibrium models and simplical search algorithms. *Journal of Urban Economics* **1**, 161–183.

Peterson, G. E. (1977). Federal tax policy and urban development. Testimony before the Subcommittee on the City of the House Banking Committee, June 16.

Polinsky, A. M., and Shavell, S. (1976). Amenities and property values in a model of an urban area. *Journal of Public Economics* **5**, 199–229.

Quigley, J. M. (1976). Housing demand in the short run: An analysis of polytomous choice. *Explorations in Economic Research, Winter,* 1976, 76–102.

Reuter, F. (1973). Externalities in urban property markets: An empirical test of the zoning ordinance of Pittsburgh. *Journal of Law and Economics* **16.**

Rose-Ackerman, S. (1975). Racism and urban structure. *Journal of Urban Economics* **2**, 85–103.

Schnare, A. B. (1976). Racial and ethnic price differentials in an urban housing market. *Urban Studies* **13.**

Segal, D. (1977). *Urban Economics.* Richard D. Irwin, Homewood, Illinois.

Shevky, E., and Williams, M. (1949). *The social areas of Los Angeles: Analysis and typology.* University of California Press, Berkeley.

Stull, W. J. (1975). Community environment, zoning, and the market value of single family homes. *Journal of Law and Economics* **16.**

Symposium on the new economics. (1973). *Bell Journal of Economics and Management Science* **4**, 591–651.

Yin, R. K. (1977). What a national commission on neighborhood could do. *Journal of The American Real Estate and Urban Economics Association* **5**, 255–278.

Yinger, J. (1976). Racial prejudice and racial residential segregation in an urban model. *Journal of Urban Economics* **3**, 383–396.

Yinger, J. (1979). Prejudice and discrimination in the urban housing market. In *Current issues in urban economics,* P. Mieszkowski and M. Straszheim (eds.). Johns Hopkins Press for Resources for the Future, Baltimore.

II

DEMAND FOR NEIGHBORHOOD

A Logit Model of Demand for Neighborhood

ROBERTON C. WILLIAMS, JR.

Few people would argue that a family does not consider the quality of its potential neighborhood or the menu of public services provided to that neighborhood in its decision concerning what housing unit it will reside in. Yet existing empirical studies of housing demand universally ignore the influence of these neighborhood variables on the family's residential choice. For many studies (see, e.g., de Leeuw and Ekanem, 1971) this omission results from the assumption that housing services are perfectly homogeneous, and hence that no account need be taken of the different attributes of housing units which contribute to the quantity of housing services provided. While such an approach is necessitated if only aggregate housing data are available, it ignores the fact that people do in fact care about the different attributes of the residence they choose. If supply is not perfectly elastic, as is likely the case in the short run, the homogeneity assumption fails to capture this essential characteristic of housing markets.

Those relatively few, more recent studies which utilize data on individual households do attempt to incorporate the multidimensiona-

THE ECONOMICS OF NEIGHBORHOOD

lity of housing by examining the demand for different attributes, either through the use of hedonic prices (see, e.g., Straszheim, 1973) or by estimating the relative probabilities of a family's choosing particular types of housing units that are defined as discrete bundles of housing attributes (see, e.g., Quigley, 1976). Yet even these studies fail to include measures of neighborhood quality as determinants of housing demand.

This chapter is an attempt to remedy that failing. It is based on research conducted in 1974–1975 to estimate housing demand functions for use in the National Bureau of Economic Research Urban Simulation Model, and incorporates many of the assumptions of that model concerning the operation of housing markets. First, it recognizes the importance of workplace location in a household's residential choice by incorporating the costs of commuting into the price of any particular housing unit. Unlike many models, however, it does not assume that all employment is located in the center of the city, but rather allows for multiple workplace locations. Secondly, the model involves a short run framework in which the stock of housing is taken to be fixed with regard to quantity, location, and characteristics of individual housing types. Households are assumed to choose from this existing stock based on their tastes for different housing attributes and the costs associated with particular housing units in terms both of the price of the unit and the commuting costs due to its location. Finally, it is assumed that one of the housing attributes which influences residential choice is the quality of the neighborhood in which the dwelling unit is located. It is the inclusion of this assumption that differentiates this study from previous work.

The model is empirically estimated using conditional logit analysis, and is based on data concerning the residential choices of 5823 Pittsburgh households who changed residence between 1962 and 1967. The results are generally consistent with prior expectations concerning the influence of the explanatory variables. In particular, measures of neighborhood quality exhibit fairly consistent and significant effects on residential choice.

The first section of the chapter lays out the theoretical model upon which the demand estimations are based. The dimensions of the model are described in the second section, while the third section discusses the possible variables considered in the search for an adequate measure of neighborhood quality and that measure actually employed in the analysis. The empirical results are presented in the final section along with a discussion of their interpretations.

1. THE THEORETICAL MODEL[1]

In choosing a residence, a household considers both the costs associated with a particular housing unit and its tastes for the housing attributes incorporated in the unit. The costs of a particular unit are assumed to be of two kinds, the price of the unit itself (expressed as a monthly rental price) and the accessibility costs associated with the residential location and those sites to which the household commonly travels. Because housing units are locationally fixed and both supply and demand for a particular housing unit will vary across locations, the prices of housing units will also vary across the metropolitan area. Similarly, accessibility costs will differ across locations. Because most household travel other than commuting is to ubiquitous destinations, frequently close to home, accessibility costs are assumed to vary with location only insofar as commuting costs vary. Thus, accessibility costs are measured by the costs of worktrips, both in terms of out-of-pocket and time costs. Since workplaces are taken as given, these accessibility costs for a particular household will vary across residential locations. The full cost, or gross price, of a particular type of housing located at a particular location for a given household is thus taken to be the sum of the price of that housing type plus the commuting costs for that household from that location. Thus,

$$GP_{ijsy} = P_{is} + C_{sj} + T_{sj}(y),\qquad(1)$$

where GP_{ijsy} is the gross price of housing type i at location s to a household with income y and workplace j; P_{is} is the price of housing type i at location s; C_{sj} is the out-of-pocket commuting cost between residential location s and workplace j; and $T_{sj}(y)$ is the value of time spent commuting, assumed to depend on income y. It is this gross price of any given housing unit which influences the household's residential choice. Beyond the effects of this gross price, however, households are assumed to be indifferent between different units of the same housing type. This implies that the relevant price for any type of housing is the lowest gross price as viewed by the household for that housing type.

Given the gross prices for different housing types, the household will attempt to maximize its utility obtained through the consumption of housing and nonhousing goods, subject to an income constraint.

[1] The theoretical model presented here is virtually identical to that used in Quigley (1976). Both models were developed as parts of research conducted for the National Bureau of Economic Research.

Assuming that each household occupies only one dwelling unit, this utility maximization can be written as

$$\text{maximize } U(H_i, Z) \qquad \text{subject to} \qquad GP_i + Z \cdot P_z \leq Y, \qquad (2)$$

where Z and P_z are, respectively, the quantity and price of nonhousing goods. Furthermore, since the choice of a particular housing unit fully determines the income available for the purchase of nonhousing goods and therefore the quantity of nonhousing goods that will be consumed, the maximization function can be rewritten as

$$\text{maximize } V(H_i, GP_i), \qquad (3)$$

given the household's income and workplace. The household's choice is thus reduced to the question of picking that particular housing type which maximizes the household's utility.

In order to estimate housing demand functions based on this utility maximization approach, the data describing actual housing choices must be stratified into groups of households which would be expected to have similar utility functions. While we can readily identify households based on characteristics which would be likely to influence tastes for housing and nonhousing goods, such as size of household and age of head, it is not possible to observe all factors that influence a household's utility function. Therefore, it is assumed that a particular household's utility from consuming a given bundle of goods is given by an average utility for households of similar size and age of head, plus a stochastic term

$$V_F(H_i, GP_i) = W_F(H_i, GP_i) + \varepsilon_F, \qquad (4)$$

where W_F is the average utility function for household type F, and ε_F represents all unobserved factors influencing a particular household's utility function.

A household will choose a housing unit of type i as long as the consumption of that housing unit yields a level of utility greater than that derived from any other housing type; that is, housing type i will be selected if and only if

$$V_F(H_i, GP_i) > V_F(H_j, GP_j), \qquad \text{for all } j \neq i. \qquad (5)$$

With the stochastic component of the utility function taken into account, the household's housing choice cannot be ascertained with certainty. Rather, the probability of a household of a given type choosing housing type i is equal to the probability that

$$V_F(H_i, GP_i) > V_F(H_j, GP_j), \qquad \text{for all } j \neq i, \qquad (6)$$

or the probability that

$$(\varepsilon_{Fj} - \varepsilon_{Fi}) < [W_F(H_i, GP_i) - W_F(H_j, GP_j)], \qquad \text{for all } j \neq i. \quad (7)$$

This indicates that the probability of a household's choosing any particular housing type depends on the characteristics and prices of all housing types and on a set of stochastic elements.

Given certain assumptions concerning the independence and distribution of the stochastic terms (see Quigley, 1976, pp. 82–84), the multinomial logit model can be used to describe the housing choice problem.[2] For the model described above, the logit formulation specifies that the probability of a household of type F choosing housing type i is

$$p_{Fi} = \frac{\exp[W_F(H_i, GP_i)]}{\Sigma \exp[W_F(H_j, GP_j)]}, \quad (8)$$

where the summation is over all housing types. If it is further assumed that the utility function is linear in the gross price and the attributes defining the housing type, the formulation can be be reduced to

$$\log(p_i/p_j) = \sum_k b_k(x_{ik} - x_{jk}) + c(GP_i - GP_j), \quad (9)$$

where the xs are values of particular housing attributes and the subscript k runs over all attributes defining housing types. Estimation of the parameters b_k and c can be accomplished utilizing a maximum likelihood approach.

2. DIMENSIONS OF THE MODEL

In order to estimate empirically the model just described, we must define both the attributes of housing that are expected to influence the consumer's choice and the characteristics of households which are most likely to determine the tastes and needs, and therefore the utility functions, of the households. Because the size of the model, and therefore the difficulties of estimation, rise geometrically with the dimensions over which housing units and households are defined, these dimensions are limited to those few which are felt to be most important to residential choice. Arguably significant omissions have been allowed in order to preserve the estimability of the model.

---

[2] A brief and general discussion of the logit model is presented in the Appendix.

2.1. Housing Types

Housing units are distributed into 50 distinct groups, classified by three basic dimensions: structure type, size, and neighborhood quality. Structure type is a proxy for immediate residential density, offering a measure of the degree of privacy provided in the dwelling unit. Units are defined as small-lot single-family (with lot size of one-quarter acre or less), large-lot single-family (with lot size greater than one-quarter acre), small multifamily (units in structures containing from two to seven separate units), and large multifamily (units in structures containing eight or more individual dwelling units). The size of the individual unit is measured by the number of bedrooms, since preferable data on floor space or total rooms are not available in the sample used to estimate the model. For single-family homes, three bedroom categories are used (two or fewer, three, and four or more), while only two categories are used for multifamily units (none or one, and two or more). Individual unit characteristics thus define ten housing classifications: six single-family and four multifamily.

Housing unit types are further defined by five classes of neighborhood quality. (A complete discussion of this dimension of the housing bundle is deferred to the next section.) In conjunction with the 10 structure–bedroom combinations, this yields a total of 50 distinct types of housing from which consumers can choose. It is assumed that each type defines a distinct housing submarket, and that households view all units within any submarket as virtually identical, while units in different submarkets are viewed as being distinctly different kinds of housing.

2.2. Household Types

Households are classified over three dimensions: number of persons, age of head, and income. In combination, the size and age of head measures are intended to distinguish households on a basis of their housing "needs" and desires and, therefore, to isolate households that might be expected to have similar utility functions, particularly with respect to the consumption of housing. For this study, three household classifications were used to define households with similar utility functions. One- and two-person households in which the head was between 30 and 60 years of age formed one group; three-person households with a 30–60-year-old head and all four-person households made up a second group; and all households with five or more members comprised the third group. (All other households were excluded from the study because they had too few observations to allow model estimation.) Within each of the three basic classifications, households were further stratified into six income classes: less than $3000, $3000–5000, $5000–7000, $7000–10,000, $10,000–15,000, and over $15,000.[3] These classifications serve two purposes. First, they allow for imposition of an income constraint without having to enter such a constraint directly into the utility maximization problem. Second, income classes further differentiate the utility functions of different households. Different incomes imply different relative valuations of particular housing attributes and of nonhousing goods, and these differences can be most readily observed if households are stratified by income class. Thus, 18 types of households are defined by income, size, and age of head, and because these households are assumed to act differently in their housing choice decisions, separate models are estimated for each household type.

2.3.   Residential Location and Gross Prices

Residential location is defined in terms of the 702 census tracts making up the Pittsburgh Standard Metropolitan Statistical Area (SMSA). For each housing type in each location, the monthly housing cost is estimated as the average rent, including utilities, for the particular type of housing in the given tract. These net prices are then transformed into sets of gross prices relevant to the household's residential choice by adding commuting costs (both out-of-pocket and time) from the given residential location to each of 70 workzones for each of six income classes. Commuting costs were calculated based on transportation studies reporting money costs and time required to travel between residence and workzones, both by private automobile and by public transportation. For each income class, the time component of travel was valued at four-tenths of the hourly wage[4] and a total dollar commuting cost was obtained for each travel mode. The chosen travel mode was assumed to be that with the lower total cost, and this cost was added to the net price of housing to provide the gross rents which enter the consumer's utility maximization calculus.

Each household is assumed to have a fixed workplace location and a fixed income. For each of the 50 housing types, the household is faced with a gradient of 702 gross rents for units viewed as identical except

[3] The means for the six income categories were assumed to be $2500, $4000, $6000, $8500, $12,500, and $17,500, respectively.

[4] The hourly wage was imputed based on income class means assuming a 2000-hour work year.

for this price term. If the household were fully aware of all 702 prices, the relevant price would be the lowest. However, households do not spend the time or money required to learn all prices for a given type of unit, nor are the prices which they do obtain necessarily accurate. Therefore, for purposes of this model, the relevant price of each type of housing is taken to be that price 5% up from the bottom of the gross rent distribution. Thus, households employed in one of the 70 workzones and which are in one of the six income classes are assumed to be faced with a single price for each of the 50 types of housing.

The more information a consumer has about a particular type of housing, both in terms of prices and location, the more likely it will be that the gross prices obtained in the foregoing procedure will accurately reflect the price measure entering the consumer's housing decision. To proxy for the amount of information available concerning a given housing type, a stock variable indicating the total number of units of that type in the entire metropolitan area has been included in the model estimation. A larger stock of a particular housing type would tend to lead consumers to be able to receive more accurate and less expensive information concerning existing rents.

The dimensions of the model are summarized in Table 1. The housing choice may be fully described as follows. A household of a particular size and age of head and with fixed income and workplace must choose 1 of 50 types of housing defined by structure type, size, and neighborhood quality. For each housing type, the relevant price is defined as the sum of the direct housing costs (rent) plus the commuting costs (both time and money), taken for that residential location for which the housing cost is 5% up from the bottom of the gross price distribution. Faced with 50 housing types and 50 associated prices, the household selects that housing unit which maximizes its utility.

3. MEASURING NEIGHBORHOOD QUALITY

The multinomial logit formulation has been utilized previously to estimate demand functions for housing (Quigley, 1976). However, while the formulations have been virtually identical to that described above, existing studies have assumed that the relevant housing attributes included only the characteristics of the dwelling unit in terms of structure type, size, and age. No study appears to have considered the quality of the neighborhood in which the housing unit is located to be a relevant attribute, although few would argue that neighborhood quality does not enter the household's utility function. The estimations pre-

Table 1
Dimensions of the Model

I. Housing unit categories: 50 types defined over three dimensions.
   A. Structure type–bedroom combinations

Structure type	Bedrooms
1. Small-lot single-family (≤.25 acre)	0–2
2. Small-lot single-family (≤.25 acre)	3
3. Small-lot single-family (≤.25 acre)	4+
4. Large-lot single-family (>.25 acre)	0–2
5. Large-lot single-family (>.25 acre)	3
6. Large-lot single-family (>.25 acre)	4+
7. Small multifamily (<8 units in structure)	0–1
8. Small multifamily (<8 units in structure)	2+
9. Large multifamily (≥8 units in structure)	0–1
10. Large multifamily (≥8 units in structure)	2+

   B. Neighborhood quality classes
      1. Low
      2. Lower middle
      3. Middle
      4. Upper middle
      5. High

II. Household categories: 18 types defined over three dimensions
   A. Household size–age of head combinations
      1. One- and two-person households, head between 30 and 60 years of age.
      2. Three-person households, head between 30 and 60 years old, *and* all four-person households.
      3. All households with five or more members.
   B. Income classes

	Mean Income
1. $0–$2,999	$2,500
2. $3,000–$4,999	$4,000
3. $5,000–$6,999	$6,000
4. $7,000–$9,999	$8,500
5. $10,000–$14,999	$12,500
6. $15,000 and up	$17,500

sented in the following section do attempt to measure the effects of neighborhood quality on the household's residential choice. Before trying to estimate such effects, however, we must discuss those variables that might be used to quantify neighborhood quality.

Neighborhood quality has many dimensions. The average dwelling unit quality, the economic well-being of the residents, the quality and quantity of local public services, and the racial composition of the population are all aspects of the quality of a neighborhood as perceived by individuals choosing a place to live. While an initial reaction is to utilize all such measures as dwelling unit attributes in order to account most fully for the effects of neighborhood quality on housing choice, such a course of action encounters three problems. First, data that provide objective measures of these variables are not available. Reporting of dwelling unit quality, for example, has proven to be so inaccurate, even when collected by trained observers, that believable data are available only in rare and isolated cases. Second, data that are available are frequently not collected at a sufficiently detailed geographical level to distinguish local neighborhoods. Measures of public services are generally available only at town or municipality levels, even though the quality and quantity of those services vary widely within local jurisdictions. Finally, even if adequate data could be found to measure all relevant dimensions of neighborhood quality, insurmountable problems of multicollinearity would be encountered. The different dimensions are highly correlated. Only by creating an index combining the different components could accurate estimates of the effects of neighborhood quality on housing demand be obtained.

Because of these difficulties involved in considering all measures of neighborhood quality as attributes of individual housing units, and because any index combining different measures must be composed in an arbitrary manner, it was decided that a single measure of neighborhood quality was called for. Initially this took the form of defining neighborhood quality based on a measure of residential density and average neighborhood income. Three density levels were created based on average lot size and the proportion of dwelling units in the neighborhood that were single-family detached units. Similarly, three income classes were utilized, both as a direct measure of neighborhood quality and as a proxy for other quality measures. These two measures were then combined to define nine distinct neighborhood quality levels.

This first approach to defining neighborhoods failed, primarily for two reasons. First, the density measure proved to be an inadequate measure of neighborhood quality. Density of a neighborhood appeared to depend primarily on when the neighborhood was developed and its distance from population centers, neither of which has a direct association with quality. Even when used in conjunction with income, density only provided a confused measure of quality that performed poorly in empirical estimations. A second problem involved interpretation of empirical results. Even had density been an adequate measure of quality, there was no a priori ordering of the nine neighborhoods defined over the two dimensions that would rank neighborhoods by overall quality. While an ex post ranking could have been created based on the desirability of neighborhoods indicated by the demand estimations, such a procedure would allow no means of evaluating the empirical results.

The second formulation of neighborhood quality, and that used in this study, dropped the density measure and expanded the use of mean neighborhood incomes to define five categories. For Pittsburgh, this involved the assignment of each of the 702 Pittsburgh census tracts to one of five neighborhood quality levels based on the mean incomes of the tract residents. The income breakdowns are given in Table 2. As was the case in the first formulation, average tract income was used both as a direct measure of neighborhood quality and as a proxy for those dimensions which were either unmeasurable with available data or too highly correlated with tract income to provide a separate measure.

As Table 2 shows, neighborhoods do not have an even geographic distribution with regard to quality. The Pittsburgh SMSA may be divided up into four sectors: the central business district (CBD), the rest of the city of Pittsburgh, the inner ring of suburbs, and the outer suburban ring. (Figure 1 shows these areas, along with aggregated work-zones from which the sectors are composed.) Over three-quarters of the CBD neighborhoods and nearly half of the neighborhoods in the rest of the city of Pittsburgh are of either low or lower middle quality, while over half of the neighborhoods in the inner suburban ring are of high or upper middle quality. In the outer suburban ring, over three-fourths of the neighborhoods fall in the middle three quality levels. Table 3 indicates that the distribution of housing units within types of neighborhoods is slightly more evenly distributed, but that the same pattern applies. Given the skewed geographic distribution, and if people do in fact consider commuting costs in their residential choices, then it would be expected that CBD workers would be more likely to live in poorer quality neighborhoods than similar individuals employed in the inner

Table 2

Neighborhood Quality Definitions for Pittsburgh SMSA Based on 1970 Census Data

Quality Class	Average Tract Income	Spatial Distribution				
		Total	CBD	Rest of Pittsburgh	Inner Suburban Ring	Outer Suburban Ring
1	≤$7900	140	19	48	29	44
2	$8000–8700	140	4	30	52	54
3	$8800–9500	142	2	29	54	57
4	$9600–10,800	140	0	29	62	49
5	≥$10,900	140	5	24	84	27

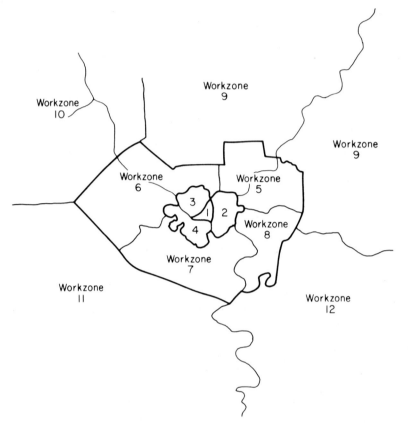

Figure 1. *Sectors and aggregated workzones for the Pittsburgh SMSA. (a) Central business district: Workzone 1. (b) Rest of city of Pittsburgh: Workzones 2, 3, and 4. (c) Inner suburban ring: Workzones 5, 6, 7, and 8. (d) Outer suburban ring: Workzones 9, 10, 11, and 12.*

suburban ring. On the other hand, if neighborhood quality is a valued attribute of housing, then individuals should be willing to incur higher commuting costs in order to live in better quality neighborhoods, and the tendency noted above might be reduced. Both hypotheses are verified by the data. For example, as Table 4 shows, for middle-aged, three-person, and all four-person households with incomes between $5000 and $7000, those with workers employed in the CBD are more likely to live in poor quality neighborhoods than those who work in the inner suburban ring. However, the table also indicates a willingness to commute to better neighborhoods, particularly on the part of CBD workers. The latter are nearly as likely to live in the better neighborhoods as are inner ring workers, despite the need to commute over

Table 3

Percentage Distribution of Dwelling Units among Neighborhoods by Sector

Neighborhood Quality Level	CBD	Rest of Pittsburgh	Inner Suburban Ring	Outer Suburban Ring	Total
1	.60	.26	.05	.15	.15
2	.18	.18	.13	.23	.18
3	.05	.20	.15	.25	.19
4	.00	.19	.24	.23	.22
5	.17	.17	.42	.14	.26

longer distances. There does indeed appear to be value placed on neighborhood quality as evidenced by willingness to incur greater commuting expenses in exchange for neighborhood.

Neighborhood quality would also be expected to vary with the size of households. Larger households should derive greater value from any particular level of neighborhood quality for two reasons. First, since neighborhood is by nature a public good, the consumption of which is nonrival, larger households, having more members to "consume" neighborhood quality, would receive greater value from a given quality level. Further, larger households are more likely to have children whose presence makes neighborhood quality more valuable, given parents' preferences to raise children in "good neighborhoods." Offsetting these two influences is the fact that larger households require more housing space, here measured in bedrooms, and therefore might be less willing to "buy" neighborhood than if space were not a factor. Table 5 indicates that larger families do in fact consume more neighborhood quality, although the degree of difference is reduced, and in some cases reversed, when income is taken into account.

Table 4

Neighborhood Quality of Chosen Residence by Workplace for Three- and Four-Person Households with $5000–7000 Income

Workplace Location	Neighborhood Quality				
	1	2	3	4	5
CBD	.147	.240	.160	.227	.227
Rest of Pittsburgh	.225	.226	.139	.215	.198
Inner suburban ring	.084	.178	.246	.235	.257
Outer suburban ring	.198	.208	.241	.252	.100

Table 5
Neighborhood Quality of Chosen Residence by Household Size

Household Size	Neighborhood Quality				
	1	2	3	4	5
One- or two-persons	.12	.16	.16	.22	.33
Three- or four-persons	.08	.13	.17	.25	.38
Five or more persons	.09	.13	.15	.24	.38

A final piece of evidence that the measure of neighborhood quality used in this study behaves as we would expect is given by the variation in neighborhood quality over income classes. This evidence is weakened, however, given the means by which neighborhood is defined. Since better neighborhoods are defined as those whose residents have a higher average income, it would appear tautological to argue that, because those with higher incomes do live in the better neighborhoods, the quality levels are in fact measuring how good a neighborhood is perceived to be. However, the tautology is broken in three ways. First, high average tract income does not mean that all residents will have high income. While there is a greater tendency of those with higher incomes to live in better neighborhoods, the relationship is not exact. Second, neighborhoods were defined based on 1970 census data, while the data on who lived where came from 1967 survey data. While there will be some correlation between tract income in 1970 and that in 1967, the relation is again not precise. Finally, and most importantly, the data on consumption of neighborhood are based on a sample of households that had moved within the preceding five years. Although such individuals would influence tract income, they would generally have only a small influence and their arrival would not be expected to alter neighborhood quality definitions significantly. Thus, while there inherently will be a correlation between income and chosen neighborhood quality, the inherent correlation is not exact. A very high degree of correlation in the observed data would add to the evidence that the neighborhood quality index does measure what is meant by neighborhood quality. As Table 6 shows for three- and four-person households, low-income households are extremely likely to live in low-quality neighborhoods while high-income families live in high-quality neighborhoods. Thus, households behave as we would expect if we were properly measuring neighborhood quality.

Table 6
Neighborhood Quality of Chosen Residence by Income Class for Three- and Four-Person Households

Income Class	Neighborhood Quality				
	1	2	3	4	5
1	.36	.21	.11	.25	.07
2	.16	.25	.19	.26	.15
3	.14	.20	.22	.25	.18
4	.08	.13	.19	.28	.32
5	.01	.06	.11	.23	.59
6	.00	.03	.05	.12	.80

4. ESTIMATION OF THE MODEL

In this section, the model defined in Eq. (9) will be estimated for the choices from among the 50 types of housing by each of the 18 classifications of households. This multinomial logit model (see the Appendix for a complete description) hypothesizes that the logarithm of the odds of choosing one type of housing rather than another is a linear function of the differences between respective attributes defining the two housing types and between the prices and available stocks of the two types of housing. The actual model estimated is

$$
\begin{aligned}
\log(p_i/p_j) = {} & b_1(LLS_i - LLS_j) + b_2(SM_i - SM_j) + b_3(LM_i - LM_j) \\
& + b_4(BR_i - BR_j) + b_5(N1_i - N1_j) + b_6(N2_i - N2_j) \\
& + b_7(N4_i - N4_j) + b_8(N5_i - N5_j) + b_9(GP_i - GP_j) \\
& + b_{10}(ST_i - ST_j),
\end{aligned}
\tag{10}
$$

where i and j are types of housing; LLS_i is a dummy variable with a value of 1 if i is a large lot, single family unit; SM_i is a dummy variable with a value of 1 if i is in a small multifamily structure; LM_i is a dummy variable with a value of 1 if i is in a large multifamily structure; BR_i is an index measuring the number of bedrooms in housing unit i; $N1_i$, $N2_i$, $N4_i$, and $N5_i$ are dummy variables with values of 1 of i is in a neighborhood of quality level 1, 2, 4, or 5, respectively; GP_i is the gross price of i, measured relative to that of a small-lot, single-family unit with fewer than three bedrooms in a middle-quality neighborhood, and given the household's workplace and income; and ST_i is the number of housing units of type i in the sample. Equation (10) is estimated using a maximum likelihood approach in an iterative process. Parameters are estimated separately for each of the 18 household classifications.

Several hypotheses may be offered concerning the values of these parameters. For a given class of households, better neighborhoods should be preferred to poorer neighborhoods. Hence, b_5 and b_6 would be expected to be negative with $b_5 < b_6$, while b_7 and b_8 should be positive with $b_7 < b_8$. Furthermore, the coefficients on low neighborhood quality, b_5 and b_6, should be more negative for higher income households, while b_7 and b_8, the parameters for better quality neighborhoods, should increase with income, as wealthier households should purchase more neighborhood quality. Similarly, since more bedrooms should be preferred to fewer, b_4 should be positive. For a given class of households, b_4 should increase with income, since higher income households would tend to live in larger units. Finally, in order to have a negative own-price elasticity and positive cross-price elasticities, the price coefficient b_9 should be negative.[5]

Table 7 presents the estimated coefficients for Eq. (10) for 16 of the 18 household type–income classifications.[6] The sample size is given for each estimated equation, and asymptotic standard errors appear in parentheses. For households with five or more members, income classes 1 and 6 had no observations in large multifamily units, so that variable had to be dropped from the estimated equation.

The neighborhood quality coefficients generally conform with the hypotheses concerning them. Half of the coefficients on the poorer quality neighborhoods have negative signs and nine others are positive but less than their standard errors. Of the 32 coefficients on better quality neighborhoods, all but 3 had expected positive signs. In addition, within each household type, the coefficients tend to decline with income for the poorer neighborhoods, while they rise with income for the better neighborhoods. The probability of a household's choosing a home in a good neighborhood is slightly higher if the household is larger, although seemingly random variations do occur within the coefficients. Table 8 shows the predicted probabilities of neighborhood quality of the chosen unit, holding all other attributes of the unit constant.

The bedroom coefficients also follow the expected pattern. Table 9 shows the probabilities of given households selecting units with given numbers of bedrooms. Larger households tend to choose units with more bedrooms, controlling for income. For example, for income class

---

[5] Own-price elasticity is $N_{ii} = GP_i b_9 (1 - p_i)$, while the cross-price elasticity is $N_{ij} = -GP_j b_9 p_j$.

[6] For three- and four-person households the estimation technique failed to converge for income classes 1 and 6 owing to small sample size. Regression results are therefore not reported for these two household-type–income combinations.

3, only 2% of small households are predicted to select large units, while 4% of medium sized households and 15% of large households select large residences. Similarly, within a given household type, the probability of selecting a larger unit rises with income. While a low-income, large household will select a large unit only 14% of the time, a middle-income, large household has a 25% probability of choosing the large unit, and a high-income, large household has a probability of .56. Eleven of the bedroom coefficients are significant at the 5% level, and all but one are larger than their standard errors.

The gross price coefficients are all of the proper sign and over half are highly significant, while all but two exceed their standard errors. While there is no consistent pattern in the magnitudes of these coefficients, they tend to be larger in absolute value for households with less income. This suggests that poorer families are more responsive to housing prices, most likely because their incomes require that they be more price conscious. There appears to be little pattern among the price coefficients across different types of households.

There is also little pattern to the coefficients on the different structure types across income classes, although higher income households are slightly more likely to reside in single-family homes than their lower income counterparts. Household size does affect choice of structure type, however. As Table 10 shows, larger households are more likely to reside in single-family structures, and large-lot units are more common among larger households. Smaller households, by contrast, are more likely to be residents of multifamily structures, although only for the lowest income level are they more likely to live in multifamily units rather than in single family houses.

Overall, the model provides a believable picture of residential choice. Small households are predicted to pick small housing units and are more likely to live in multifamily structures, while large households select more bedrooms in single-family houses. Income plays a constant role with higher income being associated with larger units in less dense structures and better quality neighborhoods. Increased housing costs have a dampening effect on the probability of a household's choosing any particular type of housing, with a greater effect for lower income households, but there was no observable pattern in the magnitudes of the price effects across household sizes.

Foremost, however, the model provides some estimates of household demand for neighborhood quality. Neighborhood quality, as measured by the average income of the residents, is an attribute of housing which households do take into account in deciding where to live. Households with higher income tend to purchase better quality neigh-

Table 7
Estimated Coefficients by Income Class and Household Type

Income Class	Observations	LLS	SM	LM	BR	N1	N2	N4	N5	GP	ST
				One- and two-person households, head between 30 and 60 years old							
1	44	.271 (.933)	-.257 (.296)	-.836 (1.28)	-.936 (.536)	1.418 (.744)	1.599 (.644)	.604 (.774)	.298 (1.06)	.605 (.490)	-.004 (.027)
2	174	-.282 (.435)	-.566 (.352)	-1.516 (.674)	-1.092 (.291)	-.353 (.281)	-.246 (.242)	.243 (.295)	.815 (.420)	.779 (.233)	-.038 (.013)
3	238	-.316 (.280)	-.790 (.247)	-.398 (.411)	-.842 (.174)	.048 (.229)	-.096 (.212)	.285 (.235)	.677 (.333)	.967 (.161)	-.023 (.008)
4	353	.242 (.188)	-.639 (.207)	.213 (.319)	-.588 (.131)	-.107 (.217)	.028 (.189)	.716 (.191)	1.024 (.259)	1.097 (.119)	-.025 (.006)
5	232	-.212 (.196)	-.663 (.259)	.387 (.354)	-.373 (.145)	-.791 (.414)	-.186 (.299)	.809 (.253)	1.478 (.317)	.923 (.124)	-.011 (.006)
6	109	.306 (.275)	.906 (.505)	2.645 (.606)	.410 (.218)	-.085 (.815)	-.737 (.791)	.267 (.446)	1.461 (.511)	.989 (.211)	-.010 (.009)
				Three-person households, head between 30 and 60 years old, and all four-person households							
2	151	.820 (.603)	-.906 (.560)	-.707 (1.23)	-.495 (.366)	.393 (.565)	.430 (.497)	1.317 (.566)	1.865 (.864)	1.755 (.431)	-.051 (.021)

3	592	-.118 (.268)	-1.058 (.260)	-1.315 (.583)	-.638 (.154)	.312 (.263)	.250 (.232)	.311 (.263)	.348 (.402)	1.039 (.164)	-.016 (.009)
4	949	.231 (.185)	-.544 (.223)	.231 (.421)	-.245 (.118)	-.232 (.233)	-.354 (.204)	.516 (.188)	.578 (.293)	1.414 (.127)	-.022 (.006)
5	554	.318 (.191)	.368 (.354)	.435 (.656)	.189 (.165)	-.363 (.477)	-.377 (.382)	.795 (.299)	1.472 (.388)	1.399 (.158)	-.012 (.007)

All households with five or more persons

1	18	1.070 (1.21)	.671 (1.07)	—	.170 (.760)	.506 (.942)	-.107 (.911)	.527 (1.01)	.173 (1.57)	.685 (.819)	-.028 (.047)
2	111	.182 (.413)	1.279 (.427)	1.422 (1.07)	.714 (.229)	.462 (.323)	.156 (.296)	-.545 (.439)	-.207 (.549)	.835 (.213)	-.016 (.012)
3	533	.154 (.152)	.579 (.194)	.558 (.773)	.535 (.090)	.512 (.157)	.221 (.139)	.250 (.152)	-.305 (.267)	1.330 (.100)	-.015 (.005)
4	825	.220 (.102)	.891 (.192)	1.005 (.517)	.933 (.081)	.040 (.156)	-.020 (.127)	.175 (.124)	.282 (.200)	1.380 (.081)	-.012 (.004)
5	515	.191 (.111)	.843 (.357)	1.343 (.713)	1.300 (.126)	-.174 (.306)	-.123 (.238)	.638 (.194)	1.367 (.277)	1.324 (.114)	-.009 (.004)
6	177	.659 (.186)	1.425 (.957)	—	1.344 (.374)	.065 (.707)	.203 (.563)	1.096 (.466)	3.121 (.601)	.597 (.302)	-.014 (.007)

Table 8
Predicted Neighborhood Quality Choice by Income Class and Household Type

Income Class	Neighborhood Quality Level				
	1	2	3	4	5
One- and two-person households, head between 30 and 60 years old					
1	.27	.38	.08	.15	.12
2	.59	.12	.11	.09	.09
3	.43	.13	.14	.14	.16
4	.37	.12	.12	.19	.20
5	.06	.09	.12	.25	.48
6	.07	.05	.11	.15	.62
Three-person households, head between 30 and 60 years old, and all four-person households					
1	.92	.02	.03	.03	.00
2	.82	.04	.03	.06	.05
3	.31	.18	.16	.20	.16
4	.28	.10	.16	.25	.21
5	.05	.06	.10	.25	.54
6	.00	.06	.07	.10	.77
All households with five or more persons					
1	.46	.12	.15	.19	.09
2	.32	.22	.21	.11	.14
3	.23	.19	.18	.26	.15
4	.10	.13	.17	.26	.33
5	.03	.06	.09	.22	.60
6	.03	.04	.04	.11	.77

borhoods, even at higher prices. However, evidence was presented to demonstrate that there was a limit to how much households would be willing to pay, particularly in terms of commuting costs, to reside in better neighborhoods. Furthermore, larger households appear to place more importance on neighborhood quality, and are more likely to choose housing in better neighborhoods. Neighborhood quality is thus a superior good which enters the household's utility function. Even though it is difficult to measure with accuracy, its exclusion from housing demand estimations is likely to result in inaccurate predictions of residential location.

Table 9
Predicted Number of Bedrooms Chosen by Income Class and Household Type

Number of Bedrooms	Income Class					
	1	2	3	4	5	6
	One- and two-person households, head between 30 and 60 years old					
0–2	.73	.92	.82	.76	.54	.40
3	.24	.07	.16	.21	.38	.43
4+	.03	.01	.02	.03	.08	.17
	Three-person households, head between 30 and 60 years old, and all four-person households					
0–2	.90	.92	.67	.58	.30	.18
3	.03	.07	.29	.37	.58	.51
4+	.07	.01	.04	.05	.13	.31
	All households with five or more persons					
0–2	.60	.37	.35	.19	.08	.09
3	.26	.40	.50	.57	.53	.35
4+	.14	.22	.15	.25	.39	.56

APPENDIX.   THE LOGIT MODEL

The logit model provides a method of estimating models with discrete dependent variables which avoids the problems of predicted values being outside the permissible range, lack of independence of the error terms, and loss of efficiency which beset linear least squares techniques.[7] This Appendix will briefly describe the theoretical basis of the logit model and how it can be estimated through either generalized least squares or maximum likelihood approaches. Most of the discussion will consider models with only two possible values for the dependent variable, but extension to the polytomous case will be considered briefly.[8]

The basic logit model assumes that the probability of the depend-

[7] For a discussion of these problems, see, for example, Hanushek and Jackson (1977) and Pindyck and Rubinfeld (1976).

[8] Discussions of the basic logit model appear in nearly all recent econometrics textbooks. See, for example, Hanushek and Jackson (1977) and Pindyck and Rubinfeld (1976). Probably the most definitive reference is McFadden (1974).

Table 10

Predicted Structure Type Chosen by Income Class and Household Type

Structure Type	Income Class					
	1	2	3	4	5	6
One- and two-person households, head between 30 and 60 years old						
Small-lot single-family	.31	.63	.59	.59	.50	.35
Large-lot single-family	.16	.03	.07	.12	.19	.27
Small multifamily	.46	.31	.27	.22	.18	.18
Large multifamily	.07	.03	.07	.07	.12	.20
Three-person households, head between 30 and 60 years old, and all four-person households						
Small-lot single-family	.93	.89	.64	.65	.52	.41
Large-lot single-family	.03	.04	.13	.16	.31	.43
Small multifamily	.04	.07	.21	.16	.15	.15
Large multifamily	.00	.00	.02	.03	.02	.02
All households with five or more persons						
Small-lot single-family	.48	.48	.63	.61	.57	.36
Large-lot single-family	.25	.18	.17	.27	.38	.54
Small multifamily	.25	.29	.19	.11	.04	.09
Large multifamily	.03	.05	.01	.01	.01	.01

ent variable (Y) taking on a given value is a function of a vector of independent variables (X) defined by the distribution function:

$$P = \text{probability } (Y = 1) = 1/(1 + e^{-X\beta}), \qquad \text{(A-1)}$$

and consequently,

$$1 - P = \text{probability } (Y = 0) = 1/(1 + e^{X\beta}). \qquad \text{(A-2)}$$

This distribution yields an extremely simple expression for the logarithm of the odds of Y being equal to one (called the logit):

$$L = \log \left(\frac{P}{1 - P}\right) = \log \left(\frac{1}{1 + e^{-X\beta}}\right) - \log \left(\frac{1}{1 + e^{X\beta}}\right) = X\beta, \quad \text{(A-3)}$$

that is, the logit is a linear function of the independent variables. This formulation has three major attractions. First, while the probability function is restricted to the (0, 1) interval, both the logit and the independent variables have unlimited ranges, and no problems of predicted values being out of range can occur. Second, the probabilities are nonlinear functions of the independent variables and automatically incorporate interactions among the X's in that the effect on P of changing any one of the X's depends on the values of all other independent variables. Finally, the logit formulation readily lends itself to statistical estimation, either through least squares or maximum likelihood techniques. It is to this latter issue that we now turn.

A major difficulty with estimating the model described by Eq. (A-3) is the fact that P cannot be observed. Instead we know only whether each sample observation had Y taking on a value of 1 or 0. One solution to this problem involves grouping observations based on values of the independent variables.[9] If the observations in each group are independent, then the fraction of each group for which $Y = 1$ (denoted by $\hat{P}_x$) provides an estimate of P for the group x. $E(\hat{P}_x) = P_x$ and $\text{var}(\hat{P}_x) = P_x(1 - P_x)/N_x$, where N_x is the total number of observations making up group x. Defining $\hat{L}_x = \log[P_x/(1 - P_x)]$, we have

$$\hat{L}_x = X_x\beta + U_x, \qquad \text{where} \quad U_x = \hat{L}_x - L_x. \qquad \text{(A-4)}$$

It can be shown that $E(U_x) = 0$ and $\text{var}(U_x) = 1/[N_x P_x(1 - P_x)]$. The model in Eq. (A-4) is thus heteroskedastic and so must be estimated using generalized least squares (GLS).

While the model can be readily estimated, this approach encounters a variety of problems. First, accurate estimation of the $\hat{P}$s and of the variance matrix of the Us needed to correct for heteroskedasticity requires that each grouping be composed of a large number of observations. Often this will not be the case, particularly when the entire sample is partitioned into many groupings. A second problem is posed by the assumption that each observation in a given grouping had the same probability of having $Y = 1$. If this is not the case, $\hat{P}_x$ does not provide an unbiased estimate of P_x, and the GLS technique will yield biased (as well as inefficient) estimates of the βs. It may well be the case that P_x is not constant within a data grouping, either because not all causal factors are accounted for in partitioning the data into groups or because categorization of the independent variables masks the true relationships. This points up a third difficulty: aggregation into groups results in a loss of information and thus leads to a loss in efficiency of estimation. Thus, while the GLS approach is accurate under the proper circumstances, it may encounter serious problems and should be used with due caution.

The problems involved in grouping data are avoided in a more recently developed maximum likelihood approach.[10] The distribution

[9] For a discussion of the aggregative GLS approach see Theil (1970).

[10] The maximum likelihood approach is presented in McFadden (1974) and Nerlove and Press (1973).

function given by Eqs. (A-1) and (A-2) is again used, but each observation is considered independently. The parameters of the distribution function are chosen so as to maximize the probability of observing the pattern of outcomes of the dependent variable revealed in the data. This probability is given by the product of the probabilities of observing each individual case, or

$$\Lambda = \prod_{t=1}^{T} P_t{}^{Y_t}(1 - P_t)^{1-Y_t}, \qquad \text{where } t \text{ ranges over all observations.} \quad \text{(A-5)}$$

Because it is more tractable mathematically, the logarithm of the likelihood function is maximized:

$$\Lambda^* = \log \Lambda = \sum_{t=1}^{T} Y_t \log P_t + \sum_{t=1}^{T} (1 - Y_t)\log(1 - P_t). \qquad \text{(A-6)}$$

Manipulation of Eq. (A-6) and substitution of the distribution function given by Eq. (A-1) reduces the log-likelihood function to (see Hanushek and Jackson, 1977, for a derivation of the following equation):

$$\Lambda^* = \sum_{t=1}^{T} Y_t X_t \beta - \sum_{t=1}^{T} \log(1 + e^{X_t \beta}). \qquad \text{(A-7)}$$

The maximizing values of β are then found by setting all of the first derivatives of Λ^* with respect to the βs equal to zero, and solving (iteratively, because of the mathematical complexity.) While the approach solves the problems encountered in grouping of data described above, it encounters a problem of its own in that it assumes that the probability distribution is exactly that given by Eq. (A-1), with no variance allowed for individual observations. However, this is minor compared with the difficulties of the GLS approach.

The above analysis of the case of a dichotomous dependent variable can be readily extended to situations in which the dependent variable can take on multiple values. The logit expression of Eq. (A-3) must be replaced by a set of conditional logits denoting the logarithm of the odds of Y taking on one given value rather than another particular value. If the probability of $Y = i$ is given by

$$P_i = \frac{e^{X_i \beta}}{\sum_{j=1}^{N} e^{X_j \beta}} \qquad \text{where } N \text{ is the number of possible values} \quad \text{(A-8)}$$

for Y,[11] then the conditional logit for choices i and j is

$$L_{ij} = \log(P_i/P_j) = (X_i - X_j)\,\beta; \qquad \text{(A-9)}$$

[11] Note that $\Sigma P_i = 1$ so this is a valid probability function.

the log of the conditional odds of the dependent variable taking on one value rather than another is a linear function of the differences between the values of the independent variables. This formulation is amenable to solution by either the grouping GLS method or the maximum likelihood technique described above (see McFadden, 1974). The difficulties outlined for the dichotomous cases also apply when the dependent variable can take on more than two values.

ACKNOWLEDGMENTS

This chapter is based on work done at the National Bureau of Economic Research during the summers of 1974 and 1975 as part of the NBER Urban Simulation Model. The research was funded by a grant from the Department of Housing and Urban Development. The author wishes to acknowledge the assistance of Bill Apgar.

REFERENCES

de Leeuw, F., and Ekanem, N. P. (1971). The demand for housing: A review of the cross-section evidence. *Review of Economics and Statistics* 53(1), 1–10.

Hanushek, E. A., and Jackson, J. E. (1977). *Statistical methods for social scientists.* Academic Press, New York.

McFadden, D. (1974). Conditional logit analysis of qualitative choice behavior. In *Frontiers of econometrics,* P. Zarembka (ed.). Academic Press, New York.

Nerlove, M., and Press, S. J. (1973). *Univariate and multivariate log-linear logistics models.* The Rand Corporation, Santa Monica, California.

Pindyck, R. S., and Rubinfeld, D. L. (1976). *Economic models and economic forcasts.* McGraw-Hill, New York.

Quigley, J. M. (1976). Housing demand in the short run: An analysis of polytomous choice. *Explorations in Economic Research* 3(1), 76–102.

Straszheim, M. R. (1973). Estimation for the demand for urban housing services from household interview data. *Review of Economics and Statistics* 55(1), 1–8.

Theil, H. (1970). On the estimation of relationships involving quantitative variables. *American Journal of Sociology* 76, 103–154.

3

A Probability Model for Analyzing Interneighborhood Mobility

JONATHAN H. MARK
THOMAS P. BOEHM
CHARLES L. LEVEN

1. INTRODUCTION

Studies dealing with intraurban mobility abound in both the economics and sociological literature. In most studies, however, the data that have been utilized has been generated over individuals without regard to their location. Accordingly, the explanatory variables investigated are primarily confined to characteristics of the moving family itself. In virtually every study the neighborhood situation of a household and its effect on the mobility decision have been ignored. Here, however, we draw on an atypical and propitious data source, surveys of 505 households initially living in two neighborhoods which were undergoing a dramatic change in income and racial composition during the period under study. Utilizing this data source, this chapter will incorporate measures of neighborhood characteristics into a conventional mobility framework to observe the nature of the relationships in a more fully specified model. In particular, we examine the effects of the neighborhood situation on the decision to move.

Because we use the existing literature as a base on which to build, we begin with a brief review of the theoretical underpinnings and

THE ECONOMICS OF NEIGHBORHOOD

empirical work associated with conventional mobility studies. Whether we are discussing the seminal works of Rossi (1955), Chevan (1968), or the more recent analyses of such authors as Kain and Quigley (1975) or Fredland (1974), the theory which underlies all the mobility literature, either implicitly or explicitly, can be adequately expressed by the following scenario.

Assume that consumers are traditional utility maximizing households. Utility is yielded by the bundle of housing services H, and a number of other goods represented by the vector X_i,

$$U = U(H, X_i) \qquad i = 1, \ldots, n. \tag{1}$$

The household maximizes utility subject to the budget constraint

$$Y = P_h H + \sum_{i=1}^{n} P_i X_i, \tag{2}$$

where P_h is the price of housing, P_i are the prices of the n other goods, and Y is income. The following resultant conditions must obtain if the individual is maximizing utility:

$$(\partial U / \partial H) - \lambda P_h = 0 \tag{3}$$

$$(\partial U / \partial X_i) - \lambda P_i = 0 \qquad i = 1, \ldots, n \tag{4}$$

$$Y - P_h H - \sum_{i=1}^{n} P_i X_i = 0. \tag{5}$$

The above results imply that in equilibrium,

$$(MU_h / P_h) = (MU_1 / P_1) = \cdots = (MU_n / P_n) \tag{6}$$

must hold, where MU_i is the marginal utility associated with the ith good. It must be kept in mind that we are considering conventional utility maximization in a market in which significant adjustment costs exist, where adjustment costs are defined to include not only the physical transportation of possessions, but also transactions and search costs, and the psychic cost associated with moving away from familiar surroundings.

Over time the household may move from an equilibrium position to one of disequilibrium, even if no actual move takes place. This can occur in one of three basic ways. Either the relative prices of housing and other commodities can change, the characteristics of the goods in the utility function might change, or the utility function itself might shift. We would expect a move to occur if the present discounted sum of the expected losses due to the resulting disequilibrium situation exceeds adjustment costs. Conventional mobility studies concentrate on this last change, primarily as a function of the family's progression through the various stages of its life cycle.

Since the dependent variable is a discrete binary choice (whether to move or not), a linear probability model of some sort is normally estimated regardless of the precise nature of the underlying theory being tested. (For a discussion of logistic analysis, see the discussion by Williams, Chapter 2 of this volume.) The independent variables are chosen to convey information about the family's changing housing needs; normally this includes variables such as the age, marital status, and sex of the household head, as well as changes in the household size, or some measure of crowding. Also, race, the distance to work, and prior tenure are generally included.

This synopsis represents the traditional approach taken in mobility studies. While theoretically some of the more recent contributors have more clearly discussed the causal influences on this decision, their empirical specifications are not significantly different than those of earlier authors.[1]

In none of these studies are the interurban movements which result from changes in the neighborhood characteristics of the housing bundle expressly considered. It could be argued that this obvious underspecification is justified if the observations were taken from a sample that is very dispersed geographically, such as a national sample; this is true in a study like that of Goodman (1974). However, many studies, such as that of Kain and Quigley (1975), are conducted for only one housing market. The obvious advantage of this type of analysis in comparison with one of national scope is that it provides the opportunity to control for the effect which the size and composition of the housing stock might have on the decision to move. On the other hand, when dealing with one market it is obvious that much of the unexplained variance which remains when only families' "life-cycle" characteristics are included in the estimation is due to the differential neighborhood situations of these households. In contrast to earlier works, we have available to use a data base which allows the specification of a number of objective neighborhood characteristics, as well as the inclusion of certain subjective perceptions of the individual's housing bundle.

---

[1] For an in-depth review of the mobility literature see Goodman (1974).

2. DATA BASE

The primary data base for this study was obtained by interviewing 505 households that resided in University City or Walnut Park in 1967. University City, an inner ring suburb of St. Louis, Missouri, had virtually no nonwhites in 1960; the proportion of nonwhites had increased to 20% by 1970. Walnut Park, an area in the northwest corner of the City of St. Louis, experienced even greater transition than had University City. In 1960, it too had virtually no nonwhites, while in 1970 the proportion had reached 30%. Observation suggests that racial transition continued to occur in both areas after 1970.

Several aspects of this data set should be pointed out. First, the interviews were actually conducted in 1973, though they allowed us to determine whether the households had stayed in or moved out of their neighborhoods between 1967 and 1970. Also, the sample of outmover families from each neighborhood is limited to households that stayed within the St. Louis metropolitan area after their move. This sample limitation substantially increases the probability that the observed moves are not made solely or even mainly as a result of changes in job location. Also, if we examine Table 1, which shows the distribution of households by mobility status, race of the head, and original neighborhoods, we see that 95% of the households in our sample are white. However, this figure should not be misinterpreted. In fact, it is quite representative of the populations in these respective areas at the beginning of the 1967–1972 period. In any case, this does imply that any generalizations of our results to mobility in other areas must be qualified.

The interview data contain extensive information on household characteristics, housing unit characteristics, and household attitudes.

Table 1
Sample Composition

	White	Black	Total
University City			
Stayers	102	8	110
Outmovers	160	2	162
Total	262	10	272
Walnut Park			
Stayers	56	9	65
Outmovers	162	6	168
Total	218	15	233
Total	480	25	505

Table 2
Variable Names and Definitions

MOVE	dummy variable for mobility, 1 = outmover, 0 = stayers
RACE	dummy variable for race of the head, 1 = black, 0 = white
SEXHEAD	dummy variable for sex of the head, 1 = male, 0 = female
TENURE	dummy variable for tenure, 1 = owner, 0 = renter
MARITAL	dummy variable for marital status, 1 = married, 0 = otherwise
YINDEX	household income divided by census tract median family income
DVSCHKID	dummy variable for presence of school age children, 1 = present, 0 = not
DVEDCOLL	dummy variable for education of head, 1 = college or more, 0 = other
DVAGE345	dummy variable for age of head, 1 = age between 30 and 60, 0 = other
DVAGE678	dummy variable for age of head, 1 = age between 60 and 90, 0 = other
RMPERJBM	ratio of rooms to number of people in the household
CRIMRATE	FBI indexed crimes per 10,000 population
MEANVAL	mean value of owner-occupied housing units in $1,000's
NWPC	proportion of the population who are nonwhite
DVCONVEN	dummy variable for convenience of getting to work, 1 = inconvenient, 0 = other
DVSATH	dummy variable for satisfaction with housing, 1 = dissatisfied, 0 = other
DVCRIME	dummy variable for rating of crime situation, 1 = poor, 0 = other

Because we believe that housing must be considered a multidimensional bundle of commodities (Little, 1976), the interview items describe not only the housing unit in which the household resides, but also the access, public service, and neighborhood characteristics associated with the housing unit. To supplement the interview data, we employ census data as well as local public service information to describe the neighborhood in which the unit is located. A complete list of the variables used in the analysis is found in Table 2.

It will be noted that the number of neighborhood variables used in the analysis is quite limited, particularly in contrast with those incorporated in an earlier study by Leven and Mark (1977) which analyzed the same primary data base. In that study, principal component analysis was employed because of the high correlations between a number of the neighborhood variables. In this analysis, we have chosen an alternative strategy to handle this multicollinearity. Here, if several variables describing the neighborhood are highly correlated, only one was employed in the analysis. Thus we must acknowledge the fact that the coefficients of such variables as nonwhite population, for example, measure the impact of that variable as well as others correlated with it. In general, this is undesirable in an analysis where the stated goal is the achievement of the best possible specification of the model, while properly handling the estimation of the system's parameters. At the present time, we must simply acknowledge the possibility that specification bias remains due to the inclusion of only a few neighborhood variables.

3. EMPIRICAL RESULTS

As noted earlier, most probability studies emphasize life-cycle variables as determinants of mobility. Accordingly, for comparative purposes, we first present our version of the standard life-equation. Following a discussion of that specification, we add neighborhood variables and present results for a more fully specified equation.

As the results of the conventional specifications are discussed, it must be remembered that our data set is drawn from two neighborhoods undergoing racial and income transition. Because of the nature of our sample, the specific hypothesized signs may differ from those of conventional studies. For example, given the nature of the transition taking place in these two areas, we would expect whites to be more mobile than blacks, and this is what we find—see Eq. (1) of Table 3.

Table 3
Dependent Variable: MOVE

Variable	Units	Eq. (1)	Eq. (2)	Eq. (3)
CONSTANT		.296 (.6)[a]	.377 (1.0)	.081 (.3)
RACE	1,0	−.572 (4.6)	−.695 (5.0)	−.575 (4.6)
SEXHEAD	1,0	.223 (1.7)	.188 (1.5)	.193 (1.6)
TENURE	1,0	−.562 (5.9)	−.563 (5.9)	−.525 (6.1)
MARITAL	1,0	.414 (3.6)	.379 (3.4)	.371 (3.5)
YINDEX		.046 (1.3)	.058 (1.7)	.056 (1.6)
DVSCHKID	1,0	.214 (3.4)	.234 (3.8)	.196 (3.2)
DVEDCOLL	1,0	−.263 (3.9)	−.069 (1.0)	−.045 (.7)
DVAGE345	1,0	−.614 (1.4)	−.635 (1.9)	−.347 (1.4)
DVAGE678	1,0	−.959 (2.2)	−.916 (2.7)	−.634 (2.5)
RMPERJBM	rooms per person	.258 (7.6)	.274 (8.4)	.258 (8.4)
CRIMRATE	per 10,000 population		.0028 (1.4)	.001 (0.6)
MEANVAL	$1000		−.206 (3.4)	−.186 (3.2)
NWPC	%		.0032 (2.0)	.003 (1.6)
DVCONVEN	1,0		.054 (.5)	.090 (.8)
DVSATH	1,0		.310 (3.2)	.273 (3.2)
DVCRIME	1,0			.301 (4.4)

[a] *t*-values in parentheses: $t > 2.326 \rightarrow$ significant at .01 one-tailed test; $t > 1.645 \rightarrow$ significant at .05 one-tailed test; $t > 1.282 \rightarrow$ significant at .10 one-tailed test.

While this result has been found in several other studies, it is not the only result which could be sensibly anticipated. Similarly, in the studies limited to life-cycle variables, married, male-headed households with school age children are relatively immobile. In our sample, however, it is precisely these households that we would expect to be most likely to move. This is caused by a desire to move their children to schools which are less integrated, and perhaps in their minds, schools which are of a higher quality. As Table 3 indicates, this is what occurs with the coefficients of SEXHEAD, MARITAL, and DVSCHKID. On the other hand, households with elderly heads would be less likely to move because older people are perhaps more hesitant to change and because their discounted future stream of benefits derived from such a move would be lower than for other groups. This is often found to be the case in conventional mobility analyses. Our finding that homeowners are less likely to move than are renters is similar to those in the traditional analyses; probably, we conjecture, because of the added transaction costs associated with ownership.

A result for which we have no definite explanation is that for DVEDCOLL. Traditionally, we expect that more highly educated individuals are more able to deal with the psychic costs of movement. Thus, relative to individuals of other education levels, we would expect educated persons to be more likely to move. We do not find this expected result; however, the coefficient we do obtain is insignificant in two of the three specifications. This result may be due to the nature of our data in that the more highly educated households are likely to be associated with Washington University (which borders University City) and thus, they are less likely to move.

In addition to the variables already mentioned, many mobility studies include a variable, such as rooms per person as a measure of disequilibrium in the housing situation, which arises due to changes in the family size thereby necessitating different structural requirements by the household. If the disutility associated with the disequilibrium exceeds the adjustment cost in the market, we would anticipate a move. Thus if family size increases and crowding becomes too great, or if family size decreases and excessive space results, we might anticipate the household's movement. Consequently, in the conventional framework the anticipated sign on this variable is ambiguous. However, in our analysis we find a strongly significant, positive effect for this variable. Once again, we can gain insight into this result by examining the nature of our sample. In our sample, 82% of the households are initially homeowners. Often it is the case that homeowners wish to remain owners after moving. For those who do want to buy again, one of the major considerations is whether sufficient wealth is available to them. This needed wealth will come not only from income but also from the equity embodied in their current dwelling. (This is the reason that current ownership is always so highly correlated with previous ownership in the tenure choice and housing demand models.) With this in mind, we must realize that as transition has taken place in these neighborhoods, housing values may have suffered, or at least households may perceive a decline in values. As a result, a given structure in this area would sell for much less than a comparable unit in another community with a preferred neighborhood environment. This leads to the conclusion that of those owners who wish to make an adjustment, only those who wish to move to a smaller dwelling will have the equity in their current home to allow them to make the desired move. This could account for the significant outmovement that is associated with an increase in RMPERJBM in our model.

Finally, one variable which is unique to our analysis is the income index created to replace the conventional current income variable. In past studies, the postulated effect of income on movement has been an ambiguous one. It is hypothesized that higher income households have a greater ability to move. On the other hand, it is also probable that higher income individuals are more likely to have already moved to a living situation which is desirable. Thus, the net effect of income in a mobility equation is ambiguous. In an attempt to circumvent this problem, we have created a variable that is defined to be the ratio of the individual's personal income to the median income of the census treat in which the initial housing unit is located. We expect that the higher the ratio of personal income a family has relative to its neighbors income, the greater its ability to move and also the greater the potential desire to move. The lower this ratio is, the less would be the desire to move. The positive coefficient suggests that our hypothesis is confirmed, and thus, this variable performed better as a predictor of movement than does the absolute income level which we tried in earlier specifications.

In summary, although we have obtained certain results which are unique to a study of mobility in a transition area, we have established the foundation for our further analysis in the spirit of the traditional specification. Furthermore, from all indications we have predicted mobility as well as do the conventional studies.

We turn now to the examination of a more complete specification of our model, where several neighborhood variables are added to the previous specification. As mentioned earlier, only a limited number of these variables are included because of collinearity among them. At the outset, it should be noted that no public service variables are included in the final specifications. Three variables—expenditure per pupil in the school district, pupil–teacher ratio in the school, and average residential tax rate for the census tract—were tried; however, the results were unsatisfactory. We feel this occurs primarily because of a lack of variation in those variables for the areas under consideration. We do not believe that this implies that public service variables are unimportant, particularly given the implicit concern for them as demonstrated by the increased potential for mobility of households with school age children.

We have chosen four objective census measures and three subjective responses to include in our analysis. The objective variables are the mean value of owner-occupied homes in the census tract, the percentage of people in the tract who are nonwhite, the crime rate, and the median family income for the tract (which enters through YINDEX, discussed earlier). The attitudinal dummy variables indicate if the individual is dissatisfied with the structural dwelling unit, if the individual feels it is inconvenient to get to work, and if the household feels that the crime situation is poor. Each of these variables affects the mobility decision as we would anticipate. We expect that the higher the mean value of owner-occupied housing in a given tract, the better would be the maintenance of structures in the area, and also the better would be the condition of the neighborhood in general. These factors suggest that as mean value increases, so would the desirability of the neighborhood. Thus, the higher the mean value, the lower the probability of movement. If racial prejudice by whites exists in the areas under study, or if individuals have gathered income information by observing the racial mix of their neighborhoods, then we would expect a higher proportion of nonwhites in an area to imply a higher probability of movement.

Another characteristic of the housing bundle that we would expect to affect movement is dissatisfaction with the structure itself. Questions concerning such attitudes were asked of the households in our interviews. Our analysis reveals the anticipated result that people who are dissatisfied with their housing are more likely to move than those who are not. Similarly, we would expect that households that feel that getting to work is inconvenient would be more likely to move than those who do not feel that way. The interview data allow us to test that hypothesis, and it is verified to the extent that the coefficient of DVCONVEN is positive. While it is not significant in this particular specification, in all other specifications tried it is always positive and in many instances it is significant at the 5% level.

The crime rate is also included because it is an important aspect of the neighborhood situation. In our sample, CRIMRATE has only a small amount of variance because data is not available for individual tracts in University City. The estimated coefficients for this variable are of the correct sign; however, they are not significant. An interesting development occurs when a dummy variable is included which indicates whether or not people felt that there was a poor crime situation in their neighborhood. By examining Eq. (3) in Table 3 we observe that while holding our objective measure of crime (CRIMRATE) constant, the household's feelings that crime in the neighborhood is a problem still has a significant impact on the decision to move. If we make the assumption that preferences of movers and stayers concerning crime are similar (this is not an unwarranted assumption, given the findings of Leven and Mark which suggest that preferences are similar), then it implies that movers and stayers as a group perceive the crime situations differently and act accordingly. While we are constrained with respect to any further pursuit of this problem here due to data limitations, it is apparent that an individual's perceptions of other neighborhood characteristics may differ significantly from objective measures of the actual situation. This in turn would lead us to the conclusion that to retard outmovement from an area we need to work not only on improvement of the actual situation, but also to change the information and attitudes people have about that neighborhood. At any rate, we see this as an area where additional work seems warranted.

To this point, there has been no discussion of the magnitudes of the estimated marginal probabilities. For all but three of the variables listed in Table 3, the coefficients are relatively stable across specifications. The coefficient of DVEDCOLL is much smaller in Eqs. (2) and (3); however, it is insignificant in those two regressions. For the two age dummy variables—DVAGE345 and DVAGE678—the coefficient in Eq. (3) is much smaller than the comparable coefficients in Eqs. (1) and (2). We have no explanation for this occurrence, especially since the correlation coefficients between DVCRIME (the only difference in specification between Eqs. (2) and (3)) and the other two variables is less than .05.

The coefficients indicate that, ceteris paribus, the probability that an owner will move (out of our transitional neighborhoods) is approximately .55 less than for a renter. Similarly, a black vis-à-vis a white has approximately a .6 lower probability of moving. All other factors remaining constant, the probability of a moving is between .6 and .95 less for a household headed by an elderly person than for a household headed by someone less than 20. With regard to DVSATH, a similar interpretation suggests that the probability of movement will be .3 higher if there is dissatisfaction with the house, relative to the situation in which the household is satisfied. As a final example of how these coefficients may be interpreted, consider those for MEANVAL. Ceteris paribus, there is a .2 lower probability that a household will move if there is a $1000 increase in the mean value of owner-occupied homes in the neighborhood. This suggests that one key to stabilizing neighborhoods is maintaining at least a floor on property values.

4. CONCLUSION

This chapter has sought to extend the current mobility literature in two significant ways. To begin with, we have provided additional insights as to how certain traditionally specified variables may effect mobility quite differently in transitional areas than they do in general. One clear example of this can be seen if we consider a married individual with school age children. Normally, such a family would be unlikely to move, however in a transitional neighborhood this family becomes the most likely to move. Second, and more important, this study reveals that neighborhood characteristics are a vital component in the proper specification of any model purporting to explain intraurban mobility. If our goal is to understand clearly what motivates this movement and why it appears more volatile in some areas than others, we must analyze this decision in greater depth than most previous mobility studies have seen fit to undertake. This is particularly important because some neighborhood and most public service characteristics can be manipulated by local public officials, and thus are potential objects of policies for neighborhood stabilization.

APPENDIX 1 COMPARABLE
ORDINARY LEAST SQUARES RESULTS

For the purposes of comparing ordinary least squares (OLS) and logit results, we include here Table A.1 which presents the coefficients obtained by estimating the specifications listed in Table 3 using OLS. Further, we present Table A.2, which compares the predicted values of MOVE with the actual values of MOVE.

As expected, when using OLS techniques to estimate this type of equation, some of the predicted values fall outside the 0–1 interval (which is theoretically impossible). For Eq. (1), 12.7% of the total number of observations fall into this category, while the comparable

Table A.1
OLS Regression Results

Variable Constant	Eq. (1) .474	Eq. (2) .459	Eq. (3) .463
RACE	−.396 (5.0)[a]	−.459 (6.0)	−.413 (5.5)
SEXHEAD	.104 (1.3)	.101 (1.3)	.105 (1.4)
TENURE	−.329 (7.0)	−.317 (7.0)	−.322 (7.3)
MARITAL	.315 (4.3)	.300 (4.3)	.282 (4.1)
YINDEX	.028 (1.2)	.044 (2.0)	.048 (2.2)
DVSCHKID	.151 (3.5)	.163 (4.0)	.130 (3.2)
DVEDCOLL	−.185 (4.0)	−.080 (1.8)	−.055 (1.2)
DVAGE345	−.146 (1.3)	−.150 (1.4)	−.118 (1.2)
DVAGE678	−.422 (3.7)	−.378 (3.5)	−.351 (3.3)
RMPERJBM	.160 (9.9)	.176 (11.5)	.165 (10.9)
CRIMRATE		.001 (1.4)	.0006 (.6)
MEANVAL		−.014 (3.4)	−.013 (3.3)
NWPC		.002 (2.2)	.002 (1.7)
DVCONVEN		.043 (.7)	.054 (.8)
DVSATH		.164 (3.5)	.129 (2.8)
DVCRIME			.190 (4.9)
R^2	.382	.463	.488
F-statistic	$F(10,494) = 30.6$	$F(15,489) = 28.1$	$F(16,488) = 29.1$

[a] t-values in parentheses: t-values > 2.326, significant at .01, one-tailed test; t-values > 1.645, significant at .05, one-tailed test; t-values > 1.282, significant at .10 one-tailed test.

figures for Eqs. (2) and (3) are 17.7 and 18.4%, respectively. It is comforting, however, to note that for each of the three equations, a vast majority of the stayers have predicted values less than .5 (65.2, 73.7, 74.9%, respectively) while a vast majority of the movers have predicted values greater than .5 (90.0, 93.0, 93.9%, respectively).

Table A.2
OLS Predicted and Actual Values of MOVE

	Predicted					
Actual	<0	0−.25	.25−.50	.50−.75	.75−1.0	>1.0
Eq. (1)						
Stay (0)	10.3[a]	16.6	38.3	28.6	5.7	.6
Move (1)	.0	.3	9.7	38.2	38.2	13.6
Eq. (2)						
Stay (0)	10.9	22.3	40.6	22.3	2.9	1.1
Move (1)	.0	.3	6.7	32.1	40.3	20.6
Eq. (3)						
Stay (0)	9.1	22.9	42.9	21.1	3.4	.6
Move (1)	.0	.3	5.8	29.7	41.2	23.0

[a] Entries are row percentages.

APPENDIX 2   COMPARISON OF PREDICTED AND ACTUAL VALUES OF *MOVE* FROM LOGISTIC ANALYSIS

As noted in Appendix 1, one of the problems in using OLS to estimate an equation in which there is a dichotomous dependent variable is that the predicted values will fall outside the 0–1 interval. Using logistic analysis remedies this situation, as may be seen by examining Table A.3 which contains a cross tabulation of actual and predicted values of MOVE. There are no observations for which the predicted value of MOVE lies outside the 0–1 interval. Furthermore, it is clear that as the predicted value of MOVE increases, it becomes more and more probable that the actual value of MOVE is one. Alternatively stated, the majority of the stayers have predicted values less than .5, while the majority of the movers have predicted values greater than .5.

Table A.3
Logit Predicted and Actual Values of MOVE

Actual	Predicted					
	<0	0–.25	.25–.50	.50–.75	.75–1.0	>1.0
Eq. (1)						
Stay (0)	.0[a]	41.1	25.1	20.6	13.1	.0
Move (1)	.0	1.5	8.2	22.1	68.2	.0
Eq. (2)						
Stay (0)	.0	57.1	20.6	11.4	10.9	.0
Move (1)	.0	1.5	7.6	12.7	78.2	.0
Eq. (3)						
Stay (0)	.0	59.4	16.0	17.7	6.9	.0
Move (1)	.0	2.1	6.1	14.2	77.6	.0

[a] Entries are row percentages.

REFERENCES

Chevan, A. (1968). Moving in a metropolitan area. Unpublished Ph.D. dissertation, University of Pennsylvania, Philadelphia.

Fredland, D. (1974). *Residential mobility and home purchase.* D. C. Heath and Company, Lexington, Massachusetts.

Goodman, J. (1974). *Local residential mobility and family housing adjustments.* Ph.D. dissertation, University of Michigan, University Microfilms, Ann Arbor.

Kain, J., and Quigley, J. (1975). *Housing markets and racial discrimination: A microeconomic analysis.* National Bureau of Economic Research, New York.

Leven, C., and Mark, J. (1977). Revealed preferences for neighborhood characteristics. *Urban Studies* **14,** pp. 147–159.

Little, J. (1976). Residential preferences, neighborhood filtering and neighborhood change. *Journal of Urban Economics* **3,** 68–81.

Rossi, P. (1955). *Why families move.* Free Press, Glencoe, Illinois.

4

A Quasi-Loglinear Model of
Neighborhood Choice

DAVID SEGAL*

There is no safety in numbers, or in anything else.
—JAMES THURBER, "The Fairly Intelligent Fly,"
in *Fables for Our Time.*

1. INTRODUCTION

This chapter is an effort to learn about the determinants of neighborhood choice, and to see how both chooser and choice attributes, as well as interactions among them, affect this choice. The work is primarily economics in the sense that it concerns utility maximizing households whose neighborhood selection process is constrained by their budgets. The price of a standardized bundle of housing services varies from one neighborhood to the next, as do the levels of neighborhood goods; and households select that neighborhood that maximizes overall utility, subject to their budget constraints.

The analysis is performed on a special census tabulation of 15,483 households that moved into the Wilmington, Delaware, area from outside the Standard Metropolitan Statistical Area (SMSA), between 1965 and 1970. Attention is centered on which neighborhoods were chosen

* A grant from the National Institute of Education helped to support the research.

by the households—neighborhoods are defined as the 11 school districts in the northern part of New Castle County (Wilmington and its close-in suburbs). Neighborhoods are not viewed qua neighborhoods, but as bundles of characteristics; and households moving to them are seen as revealing preferences for these characteristics. The small number of neighborhood types in the study necessarily limits the number and quality of inferences that can be made concerning taste for neighborhood. A much larger study, of 70 Cleveland-area neighborhoods, is currently being conducted by the author.[1] The study reported here is in the nature of a pilot.

The data that are studied are a tabulation of household counts, cross classified by neighborhood of location and category of socioeconomic characteristics. The object of the analysis is to learn how the taste for different neighborhood goods varies across household categories, that is, how the demand for neighborhood goods varies across households.

The empirical technique used here and in the forthcoming Cleveland study is relatively new to economics. It looks at the distribution of households, one stratum at a time, across neighborhoods, where neighborhoods are positioned in a multiway table of neighborhood variables (dimensions of the table are school quality, racial composition, etc.).[2] The multiway table in fact contains two types of variables: *response* variables, one for each category of neighborhood quality, and *explanatory* variables, one for each demographic category (household income, family size, race, etc.). It may actually be thought of as a chain of subtables, in which each subtable consists exclusively of response variables and each link represents a household category.

The tables are incomplete in the sense that only some combinations of neighborhood categories are represented by actual neighborhoods and have counts in them. The household counts for other combinations are structural zeros—neighborhoods that cannot be chosen for logical reasons (i.e., they simply do not exist and hence are unavailable to households in Wilmington). Because the subtables representing each of the different household strata are thus incomplete, a "quasi-loglinear" model must be used to fit them. Of interest to us is not only how well different model specifications fit the data but how the parameters we

---

[1] In addition, Martin Katzman is using similar techniques to study household choice behavior among 44 neighborhoods in the Dallas area.

[2] Two papers using *complete* multiway tables of counts are Li (1977) and Apgar (1977). In addition, a study of business projections, business investment and unemployment in Germany is currently being made by Marc Nerlove and Heinz König.

estimate for such models vary from one household group to the next, across income groups, households of varying size, and so on.

As the estimating technique is discrete multivariate, a reasonable question is whether such an approach is suitable for data that may be continuous. The answer has two parts. First, census data tend to be categorical. Thus all of our household data are categorical, and only the neighborhood variables are not. Even so, the observed levels of neighborhood variables tended to form clusters, so the categorization we performed was not entirely artificial. Second, and more basic, is the greater modeling flexibility and ease of parameter estimation that are afforded by discrete multivariate analysis. When independent variables are continuous in an estimating equation, only slopes and intercepts tend to be reported. (To be sure, various algebraic specifications can be attempted to improve fit, but this too can be artificial.) If instead these variables are categorized, then typically a larger number of parameters may be estimated—ones for each of the levels of the categories as well as any interactions among them that may be important.[3] The possibilities for exposing significant nonlinearities among the variables, inherent in the data set, are thus increased.

The remaining sections of the chapter discuss the economics of neighborhood choice, the estimation technique, the data, and the findings.

2. AN ECONOMIC MODEL OF NEIGHBORHOOD CHOICE

While the empirical section of the chapter considers mainly those households migrating into a metropolitan area from the outside, the model of this section is broadened to cover those already in the area as well. Structurally the choice descision is identical for the two household categories. In the one case neighborhood choice is conditioned on prior location in a neighborhood inside the metropolitan area; in the other it is conditioned on prior location outside the area.

For households already in a city we are interested in two decisions that occur jointly: whether a household will move to a new neighborhood within a metropolitan area, and what neighborhood it will choose

---

[3] It has been found that the use of categorical (instead of continuous) independent variables with as few as four or five levels per category, results in very little loss of information when the underlying variable structure is linear. When it is nonlinear, however, there may be actual gains in information. See Aigner *et al.* (1975).

to live in. If the household chooses not to move, its choice of neighborhood is simplified: It remains in the same neighborhood. But if it decides to move then either it may move to a new location in the same
neighborhood or it may locate in any of the existing alternative neighborhoods. In actual fact a third decision is made jointly with the first
two—which house to occupy. And a fourth choice is open as well,
namely what kind of tenure to opt for.[4] We shall be concerned primarily
with the first two choices and suppress, to a degree, the third and
fourth.

Imagine that a household tries to maximize a utility function that
includes as arguments the quantity of housing services it consumes,
the bundle of neighborhood goods it consumes, and quantities of all
other goods, subject to its budget constraint—the household's income,
the prices of the physical attributes of housing, the prices of neighborhood goods, and the costs of making a move.

If a metropolitan area has J neighborhoods any one of which may
be designated as j, the household will maximize utility by finding the
function

$$\max U(h, q_j, q_z) + \lambda(y - p_j q_j - r_j h - p_z q_z - m), \tag{1}$$

where the first term is the utility function, the second is the budget constraint, and λ is a Lagrangian multiplier; where h may be thought of as a
vector of the physical attributes of housing, q_j is a vector of neighborhood goods; and where y is the household's income (or annualized
wealth), p_j is a vector of prices which price neighborhood goods in
neighborhood j, u_j is similarly a price vector for the physical attributes
of housing in j, p_z is a vector of the prices of all other goods (equiva-
lently, the scalar $p_z q_z$ may be thought of as the sum spent on a composite good), and m are the costs of moving. We assume for convenience
that m is constant for all circumstances in which a move is made, and
zero otherwise.

Suppose now that the households of a city are divided into I distin-
guishable subgroups, according to characteristics such as income, family size, age of the head, and workplace locations, and that all households *within* any given subgroup i are assumed to have identical utility
functions. During estimation we assume that utility functions are
stochastic—that because of error in measurement and/or specification,
households observed to have similar attributes wind up in different

---

[4] Pollakowski (1975) has developed a model in which he focuses on choices two
through four. He believers the tenure choice is the initial one, and that following the
course of a decision tree, a household will select neighborhood and house only after the
tenure question has been resolved.

neighborhoods. Assume further that, because tastes are identical within subgroups, the bundle of physical housing attributes needed by a household h_i (now subscripted to allow for differences among subgroups) is fixed. The utility function as described in Eq. (1) above may thus be rewritten for members of any given population subgroup:

$$U_i(\overline{h}_i, q_j, q_{iz}) + \lambda(\overline{y}_i - p_j q_j - r_j \overline{h}_i - p_z q_{iz} - \overline{m}), \tag{2}$$

where $\overline{h}_i$ and $\overline{m}_i$ are fixed by assumption and $\overline{y}_i$ by definition for all members of a subgroup; q_j is subscripted by neighborhood only, reflecting the public good character of neighborhood goods; r may or may not be subscripted by j (here it is), depending upon whether the prices of structure characteristics are priced in markets that are city-wide or that vary from one submarket (neighborhood) to the next; and $\overline{m}_i$ is allowed to vary among subgroups (it is more expensive for a nuclear family with four dependents to move than for a young bachelor).

We can exploit the assumptions of the fixed $\overline{y}_i, \overline{h}_i,$ and $\overline{m}_i$ in order to simplify the utility function. Because we assume $\overline{h}_i$ will be consumed whichever neighborhood is selected, we may think of the amount of income left over once a neighborhood has been picked as being expended entirely on the composite good, q_{iz}. We may now designate the cost of housing for any given subgroup as $c_{ij} = p_j q_j + r_j \overline{h}_i + \overline{m}_i$, where, as earlier, $\overline{m}_i = 0$ if a move is not made or if, as in the case of new inmigrants, moving costs are sunk in the decision to leave the previous location. c_{ij} is subscripted with a j as well as an i because, for a household belonging to any particular subgroup i, its level depends only upon the neighborhood selected. A household's income is thus totally allocated to housing, at a cost of c_{ij}, and to the composite good, q_{iz}. More spent on one means that less is available for the other.

This in turn means that because q_{iz} and $(\overline{y}_i - c_{ij})$ represent equally well the amount of income left over after housing expenses are deducted, we may replace q_{iz} by c_{ij} in the utility function of a household: $\overline{y}$, a constant, drops out. Thus the relevant household utility function for household i considering neighborhood j may be rewritten as

$$U_{ij} = U_{ij}(q_{1j}, \ldots, q_{Nj}; c_{ij}), \tag{3}$$

where $q_{1j}, \ldots, q_{Nj}$ refer to N different neighborhood goods or attributes in the jth neighborhood, and c_{ij}, the cost of housing in j, is a variable entered negatively into the utility function.

At various points in the chapter, and in Section 5 we discuss hypotheses to be tested about household utility functions. For example, and as just mentioned, we hypothesize that the cost of housing enters negatively into the utility functions of most households, that is that $\partial U_{ij}/\partial c_{ij} < 0$. We shall also be interested in variations in the price elasticity of demand for housing among household subgroups. Primarily, however, we shall look at the manner in which neighborhood effects enter household utility functions, while we control for the price effects. For example, as household incomes increase, to what extent does demand for school quality increase? To what extent does racial mix in a neighborhood influence a household's chances of moving there? Or, conversely, to what degree does a change in the racial balance of a household's own neighborhood affect its chances of staying on? To what specific degree does a change in job location affect the likelihood of neighborhood change? We shall return to these questions in detail.

In the problem of neighborhood choice we can imagine a household currently in the city evaluating the utility function of Eq. (3) for each of the J neighborhoods of a city and selecting the neighborhood that maximizes utility. In the course of this evaluation what is relevant is a set of paired comparisons—the *ratios* of utility to be had from locating in any of the $J - 1$ neighborhoods in which a household does not live to the utility from the neighborhood in which it is currently located. That is, a household currently in neighborhood j evaluates the following ratio of utility functions, for each of $J - 1$ alternatives:

$$\frac{U_{ik}}{U_{ij}} = \frac{U_{ik}(q_{1k}, \ldots, q_{Nk}; c_{ik})}{U_{ij}(q_{1j}, \ldots, q_{Nj}; c_{ij})}, \tag{4}$$

where $j, k \in J$. The household will move to that neighborhood, k, for which this ratio is a maximum, in the event that the ratio exceeds unity for some neighborhoods, k. Otherwise the household will stay put. The household is in equilibrium when it reaches that neighborhood which maximizes utility.

Of course once a household achieves its equilibrium location it may not stay there indefinitely. Neighborhoods change and so do households. According to the Tiebout model, households shop for neighborhoods according to the different bundles of public goods offered in them, selecting the particular bundle (and hence neighborhood) which most accords with their own preferences and budgets. Once in such a neighborhood, for example j in Eq. (4), they may discover that the bundle of neighborhood goods changes. What is relevant is whether the new bundle (after a change), at the price charged for it (local taxes—which may have changed too), leaves a household better or worse off in comparison with every alternative, k. If the household is better off in comparison with its next best alternative it will have experienced a windfall gain as a result of being in j. If it is worse off, however, it may choose (1) to engage in political activity in order to "correct" the level of neighborhood goods (move it closer to its own preferences), (2) to supplement the publicly provided neighborhood goods with private outlays, or (3) to move to a a new neighborhood. In part this has been termed a question of exit, voice, and loyalty (see Hirschman, 1970).

Households change over time too, sometimes causing equilibrium locations to become disequilibrium ones. As a household's income increases or decreases, as it ages, and as its family size or job location changes it will tend to move from one household subgroup to another. Accordingly its tastes for neighborhood goods and bundles of physical housing services will change. A household maximizing utility over time may find that there is no one neighborhood that is a neighborhood for all seasons, even if neighborhood goods remain constant over time or changes in their levels were fully foreseeable. The utility maximizing outcome may involve a sequence of neighborhoods over time.

Ordinarily there will be a good deal of disequilibrium in the distribution of household locations by neighborhood—owing to the presence of moving costs, and to certain institutional quirks in the housing market. As examples of the latter, households with school age children might find it difficult to move during the months from October to May; or a buyer might be slow to take a house the sale of which is a precondition for the existing owner to move to a new neighborhood.

For reasons such as these there may be considerable lagged adjustment in the system and the households from a given subgroup that move to new neighborhoods in any given time period may represent but a fraction of those who will ultimately move. It is worth distinguishing here between our two household categories—those already in the area and those migrating in from the outside. Households in the later category may be thought of as having zero moving costs, m: The costs of moving to a different neighborhood, as noted above, are sunk in the costs of migrating to the metropolitan area in the first place, and such households will have a greater tendency to proceed directly to their optimal locations, subject to the possibility of imperfect information about neighborhoods. Adjustment is assumed to be perfect for these households in any given time period.

By contrast, and for reasons already stated, adjustment is imperfect for households already inside a metropolitan area. Elsewhere we shall speculate on the rate of adjustment at which households moving out of the central city achieve their equilibrium locations. Here we point out that a crude approximation to the adjustment parameter of a lagged adjustment model can be inferred by comparing, for any subgroup, (a) the rates at which households already in the metropolitan area relocate in new neighborhoods during a given time interval; with (b) the rates at which households entering the metropolitan area from the outside approach these same neighborhoods during the same time period. Dividing the former by the latter will suggest the adjustment parameter.

Unfortunately, given the nature of the model we can do no better than "suggest." The reason for this is that whether an adjustment rate such as we are considering here is sustained over time will depend upon a closer examination of the characteristics of households that stay behind versus those that move. We have assumed that households within given socioeconomic strata or subgroups are undifferentiated, but the weakness of this assumption may be particularly evident when we consider mover behavior. Demographers and other students of intrametropolitan mobility speak of the "cumulative inertia" or "house attachment" of households staying behind. They argue that, ceteris paribus, the probability that a household will move away from a given location is a decreasing function of time (see, e.g., Land, 1969; Siegel, 1975). A more elaborate model than that employed here might structure cumulative inertia into a lagged adjustment equation and estimate the adjustment parameter net of this phenomenon.

Let us turn in conclusion to the specific form we shall assume for the utility functions of Eqs. (3) and (4). As suggested earlier, we assume that the tastes for neighborhood for all households of a given stratum are identical. Why, if they are identical, would not all such households locate in the same neighborhood? Here we assume that while tastes may be the same among households, available information varies considerably. And as information figures heavily in determining the mobility and search threshholds of households, locational and relocational activity will tend to be similar in time and space, but not identical, for households in a given socioeconomic category.[5] So the utility functions of Eqs. (3) and (4) are assumed to be stochastic, not deterministic.

We assume the applicability of the loglinear model—that the natural *logarithm* of the expected number of households migrating to any given neighborhood from a fixed stock of households is *linear* in the effects of the arguments of the utility function of Eq. (3), all of which are response variables in our analysis.

[5] For an elaboration of the idea of a stochastic utility function in the area of mobility, see Quigley and Weinberg (1977).

By way of example, suppose that the utility function has but three arguments, that each of these are categorical neighborhood variables, and that the levels of the variables are represented by a, b, and c. The most general form of the loglinear model (Fienberg, 1977, p. 26) states that

$$\log m_{abc} = u + u_{1(a)} + u_{2(b)} + u_{3(c)} + u_{12(ab)} + u_{13(ac)}$$
$$+ u_{23(bc)} + u_{123(abc)}, \tag{5}$$

where m_{abc} is the expected number of households from a fixed total stock choosing a neighborhood whose qualities are represented by the ath level of the first variable, the bth level of the second, and the cth level of the third; u is a general mean effect, whose antilog reports the number of households that could be expected to locate in neighborhood abc in the absence of any attractant or deterrent neighborhood qualities; $u_{1(a)}$, $u_{2(b)}$, and $u_{3(c)}$ are parameters whose values report the main attractant or deterrent effects of each of the three quality variables (they scale e^u up and/or down by the multiplicative factors $e^{u_{1(a)}}$, $e^{u_{2(b)}}$, and $e^{u_{3(c)}}$); $u_{12(ab)}$, $u_{13(ac)}$, and $u_{23(bc)}$ are one-way interaction effects, reporting the effects of interactions between pairs of variables; and $u_{123(abc)}$ is a two-way interaction effect. As in all loglinear models

$$\sum_i u_{1(a)} = \sum_j u_{2(b)} = \sum_k u_{3(c)} = 0,$$

$$\sum_i u_{12(ab)} = \sum_j u_{12(ab)} = \sum_i u_{13(ac)} = \sum_k u_{13(ac)}$$

$$= \sum_j u_{23(bc)} = \sum_k u_{23(bc)} = 0,$$

$$\sum_i u_{123(abc)} = \sum_j u_{123(abc)} = \sum_k u_{123(abc)} = 0.$$

Specific models may set the two-way interaction term and/or one or more of the one-way interaction terms equal to zero.

Households in a given stratum entering a city from the outside maximize utility through a process of paired comparisons of neighborhoods; in picking the chosen neighborhood they reveal a preference for its bundle of qualities over those of all the remaining neighborhoods. Equation (5) informs us as to the results of the paired comparisons; preferences are fully revealed by it.

The analysis is somewhat different for households already in the city. As suggested earlier, households in this category are likely to move to their most preferred locations (if they are not already at them) only if the value of utility gained by a move is at least as large as the value of moving costs. There are two ways in which mover behavior—and the revealed preferences associated with it—can be modeled. First we might assume that disequilibrium households will ultimately tend to distribute themselves across neighborhoods identically to the outsiders. Over any time period, however, adjustment is partial. The adjustment parameter is then equal to the proportion of disequilibrium households who move in the given time period. The loglinear model of Eq. (5) still applies.

An alternative model relates the odds of moving to the preferred neighborhood from a disequilibrium one to the differences in a household's evaluation of utility functions (Eq. (3)) at its current location and at the preferred one. Here a linear logit model is appropriate. Using notation similar to that in Eq. (5), let us designate as m_k the number expected to move to k, the preferred location, and m_j the number expected to stay behind. The odds that a household will move to k given that it is currently in j are m_k/m_j. We can then say that the logit, or log-odds, is linear in the differences of the effects of the neighborhood variables at k over those at j:

$$
\begin{aligned}
\log(m_k/m_j) = {} & [u_{1(a)} - u_{1(a)}] + [u_{2(b)} - u_{2(b)}] + [u_{3(c)} - u_{3(c)}] \\
& + [u_{12(ab)} - u_{12(ab)}] + [u_{13(ac)} - u_{13(ac)}] \\
& + [u_{23(bc)} - u_{23(bc)}] + [u_{123(abc)} - u_{123(abc)}] \\
= {} & w_{1(a)} + w_{2(b)} + w_{3(c)} + w_{12(ab)} + w_{13(ac)} \\
& + w_{23(bc)} + w_{123(abc)}.
\end{aligned}
\tag{6}
$$

The two neighborhoods, whose qualities a household contrasts before deciding whether to move, may or may not share common levels for one or more of the neighborhood variables. If the level of but one of the variables is common to both neighborhoods, the main-effect w-term for that variable will drop out of Eq. (6). If the levels of two variables are shared, then two main-effect terms will drop out, as will the one-way interaction term between the two variables. An elaboration of the technique for transforming the loglinear model into the logit model, with a good exposition of how to interpret the logit model, is to be found in Fienberg (1977, p. 78) and Bishop *et al.* (1975, pp. 22–23). As in the example of the loglinear model of Eq. (5), one or more of the interaction terms may be set equal to zero, depending upon which model is specified.

The empirical analysis in the balance of this chapter applies only to the preferences of recent inmigrants, as described in Eq. (5) and the related text. Subsequent work will consider relocation behavior and what inferences can be made from it concerning demand for neighborhood.

3. ESTIMATION TECHNIQUE

As indicated in the previous sections, our approach is to view neighborhoods as bundles of characteristics and to see how variations in levels of these attributes are viewed by different household groups. Because so few neighborhoods are included in the study, there are insufficient degrees of freedom to examine more than a minimal amount of variation in neighborhood characteristics. The forthcoming Cleveland study addresses this difficulty.

The estimation technique involves applying the loglinear model of Section 2 to a multiway table of household counts. The multiway table is actually a grand table, composed of a set of subtables, one for each stratum. The subtables are identically dimensioned and differ only in the frequencies in their cells. Each of the dimensions of any given subtable is one of the argument variables of the utility function of Eq. (3), and each of the variables in turn is broken down into levels or categories which are used to callibrate the dimensions. Neighborhoods are thus represented as cells in the various subtables and their coordinates are the levels of the neighborhood variables that are used to define them.

Individual neighborhoods may not be entitled to cells of their own. If two or more neighborhoods are identical in the sense that they share levels of the neighborhood variables, they are treated as one: The number of household counts that enters the cell will be the aggregate of the number of households locating in the separate neighborhoods.

Similarly, it does not follow that every cell in a given subtable of counts will be occupied by at least one neighborhood. Rather, the number of theoretically possible cells will typically exceed the number of actual neighborhoods: Not all of the combinations of levels of neighborhood quality exist in real-world cities.

When certain combinations of neighborhood quality have no counterparts in the neighborhoods of a city there will, of course, be no household in the corresponding cells. However, the absence of households is a matter of logic, not of sampling. A special estimating procedure is applied to the analysis of "incomplete" multiway tables, having logical or structural zeros in them. The procedure for estimating incomplete tables is similar to that used for complete tables. An iterative proportional fitting algorithm is used for both in order to obtain goodness-of-fit statistics, maximum likelihood estimates of the counts, and the u-terms. However there are important differences. The procedure for estimating incomplete tables, which is used in Section 4, is described in detail by Fienberg (1977, Ch. 8) and Bishop *et al.* (1975, Ch. 5).

In Section 5 we describe the empirical results from estimating several models. Four variables are assumed to govern neighborhood choice: In addition to the cost of the appropriate bundle of housing, c_{ij}, we assume choice is affected by public school quality, Q; neighborhood racial mix or whiteness, W; and the availability of housing, A.[6]

As reported in Section 5 and Appendix 1, there are four levels each of housing prices and public school quality, three levels of racial mix (percentage white), and two levels of housing availability. A problem arises for us as well as for others who have researched this area in that housing prices and school quality are very highly correlated, making it difficult to separate the two variables so as to study the partial effects of each.

A quick scanning of the price and school quality variables for each of Wilmington's 11 neighborhoods in Appendix 1 shows them to be perfectly correlated across neighborhoods, except in the case of Stanton. Because the attribute bundle for Claymont $\{p_3QA_1W_3\}$ and Stanton $\{p_2Q_3A_1W_3\}$ are identical except for price, the full burden of the impact of price variation on the demand for neighborhood falls on these two neighborhoods. Crude price elasticities of demand for neighborhood may be estimated from the household observations in these cells.

Because the information on Stanton is redundant once the price variations vis à vis Claymont are captured, the Stanton cell is separated from the rest of the table. (The concept of "separability" in an incomplete multiway table is explained by Bishop *et al.* (1975, p. 212).) Once this is done, the table loses a dimension. What is left is a three-way table , $4 \times 2 \times 3$, with 24 theoretically possible cells, 10 of which are represented by (household counts in) real neighborhoods, and 14 of which do not exist.[7] A graphic representation of a typical incomplete

---

[6] Housing price and availability both belong as arguments of the utility function because information on both of them is needed to indicate whether short-run housing prices—the ones households must deal with in a given time period—are at or above long-run equilibrium prices. The former will tend to be the case when housing is abundantly available in a neighborhood. For any given price a household exposes itself to capital loss, and hence is worse off, if availability is also low.

Pollakowski (1975) offers a second explanation as to why $(\partial U/\partial A) < 0$. He argues that lesser availability implies greater search costs.

[7] Whether one is left with the price variable, the school-quality variable, or some combination of the two, once the separation procedure is complete is an important question, without an obvious answer. The signs associated with the different levels of school quality for the parameter estimates reported in Table 2 seem to indicate that the residual variable is dominated by school quality.

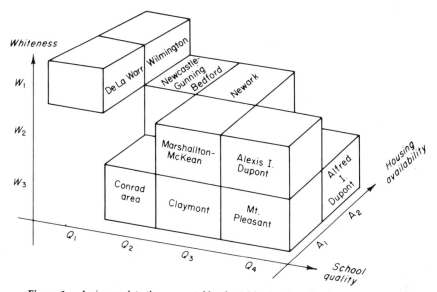

Figure 1. *An incomplete three-way table of neighborhood quality faced by a hypothetical socioeconomic group, Wilmington, Delaware, 1970.*

subtable used in our study of Wilmington is shown in Fig. 1. The grand table contains subtables such as this for households in each of the socioeconomic strata. Subscripts that go from low to high indicate values that do the same (actual values are provided in Appendix 1).[8]

A number of models are possible, specifying interactions (a) among the response variables depicted in Fig. 1 and (b) between them and the explanatory (socioeconomic) variables. As noted in the previous section [Eq. (5) and related text], a model is specified by setting one or more of the interaction terms equal to zero. As all the models are hierarchical, all lesser order interactions are implied whenever a higher order interaction is postulated. This means that in suppressing interactions one must begin with the highest order interaction—setting $u_{123(abc)}$ of Eq. (5) equal to zero—and work through lesser interactions.

Among the models that are tested in Section 5 (see Table 1) are (a) that in which no interactions among the response variables are present and (b) those in which various one-way interactions among them are present. The former postulates independence of the different neighborhood effects. It is referred to as the quasi-independence model, just as

---

[8] As we note in the closing section, whenever a $[QA]$ or $[AW]$ interaction is specified in a model, the three-way table of Fig. 1 separates into a 2×1 "two-way" table (Q, A, W and Q, A_2, W) and a $3 \times 2 \times 2$ "three–way" table (for the remaining neighborhoods). The computation of parameters and statistics for the former table is trivial.

Table 1
Statistics for Various Models Applied to 8155 Households, Age 35–64

A. TERMINOLOGY

Variable	Description	Levels
Response variables		
Q	School quality	4 (see Apendix 1 for details)
A	Housing availability	2 (see Appendix 1)
W	Whiteness	3 (see Appendix 1)
Explanatory variables		
R	Household race	2 (white; nonwhite)
Y	Household income	3 (<$6000; $6000–15,000; >$15,000)
L	Household head's workplace location	2 (work in central city; work in suburbs)
C	Children	2 (no children; some children)

B. MODELS TESTED

Model Number	Model	Degrees of Freedom	G^2
1.	[QRYLC] [ARYLC] [WRYLC]	72	847.7
2.	[QRYLC] [AWRYLC]	48	280.1
3.	[QWRYLC] [ARYLC]	48	627.6
4.	[QARYLC] [WRYLC]	24	155.7
5.	[QARYLC] [QWRYLC]	0	0
6.	[QWRYLC] [AWRYLC]	0	0
7.	[QAYLC] [QWYLC] [R]	119	2655.
8.	[QARLC] [QWRLC] [Y]	79	3457.
9.	[QARYC] [QWRYC] [L]	119	1532.
10.	[QARYL] [QWRYL] [C]	119	1705.

the class of loglinear models that are fit to incomplete tables are known as quasi-loglinear models. One of the models with interaction that better fits the data of Section 5 than the quasi-independence model is that which interacts race and housing availability. The interpretation of the greater explanatory power of the race–availability interaction involves the fact that high availability in the largely black neighborhoods of Wilmington is frequently associated with deteriorated or abandoned units, while in white neighborhoods it often means new housing. The former interaction, W_1A_2, has more of a deterrent effect than would be the case for the net effects of W_1 and A_2 separately. The symmetrically opposite effect applies to W_2A_2 and W_3A_2.

Two levels of analysis are conducted in Section 5. First, we interact a large set of socioeconomic variables with the response variables so as to make inferences about the relative importance of different household attributes. Then we compare, for a given modeling of the response variables, the parameters and statistics on a stratum-by-stratum basis.

4. THE DATA

An empirical application of the model and the discrete multivariate estimation technique of the previous two sections was made to neighborhood choice among 11 Wilmington, Delaware, school districts during the period 1965–1970. The geographic area to which the analysis is applied is shown in Fig. 2. Two districts in the southern part of Newcastle County, Appoquinimink and Smyrna, are not shown on the diagram. They are the only portion of the county not included in the analysis. They were omitted because of a lack of observations.

Just over three-fourths of the Wilmington SMSAs 1970 population of a half million lived in New Castle County, Delaware. The remainder, in suburban Maryland and New Jersey counties, was excluded. Twenty-one percent of the population of New Castle County, about 80,000, lived in the city of Wilmington.

Wilmington is a microcosm of its larger neighboring cities in the industrial Northeast: It has a balance of heavy industry, manufacturing, and service employment comparable to that, say, of Baltimore or Philadelphia. Forty-four percent of the city is black; only 4.5% of the suburban population is black. The wealthy suburbs to the north of the city, where Winterthur, the Dupont estate, is located and many of the Dupont executives live today, compare with those of any of the fashionable suburbs of other mid-Atlantic region cities.

Wilmington was chosen for the study because of the interest the National Institute of Education, funding the research, held in the city's educational system. It was once thought that among school officials in the area there was interest in a school voucher experiment, although events of the more recent past have tended to move the school system away from this possibility. In its early stages the study was aimed at estimating the impact of a voucher experiment on the spatial structure of the city: How much suburbanization might not have occurred had a voucher experiment been in effect during 1965–1970? While this feature of the analysis and empirical work remains very much in tact, the analysis has a wider reach.

The principal data used in the study were especially prepared by the Data User Services Division, Bureau of the Census, as a special tabulation of the 115,000 households in New Castle County. The tabulation emphasized mover behavior—which households moved to new locations within the county during 1965–1970 and which did not. Of primary interest in this chapter was one subset of the data—a set of 15,483 households coming into the Wilmington area from the outside—from other parts of Delaware, or from the rest of the country. Later work will

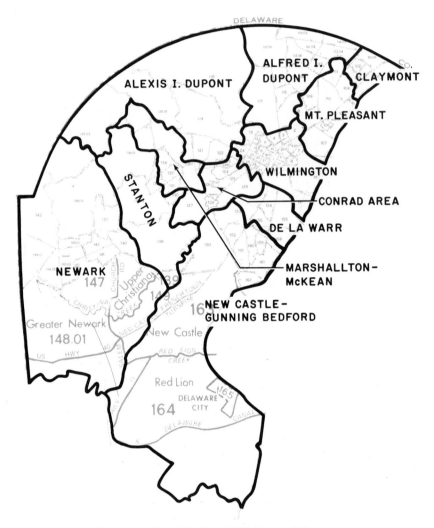

Figure 2. *School districts of Wilmington, Delaware.*

apply the logit model to observations on approximately 28,000 households that were located in Wilmington in 1965, of whom about 7000 had
relocated to suburban school districts by 1970. It would have been
useful to have had data on the interdistrict movement of households in

the suburbs, but this kind of detail is unavailable in census data for all but the largest SMSAs.[9]

The special census tabulation includes a rich variety of detail on the characteristics of moving and staying households. Emphasis was on demographic detail relevant to school district choice—household size and composition, children by type of school enrolled, the age and education of the household head, as well as race, income, workplace (central city, inner suburbs, and beyond).

While about a quarter of New Castle County's 1970 population was Wilmington-based in 1965, an equal fraction came into the county from outside the SMSA. Both data sets are drawn upon in the application of the analysis in the next section. In addition to the demographic detail cited, households are allocated between owners and renters, and school type (public, private, parochial) of their children.

Separate and apart from the special census tabulation, data were gathered on four characteristics for each of the 11 school districts: the costs of housing, the availability of housing, neighborhood racial composition, and school quality.

The technique that was employed to estimate prevailing housing costs in different neighborhoods is described elsewhere.[10] An example of these data—for a middle-income household, of age 35–64, and with 2.3 children—is provided in Appendix 1, where data for the other neighborhood variables are listed as well.

Data on housing availability for the years 1965–1970 in a given school district are the sum of (a) housing units built in the district since 1965 (Table H-2, *Census Tracts,* PHC(1)-234) and (b) the number of households migrating out of each district during 1965–1970. The use of the latter component probably leads to some overstatement of availability as two or more households may move out of the same unit during a 5-year time interval.

Census data were used on the percentage of the household in a school district that are white. Three categories of "whiteness" were distinguished: over 97.5%, 92.5–97.5%, and under 92.5% (the percentage white in the last category is actually about 60).

---

[9] Since the early 1970s the Bureau of the Census has made available information on the distribution of census tracts among school districts in SMSAs. Their correspondence was used here. In instances where a give census tract fell into two or three school districts, data from the tract were prorated among the districts according to the percentage of the tract population which the Census estimated to fall within each district.

[10] The technique followed was similar to that employed by Straszheim (1975). See also Segal (1977).

Two types of public school quality data were provided by the Department of Public Instruction, Dover, Delaware. Because they were highly correlated they were used interchangeably in the study. The measures were (a) the percentage of twelfth-grade students going to college in 1970 and (b) 1970 reading and math test scores for fifth-graders. The latter data were provided with the understanding that they not be reproduced, so only the percentage of college-going data are listed in Appendix 1.

5. THE RESULTS

Before proceeding to the results of the empirical work, a brief comment is in order on model selection—the matter of which interaction terms of Eq. (5) should be constrained to equal zero.

The question of which model best fits the data is addressed by Table 1. For each of the 10 models reported there we condition on the values of the explanatory variables. We do this because we can then use the quasi-loglinear model (a) to assess the effects of the explanatory variables on the individual neighborhood variables and at the same time (b) to determine the interrelationships among the response variables.

The results presented in Table 1 should be considered tentative, given that the study here is a pilot. Because of the small sample of neighborhoods and the confines this places on the study, the chances of a *type 1* error would seem to be high—of rejecting a given model, for example model number 4, when in fact it is true. According to the table, only the fully saturated models, 5 and 6, fit the data well. Among the first four models, the model interacting school quality and housing availablity fits the data less poorly than the others.

That each of our demographic variables belongs in the analysis can be inferred by comparing one of the saturated models, for example model number 5, with the model that emerges with one of the demographic variables omitted—models number 7–10. Income and race clearly have a powerful impact on taste for neighborhood. So do workplace location and family size, although their effect is not quite as strong.

The results improve somewhat when we confine our attention to a subset of the sample fitted by the model of Table 1, that is, to the neighborhood choice behavior of a particular socioeconomic group. We tried this for the stratum of 1932 white, middle-aged, middle-income households with children. We collapsed across the workplace variable and looked just at models testing different combinations of the response variables, setting alternative interaction terms in Eq. (5) to zero.

We could not reject the [QA] [W] model for this data set, and the quasi-independence model—[Q] [A] [W]—was just barely rejected. Because of the simplicity of interpreting the parameters of the latter model we have chosen to present them here. (In any case, the parameters for the main effects closely resemble one another for the two models.) This is done for a variety of strata in Table 2.[11]

Earlier we indicated an estimating problem that arises because of the high degree of correlation between housing prices and school quality in a neighborhood. We outlined a separation procedure for eliminating the neighborhood, Stanton, that stood in the way of perfect correlation of the P and Q variables. Because Stanton and Claymont differ only in regard to housing prices, for purposes of ascertaining price effects we may take as the MLEs of the households moving into the districts the actual counts of the households moving into them. Thus, for any given household type it is possible (a) to estimate average housing prices for the two neighborhoods (following a technique described elsewhere—see footnote 10); and (b) to consider the estimates (counts) of households moving into the districts.

If one is willing to accept certain axioms about revealed preference, then from these four numbers it is possible to estimate the price elasticity of demand for neighborhood. We did this and found the values of these estimates to range from −.54, for those households living in Wilmington in 1965, to −4.01, for those coming in from the outside. Most of the estimates were in the −1.0 to −1.6 interval: A 1% increase in the cost of living in a neighborhood, ceteris paribus, brings about a 1–1.5% decrease in the probability of locating there.

In addition to the data of Table 2, Figs. 3 and 4 provide a graphic representation of data from Table 2 on the impact of family composition

---

[11] The u-terms were estimated using LOGLIN 1.0, developed in 1976 by Donald C. Olivier and Raymond K. Neff, Health Sciences Computing Facility, Harvard School of Public Health. The standard errors were estimated using the nonlinear regression and maximum likelihood estimation subroutine of BMDP3F (1977 revision). The explanation of how to apply nonlinear least squares regression to the problem of estimating parameters and error terms for incomplete tables is found in Jennrich and Moore, (1975).

Table 2
Determinants of Neighborhood Choice, by Stratum, Wilmington, Delaware 1965–1970[a]

Equation Number	Stratum	Number in Sample	Grand Mean Effect	School Quality				Race			Housing Availability		Likelihood Ratio χ^2
				Q_1	Q_2	Q_3	Q_4	W_1	W_2	W_3	A_1	A_2	
(1)	White, middle-aged, middle-income, with children	1932	5.08	-.54 (.13)	-.19 (.0)	.60 (.07)	.13 (.08)	-.11 (.13)	-.13 (.07)	.24 (.08)	-.55 (.03)	.55 (.03)	49.52
(2)	White, middle-aged, middle-income, without children	1533	4.97	-.05 (.0)	-.02 (.04)	.33 (.04)	-.26 (.08)	-.10 (.04)	-.11 (.04)	.21 (.08)	-.52 (.03)	.52 (.03)	124.66
(3)	White, middle-aged, middle-income, work in city	960	4.58	.19 (.16)	-.09 (.10)	-.02 (.0)	-.08 (.10)	-.05 (.15)	-.13 (.08)	.18 (.10)	-.30 (.03)	.30 (.03)	41.82
(4)	White, middle-aged, middle-income, work in suburbs	2203	5.15	-.66 (.09)	-.03 (.04)	.73 (.03)	-.04 (.0)	-.14 (.06)	-.16 (.0)	.30 (.05)	-.68 (.02)	.68 (.02)	111.05
(5)	White, middle-aged, middle-income	3465	5.74	-.30 (.08)	-.12 (.05)	.47 (.0)	-.05 (.03)	-.11 (.08)	-.12 (.04)	.23 (.0)	-.54 (.02)	.54 (.02)	116.66
(6)	White, middle-aged, low-income	1573	4.92	.78 (.16)	-.26 (.0)	.14 (.08)	-.66 (.10)	-.13 (.15)	-.15 (.07)	.28 (.10)	-.62 (.03)	.62 (.03)	155.91
(7)	White, middle-aged, high-income	3105	5.16	-.59 (.0)	-.98 (.05)	.40 (.04)	1.17 (.05)	-.15 (.05)	.12 (.03)	.03 (.05)	-.77 (.02)	.77 (.02)	53.78
(8)	White, young, middle-income	6711	6.32	-.54 (.06)	-.03 (.03)	.72 (.0)	-.16 (.0)	-.12 (.06)	-.16 (.03)	.28 (.03)	-.56 (.01)	.56 (.01)	424.30
(9)	White, elderly, middle-income	160	2.77	.58 (.13)	.03 (.15)	-.51 (.17)	-.10 (.20)	-.04 (.0)	-.12 (.11)	.16 (.22)	-.32 (.08)	.32 (.08)	86.82
(10)	Black, middle-aged, middle-income	469	3.00	2.10 (.09)	-.76 (.18)	.22 (.14)	-1.56 (.0)	-.22 (.0)	-.26 (.12)	.48 (.24)	-.82 (.06)	.82 (.06)	44.77

Estimated Coefficients[b]

[a] There are two degrees of freedom for each of the equations estimated here.
[b] Main effects only (no interactions). Asymptotic standard errors are reported in parentheses.

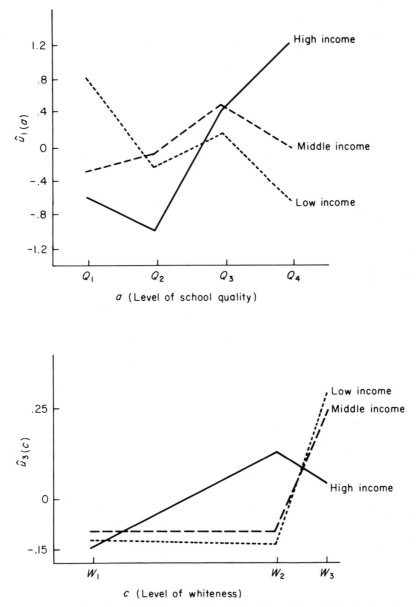

Figure 3. *Role of household income in determining demand for neighborhood quality.*

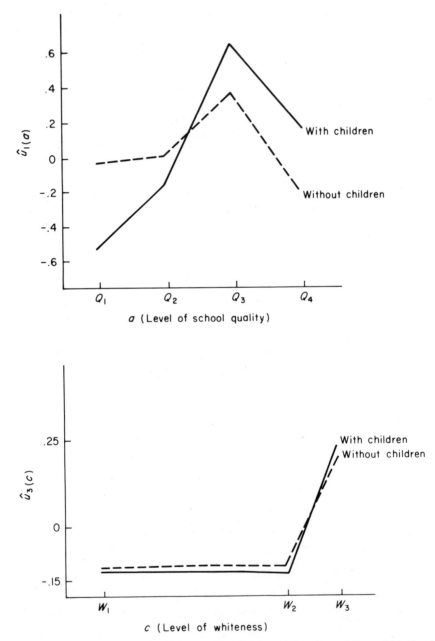

Figure 4. *Role of household composition in determining demand for neighborhood quality.*

and income on log $\hat{m}_{abc}$, the logarithm of the number of households that might be expected to locate in neighborhoods with varying levels of school quality and racial mix. The figures portray "demand functions" for varying levels of neighborhood attributes.

In the balance of the chapter we shall draw upon the data of Table 2 to review the impact of the different demographic and economic variables on the demand for neighborhood quality. We shall comment also on the way in which a school voucher program might impact the demand for neighborhood and on how households trade school quality off against racial mix in neighborhoods.

5.1. Impact of Socioeconomic Variables

The data of Table 2 and Fig. 3 reveal among both lower and upper income groups a somewhat greater taste for the lowest levels of school quality and whiteness apparently because the center-city school district, the City of Wilmington $\{Q_1, A_2, W_1\}$, includes substantial pockets of upper-income white households along with large numbers of lower income households. (Note the "hooks" in the Fig. 3 diagram on school quality, between Q_1 and Q_3, for these two income categories.) This fact should be borne in mind in the discussion below. We rejected the option of omitting the Wilmington neighborhood and its greater heterogeneity of households from the empirical analysis.

As might be expected, the presence of school-age children in white middle-income households sharply increases the demand for quality in the public schools. White middle-income households with children had, however, only a slightly greater demand for neighborhood whiteness than those without.

Again there is little surprise in the fact that households whose heads worked in the suburbs had a sharply lower chance of locating in the centrally located Q_1 and W_1 neighborhoods (Wilmington and De La Warr) than those working in the city. The elderly (heads over 65) seemed to be drawn to these two neighborhoods while young households (heads under 35) were drawn away from them. (The high attraction of Q_3 for young households probably reflects the presence of this attribute in the Newark district, where the University of Delaware is located.)

Middle-income black households, in contrast with poor blacks (not shown), exhibited a preference to locate in neighborhoods with the highest fractions of whites. They disproportionately located in neighborhoods of low school quality.

5.2. *Impact of School Vouchers*

An upper bound effect of school vouchers—free choice of schools and hence only a slight impact of public school quality in a given area—might be reckoned as follows. Consider the number of households that could be expected to migrate into the City of Wilmington under current institutional arrangements: $m_{121} = \exp(u + u_{1(1)} + u_{2(2)} + u_{3(1)})$. With freedom of choice in schooling, $u_{1(1)}$ would be revalued in the direction of zero.

For the households indicated in equation number (1) of Table 2, under current arrangements 145 would migrate into the central district, but in the presence of vouchers as many as 105 additional households might locate there. For households covered by equation number (8), the additional households (under vouchers) could go as high as 360. And when similar calculations are made for all the school districts—the central-city district versus the rest—as many as 1200 to 1500 households might have opted for the central district that instead chose higher quality school districts.

The more important effect of vouchers, as far as urban spatial structure is concerned, would probably be on households already in the city weighing whether to relocate. As noted earlier, this phase of the analysis has yet to be completed.

But indications are that under vouchers the central city's retention power over these households would probably be even greater than the attraction of the city (under vouchers) for those newly arriving.

5.3. *School Quality/Racial Mix Trade-Off*

Crude elasticity estimates can be made on the basis of the u-term estimates of the increase in school quality that, say, a white household with children would require if it were to have the same odds of locating in a neighborhood after the fraction of blacks had increased. The word "crude" is used because normally the elasticity concept is applied to variables that vary continuously, whereas here we are dealing with discrete variables.

Consider the households of Eq. (1) again, and imagine that some of them are located in a neighborhood with the characteristics of $\{Q_1, W_3\}$ for some level of A. If through increased black inmigration the racial composition falls from W_3 (over 97.5% white) to W_2 (92.5–97.5% white), then school quality would have to increase to Q_2 for white households to be kept at the same level of attraction toward the neighborhood as in the status quo ante.

The forthcoming Cleveland study, as noted earlier, extends neighborhood choice behavior to 70 neighborhoods. The fact of a data set more than six times as large as the one employed here offers opportunities for analysis well beyond those of our prototype.

APPENDIX 1. NEIGHBORHOOD QUALITY DATA AND LEVELS FOR ELEVEN WILMINGTON AREA SCHOOL DISTRICTS

| A. Data | 1970 | 1970 | 1965–1970 | 1970 |
School District	College-going (%)	Population that is White (%)	Housing Units Available (%)	Housing Costs[a]
Alexis I. Dupont	71.0	96.7	3.4	$37,150
Alfred I. Dupont	81.3	99.0	5.4	33,531
Claymont	57.9	97.7	10.6	29,755
Conrad Area	37.5	97.6	7.5	23,769
De La Warr	36.4	66.9	2.9	18,459
Marshallton-McKean	54.6	94.3	4.3	29,755
Mount Pleasant	71.4	99.2	7.3	36,361
New Castle-Gunning Bedford	40.5	95.5	8.9	22,125
Newark	50.3	96.8	17.6	29,740
Stanton	50.3	98.3	5.2	25,452
Wilmington	32.6	55.9	26.9	15,801
Weighted average for 11 school districts	52.1	86.8		

B. Neighborhood Quality Levels[b]	
Alexis I. Dupont	$p_4Q_4A_1W_2$
Alfred I. Dupont	$p_4Q_4A_2W_3$
Claymont	$p_3Q_3A_1W_3$
Conrad Area	$p_2Q_2A_1W_3$
De La Warr	$p_1Q_1A_1W_2$
Marshallton–McKean	$p_3Q_3A_1W_2$
Mount Pleasant	$p_4Q_4A_1W_3$
New Castle–Gunning Bedford	$p_2Q_2A_2W_2$
Newark	$p_3Q_3A_2W_2$
Stanton	$p_2Q_3A_1W_3$
Wilmington	$p_1Q_1A_2W_1$

[a] For household with $11,000 annual income, aged 35–64, and with 2.3 children—for details of estimation see reference in footnote 9. The figures include an assumed level of $3000 moving costs for all units except those located in Wilmington.

[b] Symbols are mnemonics for price, school quality, housing availability, and whiteness. Subscripts are levels ranging from low to high based on data in Part A of this Appendix.

REFERENCES

Aigner, D. J., Goldberger, A. S., and Kalton, G. (1975). On the explanatory power of dummy variable regressions. *International Economic Review* **16**, 503–510.

Apgar, W. C., Jr. (1977). Occupational and geographic mobility: A human capital approach. Unpublished manuscript.

Bishop, Y. M., Fienberg, S. E., and Holland, P. W. (1975). *Discrete multivariate analysis.* M.I.T. Press, Cambridge, Massachusetts.

Fienberg, S. E. (1977). The analysis of cross-classified categorical data. M.I.T. Press, Cambridge, Massachusetts.

Hirschman, A. O. (1970). Exit, voice, and loyalty: Response to decline in firms, organizations, and states. Harvard University Press, Cambridge, Massachusetts.

Jennrich, R. I., and Moore, R. H. (1975). Maximum likelihood estimation by means of nonlinear least squares. *Proceedings of the Statistical Computing Section, American Statistical Association.* Pp. 57–65.

Land, K. C. (1969). Duration of residence and prospective migration: Further evidence. Demography **6**, 133–140.

Li, M. M. (1977). A logit model of homeownership. *Econometrica* **45**.

Pollakowski, H. O. (1975). A conditional logit model of residential choice. Paper presented Annual Meeting of the Econometric Society, Dallas, December 28–30.

Quigley, J. M., and Weinberg, D. H. (1977). Intra-urban residential mobility: A review and synthesis. *International Regional Science Review* **2**, 41–66.

Segal, D. (1977). A discrete multivariate model of neighborhood choice. City and Regional Planning Discussion Paper D77-5. Harvard University, Cambridge, Massachusetts.

Siegel, J. (1975). Intrametropolitan migration: A simultaneous model of employment and residential location of white and black households. *Journal of Urban Economics* **2**, 29–47.

Straszheim, M. R. (1975). *An econometric analysis of the urban housing market.* Columbia University Press for the NBER, New York.

5

Neighborhood Choice and
Transportation Services

STEVEN R. LERMAN

1. INTRODUCTION

Transportation planners have long recognized that there exists a complex relationship between urban households' decisions about residential neighborhood and the level of service provided by the transportation system. Households must frequently trade off desired neighborhood attributes, housing prices, and better transportation service in choosing where to live and how to travel, particularly for work trips. These trade-offs may also involve other decisions, such as how many automobiles a household decides to own.

Unfortunately, the analysis tools used in planning practice have generally been large scale, comprehensive urban land use models which have, for the most part, failed to produce either behavioral insights into the nature of households' preferences or, for that matter, useful forecasts to guide investment and planning decisions (Lee, 1973). One of the major reasons for this is that existing models drastically oversimplify the relationship between neighborhood choice and travel choices. In most transportation planning models, preferences for neighborhood characteristics are totally omitted from the description of the residential location process. Furthermore, most models fail to deal adequately with either housing or automobile ownership choices, both of which play an important role in households' neighborhood/transportation trade-off.

This chapter represents some of these more subtle interactions among neighborhood, housing, automobile ownership, and mode to work decisions in a multinomial logit choice model. The model was estimated using data from a subsample of a 1968 Washington, D.C., home interview survey conducted for transportation planning purposes by the Metropolitan Washington Council of Governments. The subsample consists of single worker households who listed their employment as other than unskilled. The model treats the households' residential neighborhood, housing, automobile ownership, and mode to work decisions as jointly determined; workplace choice is assumed to be given in the decision process, although extensions of the modeling approach to include workplace choice are feasible.

Section 2 is a discussion of the issues inherent in applying multinomial logit to choice situations involving spatially distributed alternatives such as neighborhoods. [A derivation and discussion of logit appears in Williams (Chapter 2 of this volume).] In Section 3, the various attributes used in the model are discussed. Section 4 summarizes the choice set available to households. Sections 5 and 6 describe the actual functional form of the model and the estimated parameters.

Sections 7 and 8 explore some of the potential policy implications of the model results. A small, hypothetical city is developed, and the response of a number of representative, or prototypical, households to a range transportation policies is explored. The reader is cautioned that these tests only explore the nature of individuals' demand response to transportation policy; no direct inference about either the aggregate demand response or the changes in the market equilibrium (both long and short term) are possible without integrating the model described herein with other, supply-side models.

Section 9 summarizes the major methodological and empirical conclusions of the study, and details some of the potential areas for future research into neighborhood/transport interactions.

2. CHOICE THEORY AND SPATIAL ALTERNATIVES[1]

Choice theory is based on the assumption that each decision-making unit (in this case, a household) is confronted with a set of fea-

[1] The details of choice theory are explored in other references, including Charles River Associates (1972), McFadden (1974), Domencich and McFadden (1976), and Richards and Ben-Akiva (1975).

sible alternatives, one and only one of which can be selected. Each decision maker is assumed to behave as if he/she evaluated the attributes of
every alternative and selected the one yielding the greatest utility. Since
some of the attributes are unobserved and imperfectly measured, or because there is taste variation, it is impossible for an observer to determine precisely which alternative any decision maker will select. However, with suitable assumptions about the distributions of the unobserved elements or disturbances in the utility function, it is possible to
predict the *probability* with which any alternative will be selected.

These assumptions lead to a class of models termed random utility
models. The utility of any alternative i to individual t, U_{it} is expressed
as follows:

$$U_{it} = V_{it} + \varepsilon_{it},$$

where V_{it} is a systematic, or representative component of utility, and ε_{it}
is an additive random element.

Multinomial logit, the most widely used choice model, is derived
from the assumption that the unobserved, additive disturbances of the
utilities are independent and identically distributed (IID) with the Weibull distribution. The functional form derived from this assumption is
as follows:

$$P(i \in A_t) = \exp(V_{it}) / \sum_{j \in A_t} \exp(V_{jt}),$$

where $P(i \in A_t)$ is the probability that a decision-maker t will select
alternative i from the set of feasible alternatives A_t.

It is generally assumed that V_{it} and V_{jt} are linear in their parameters, permitting relatively easy estimation of the model by maximum
likelihood. Note that the set of available alternatives A_t can vary from
decision maker to decision maker. For example, it was assumed in this
study that locations which are completely racially segregated are for
practical purposes not viewed as feasible options for minority households.

Multinomial logit has been widely applied to the analysis of discrete decision problems such as mode choice; however, there are a
number of particular methodological problems which arise in using
logit when the choice set A_t involves spatially distributed alternatives.
These issues, reviewed in Lerman and Adler (1976), result from the fact
that the choice set for spatial choice problems is typically extremely
large, and it is often impossible to obtain data about the attributes of
every feasible alternative. Moreover, in decisions such as neighbor-

hood choice, it is impossible to define precisely what constitutes the set of relevant alternatives.

The theoretical approach adopted in this study is to consider every feasible housing unit (i.e., all housing units which a household could reasonably afford) as a feasible alternative. Any given group of housing units (e.g., all single family dwellings in a census tract) constitute an aggregation of alternatives, and the utility of the group is simply the maximum of the members of the group. In mathematical terms, if L is some set of alternatives and U_L denotes the utility of the group,

$$U_L = \max_{l \in L}(U_l),$$

where U_l denotes the utility of alternative l and $l \in L$ denotes all members of set L.

Under the assumption that all the U_ls are IID and Weibull distributed it can be shown (Domenich and McFadden, 1975)

$$E[U_L] = \ln \sum_{l \in L} \exp(V_l).$$

Furthermore, when all the observable characteristics of the alternatives within the set L are nearly identical to their mean value V_L, a good, first-order approximation (Lerman, 1975) of $E[U_L]$ is

$$E[U_l] = V_L + \ln N_L,$$

where N_L denotes the number of members in set L.

This result implies that as long as members of groups of alternatives are nearly homogeneous in their observable characteristics, aggregations of alternatives can be used as the set of available alternatives with the average attribute values for the group representing the characteristics of the group. In doing so, however, the natural logarithm of the group must be introduced as an independent variable with its coefficient constrained to unity.

These results make it feasible to use readily available data about the average characteristics of housing units in a group rather than detailed information about each unit. As long as the assumptions of multinomial logit and within-group homogeneity are maintained, the actual choice of which grouping to use is solely one of convenience. The models estimated in this study used census tracts as the aggregation level, with all units of a given type in a tract treated as members of a single group.

Williams (1977), Ben-Akiva and Lerman (1977), and others also explore a model termed "structured," or "nested," logit in which each aggregation of alternatives is treated as having utilities with IID Weibull disturbances, but the "within aggregation" variance of the utilities differs from (and is less than) the variance between aggregates. In these cases, the expected utility of the aggregate can also be approximated, yielding

$$E[U_L] = V_L + \delta \ln N_L,$$

where δ is a positive parameter of the model and less than or equal to one.

In the empirical results reported in Section 4, the estimation results with and without the constraint $\delta = 1$ are reported.

3. MEASURES IN THE MODEL

The attributes which effect the household's choice of a neighborhood/housing/auto ownership and mode to work bundle can be divided into six general categories. These are as follows:

1. *Transportation level of service to work*—travel time (in-vehicle and out-of-vehicle time) cost, comfort, convenience, etc., all for the work trip
2. *Automobile ownership attributes*—taxes, depreciation, registration costs, maintenance, title costs, etc.
3. *Locational attributes*—neighborhood quality, demographic composition, taxes, urban services, parking availability, local insurance rates, etc.
4. *Housing attributes*—age of structure, quality, size of unit, garages, driveways, structure type, etc.
5. *Spatial opportunities*—measures of accessibility to shopping, social, school, personal business, and recreational destinations.
6. *Socioeconomic characteristics*—income, race, household size, number of drivers, number of workers, education, marital status, age of household members, etc.

The first type of variable, *transportation level of service to work*, can be measured for both the transit and car modes. Each potential residential location is characterized by a vector of level of service measures for traveling to the workplace of the employed household member. These values influence the choice of location and the choice of mode directly, but also influence the auto ownership and housing selection through the joint structure of the decision process. For example, if transit to work is quite favorable as compared with the car mode in a given location, the household choosing to live there might have a lower probability of owning many cars and living in a housing unit with a two-car garage.

Most mode choice models have generally focused on the most directly measurable trip attributes: in-vehicle time, out-of-vehicle time, and travel cost. More recently, researchers have attempted to introduce attitudinal measures which can reflect comfort, convenience, etc. Such attitudinal measures may prove to be significant determinants of the locational decision, since, for example, shifts in the amenities associated with transit travel may greatly enhance the attractiveness of locations near transit stations. However, aside from the lack of attitudinal information in the Washington data, current understanding of the appropriate use of attitudinal information in choice modeling would appear to be too poor to make a departure from traditional measures warranted.

In addition to the three transportation level of service measures, a dummy variable that reflects the additional disutility associated with using the car mode to travel to a downtown workplace was introduced. This variable, the significance of which has been empirically verified in previous studies by Cambridge Systematics (1974), presumably measures the effect of the frustration associated with downtown congestion in the central business district (CBD) and the high variance of car travel time associated with downtown oriented trips.

Automobile ownership attributes can be measured by a number of variables. However, most of these measures such as vehicle size, horsepower, age, and fuel consumption are specific to the type of car under consideration, while the choice models to be estimated deal only with the number of autos. Automobile ownership attributes must, therefore, be greatly simplified. For this reason, only the average annual cost of auto ownership (not including location dependent factors such as insurance or tags) was used to represent auto ownership attributes in the model. This value was assumed to be $800 per auto.[2] The benefits which a household derives from owning automobiles are reflected in the structure of the spatial opportunity variables and the set of alternatives open to a household when autos are owned.

A broad range of *locational attributes* have generally been considered to be relevant in household location choice. The factors proposed include urban services, taxes, and the racial composition and quality of the neighborhood surrounding a particular residential site.

Local urban services can be measured in terms of the quality of

[2] This figure is a modification of one used by Lerman and Ben-Akiva (1975) and Burns *et al.* (1975), corrected for insurance costs, which are separated here into a distinct measure.

the entire spectrum of municipal services such as schools, police, firefighting, recreational facilities, sanitation, sewerage, road maintenance, etc. However, one service, the public schools, has been generally viewed as being of particular significance in the evaluation of location decisions. Education accounts for roughly half of all local government expenditures in the United States and is an important indicator of the quality of other services.

For this reason, annual per pupil school expenditure was used in the model.[3] However, in the District of Columbia, many residents use the extensive private school system, particularly upper status residents who can afford the relatively expensive alternative to public schools. This factor was accounted for by not including school expenditures in the utility function for sites in the District of Columbia, and by introducing an extra dummy variable for District of Columbia locations to correct for this.

Urban services are only one aspect of the effect of local government on locational decisions; the other is local taxes. Taxes imposed on real property for home owners by municipalities were included in the model for the owner-occupied single family dwelling alternatives. In addition, state income taxes as a function of household size, marital status, and income were estimated from standard tax formulas.

Other costs which vary across locations (as well as levels of auto ownership), such as automobile insurance tags and personal property taxes, were also used in the model. However, incidental expenses with only a minor location dependent component such as sales taxes were ignored.

Racial composition is of particular significance in the Washington area, where the District of Columbia is predominately black and the surrounding suburbs are predominately white. For this reason, the fraction of nonwhite households in a tract was used in the model. Obviously, this measure is perceived differently by white and nonwhite households, and this difference must be reflected in the structure of the utility functions.

Neighborhood quality is a particularly difficult attribute to measure, since it is a generic term for a complex bundle of attributes and may be perceived in many ways by different households. The measure ultimately selected is the difference between the household's income and the average tract income. One would expect that all else being

[3] Oates (1969) and others have pointed out that expenditures are actually a measure of the input to the production of public services, while households perceive the output, that is, school quality. However, virtually all empirical research into the effect of public school services on residential location preferences has had to rely on this proxy measure.

equal, people would prefer not to live in an area populated primarily with lower income residents. To some extent, they might prefer to live among those with higher incomes. However, at some point one might speculate that a household would rather not live in an area where its income was insufficient to maintain the life style of its neighbors. Experimentation with a number of forms of the income differential measure lead to the conclusion that the desire not to live with those of lower income was quite strong, while the reverse effect was ambiguous and at best quite weak. For this reason, the latter effect was eliminated from the model specification.

The final locational attribute used in the specification is the net residential density of the location. This measure in part represents the general character of the neighborhood in which a particular housing unit is located. In addition, it is a measure of average lot size, which is a housing rather than a locational attribute.

The fourth class of variables, *housing attributes*, is perhaps the most poorly represented group. Aside from a number of dummy variables for housing types and the density measure discussed above, the only housing attribute used was the unit's annual housing cost in its location. For rental housing, this was measured as the annual gross rent, estimated by the U.S. Census. For owner-occupied single-family dwellings, it was assumed that the total annual cost of any unit was 12% of the house's value (Ingram *et al.*, 1972). This cost is exclusive of property taxes described previously as a locational attribute.

Other attributes including the median number of rooms and the fraction of units which are substandard (a proxy for the probability that the particular unit chosen in a census tract is substandard) were included in the model, but yielded statistically insignificant and often counter-intuitive parameter estimates.

The fifth type of variable, *spatial opportunities*, is perhaps the most difficult class of variables to represent and measure. Since they are a composite of all nonwork trips, some way of combining the characteristics of various possible trips with the relative likelihood of the household making those trips must be found. The measures selected are the expected disutility, or generalized cost, associated with the household shopping by both transit and auto. These measures are formulated using a previously estimated mode and destination choice model (Ben-Akiva, 1973) and are described in detail in Lerman and Ben-Akiva (1975). It suffices to state here that they are weighted composite measures of the expected, or average, shopping trip for a given mode, and depend on both the alternative tract being considered and the household's annual income.

Table 1
Summary of Measures Used in the Model

Category	Measures
Transportation level of service to work	In-vehicle, out-of-vehicle time (for car and transit), car operating cost, transit fare, a CBD workplace dummy variable
Automobile ownership attributes	Assumed cost of $800/auto
Locational attributes	Per pupil school expenditures, state income taxes, real and personal property taxes, auto insurance and tag costs, fraction nonwhite, difference between average tract income and household income, net residential density
Housing attributes	Gross rents, housing values
Spatial opportunities	Generalized shopping price by car and transit
Socioeconomic characteristics	Income (after federal income taxes), marital status, household size, number of licensed drivers, presence of school-age children in household, race

Because the choice process being represented is so complex, the number of *socioeconomic characteristics* which must be considered is quite large. Simple consumer theory indicates that income after taxes should influence a household's decision. In addition, a household's stage in its life cycle alters its perception of many of the previously discussed variables. For example, households without children may not care about local school quality, since they do not benefit from it. Large households may have greater need for the space associated with single-family dwellings, while smaller ones might desire apartments. Households with large numbers of licensed drivers may prefer to own more automobiles, though the chances of a worker using one of the cars available to travel to work probably decreases when there are more drivers. As discussed previously, a household's response to the racial composition of a neighborhood depends on its own race. Finally, federal and state income taxes depend on the marital status of the head of the household.

Each of the measures discussed above are used in the specification of the utility functions defined in the following section. Table 1 presents a summary of the measures used by category.

4. DEFINITION OF CHOICE SET

Location, housing, automobile ownership, and mode of travel to work can be almost infinitely subdivided. Alternative locations can be taken to be cities, towns, census tracts, blocks, zones, or any other geographical unit. Alternatively, location can be defined simply in terms of distance from the CBD or whether a site is in the central city, urban ring, suburbia, or rural fringe. Housing can be defined along a broad spectrum of dimensions, including age of structure, lot size, architectural style, number of rooms of various types, garage space, quality and condition of unit, and type of tenure. Automobile ownership can consist of the number of autos as well as their make, age, gas mileage, horsepower, or operating cost. Finally, mode to work can be roughly classified as transit or car, or further described as bus, trolley, rail rapid transit, taxi, shared ride, paid car pool, or drive alone.

Clearly, at some level of detail the number of possible alternatives one could create is enormous. Even if suitable data were available, a model developed with such detailed alternatives would be almost impossible to estimate and apply. Some level of abstraction in defining alternatives is clearly indicated.

In the case of the location, the problem of reducing the number of alternatives can be resolved by use of aggregates of alternatives that are nearly homogeneous. As discussed previously, census tracts were used in this study.

The dimensions of housing alternatives used in this study are structure type and tenure. Four feasible choices: owner-occupied single-family house, rented single-family house, rented walk-up or garden style apartment, and high-rise dwelling were used. This choice was determined primarily by the data available from the home interview survey. For the purpose of transportation planning, where the primary focus is on the spatial aspect of neighborhood choice rather than housing, this choice set should prove adequate. However, the use of only structure type and tenure does restrict the applicability of this study to the analysis of housing policies, where issues of structure size and quality are very relevant.

The only aspect of auto ownership considered in this study was the number of autos a household selects. Transportation planners are primarily interested in how people will alter their travel behavior in response to various policies. This response is in many cases determined more by (among other factors) the number of automobiles owned by the household than the types of autos owned.[4] Thus, for the behavioral questions this study is intended to address a consideration of the number of autos should be sufficient.

The final choice dimension, mode of travel, was restricted to two

---

[4] An exception to this is when pollution control or energy reduction strategies are being evaluated. In this case the mix of cars as well as their number is critical.

modes of vehicular travel, car and transit. These two modes together constitute 93% of all work trips in the study city, Washington, D.C. (This figure does not include some very short work trips.) Thus, using only car and transit captures the choices of a vast majority of the population. In order to further limit the scope of the empirical study, only driving alone and transit modes were considered. All forms of ride sharing, representing approximately 18% of all car work trips in the Washington data, were eliminated.

Not all possible residential neighborhood–housing–auto ownership–mode to work combinations are necessarily feasible alternatives. For example, some locations are not served by transit, and consequently for households residing there using a car to get to work is essential. Similarly, some tracts have a limited range of housing options due to either zoning ordinances or market forces. Furthermore, certain households may not have some choice bundles open to them. Households without drivers do not generally own automobiles, and low-income households can only afford a limited subset of all feasible bundles. In addition to restrictions such as these, the tracts available to any particular household were limited to the set of tracts actually selected by workers (in the sample used) in the household worker's employment zone.[5]

5. SPECIFICATION OF THE UTILITY FUNCTION

Given the measures discussed in the previous section there are a virtually limitless number of possible utility function specifications which might be explored. In addition there are an extremely large number of possible neighborhood–housing–auto ownership–mode to work combinations. Thus, the number of utility functions is correspondingly great. Rather than consider each utility function individually, every variable will be defined as pertaining to *all* alternatives but as taking zero value for those utilities where it is not included. Table 2 summarizes the independent variables used in the model.[6]

---

[5] McFadden (1977) demonstrates that this procedure yields consistent parameter estimates as long as the number of observations with a common workplace is large. Some models were also estimated on smaller sets of location alternatives by randomly drawing subsets of tracts.

[6] A detailed discussion of these variables is given in Lerman (1975) and is not repeated here. Many of the nonlinear independent variables were defined from extensive empirical tests, including piecewise linearization. Other variables were specified using functional forms from previous empirical research by the author and others.

Table 2
Definition of Variables

Variable	Definition
1—DRENT1 =	1 in the rent single-family dwelling alternatives 0 otherwise
2—DRENTG =	1 in the rent garden style or walk-up apartment alternatives 0 otherwise
3—DRENTH =	1 in the rent high-rise apartment alternatives 0 otherwise
4—DAO1 =	1 in one-auto alternatives 0 otherwise
5—DAO2 =	1 in the two- or more auto alternatives 0 otherwise
6—DCAR =	1 in the car to work alternatives 0 otherwise
7—DAPTSTYL =	1 in the rent garden style, walk-up, or high-rise apartment and own less than two autos alternatives 0 otherwise
8—DSUBSTYL =	1 in the own single-family dwelling and own two or more autos alternatives 0 otherwise
9—TOTIME =	{ total two-way travel time (in minutes)
10—OVTT/DIST =	$\dfrac{\text{two-way out-of-vehicle time (in minutes)}}{\text{two-way travel distance (in miles)}}$
11—DCITY =	1 for households with downtown workplaces in the car to work alternatives 0 otherwise
12—ln Z =	{ natural logarithm of remaining income
13—AALD =	$\dfrac{\text{number of autos in alternative}}{\text{number of licensed drivers in the household}}$ in the car to work alternatives 0 otherwise
14—ILD =	0 for zero auto alternatives 1/number of licensed drivers in the one auto alternatives 2/number of licensed drivers in the two alternatives
15—GPTINV =	{ 1/generalized shopping price by transit
16—R1 =	$\dfrac{\text{expected generalized car cost for shopping}}{\text{expected generalized transit cost for shopping}}$ in the one auto alternative 0 otherwise
17—R2 =	{ same as R1 but for two auto alternatives
18—HHSIZE1 =	household size in single family dwelling alternatives (own or rent) 0 otherwise
19—INCDIFF =	squared income differential when household income exceeds average tract income 0 otherwise
20—FBFORW =	fraction nonwhite households in tract for whites 0 for nonwhites

(continued)

Table 2 (*continued*)

Variable	Definition
21—FBFORB	$= \begin{cases} \text{fraction of nonwhite households in tract for nonwhites} \\ 0 \quad \text{for whites} \end{cases}$
22—DENSITY	$= \{$ net residential density (households per acre)
23—SCHOOL	$= \begin{cases} \text{per pupil school expenditure for households with children (in} \\ \quad \text{dollars per year), except in District of Columbia} \\ 0 \quad \text{in District of Columbia} \end{cases}$
24—DOC	$= \begin{cases} 1 \quad \text{in District of Columbia} \\ 0 \quad \text{otherwise} \end{cases}$
25—$\ln N_L$	$= \begin{cases} \text{natural logarithm of the number of dwelling units in the group of} \\ \quad \text{alternatives} \end{cases}$

The first group of eight variables are constant terms in the utility function. These constants measure the so-called "pure alternative" effects, that is, the net effect of all attributes of an alternative which are not measured by the other variables.

In order to limit the number of constant terms to something less than 19, (the number of possible options aside from location minus one used as a base), some way of approximating each independent effect by a linear combination of a smaller number must be found. While Nerlove and Press (1973) explore a technique which uses pairwise associations among alternatives to test for relationships among the options, a much simpler approach was adopted here. Each choice group was given a constant term for all its members but one, and some of the interactions among choice groups that an exploratory data analysis indicated as being significant were assigned constants.

The next two variables represent the travel time aspects of the level of service to work. In mode choice studies, these variables have been expressed as simply the in-vehicle and out-of-vehicle time. More recent work by Koppelman (1975) and Cambridge Systematics (1974) has indicated that the disutility of out-of-vehicle time may be perceived as a function of the total trip length, which can be measured by travel distance. In addition to these variables, a dummy variable was defined to reflect the added disutility associated with the use of a car in the downtown area.

The 12th variable was developed because there are a large number of monetary measures in the model, including household income, federal, state, and local taxes, housing costs, auto ownership costs, and out-of-pocket travel costs for the work trip. For pragmatic reasons of statistical efficiency, one would like to avoid introducing a separate variable for each of these cost factors. The question is how can these attributes be combined into a single variable representing the money which would be available to the household if it selected each alternative. This was done by formulating a composite variable, termed for reference the Z variable.

In words, the value of Z (in dollars per year) for any particular choice is an estimate of the amount of money a household has left after the following expenses:

1. Federal taxes
2. State taxes
3. Property taxes (if applicable)
4. Housing costs
5. Direct auto ownership costs
6. Auto insurance, tags, and taxes
7. Commuting cost to work (250 annual work trips assumed).

The natural logarithm of the Z variable was used (and subsequently confirmed in piecewise linear model forms) to reflect decreasing marginal utility with increasing income.

The next variable AALD commonly appears in simple mode choice models in which auto ownership is assumed fixed, and represents the level of automobile availability which *would be obtained* if the household chose a given alternative. It is defined as specific to the car utility and a positive coefficient is expected.

Variable 14 was designed to reflect another effect of the number of licensed drivers within a household. While the number of licensed drivers impacts on choice of mode to work through the AALD variable, it also should affect the level of auto ownership directly. The more licensed drivers in the household, the more likely it should be to select a high auto ownership level, independent of the mode to work used.

As specified in Table 2, ILD is equivalent to the introduction of the inverse of the number of licensed drivers as two distinct variables made specific to auto ownership levels of 1 and 2. Tests by Lerman and Ben-Akiva (1975) with this variable indicated that the ratio of the coefficients of these two variables was insignificantly different from 2; the variable ILD reflects that result, and is equivalent to estimating both coefficients with a linear constraint.

Spatial opportunities influence the mobility decision in at least two ways. First, the absolute level of accessibility to shopping by either car or transit is probably important in many households' choice of location. This effect is represented by the variable GPTINV. (GPTINV is zero when transit is completely unavailable since transit generalized price in such areas is for practical purposes infinite.) Attempts to use a corresponding variable for the absolute level of car accessibility produced statistically insignificant coefficient estimates with an unexpected sign. This problem also occurred in a study by Wheaton (1974). He attributes the result to the high levels of externalities (noise, traffic congestion, etc.) often associated with locations with good highway accessibility.

The effect of the relative accessibility was measured by the ratio of car and transit shopping generalized costs. However, this variable does not change value for different ownership alternatives, and therefore was introduced into the utility function as two alternative specific variables.

The variable HHSIZE1 reflects the effect of household size on the desire for living in a single-family dwelling.

The next group of six variables are all locational attributes as described in the preceding section.

The first of these variables, INCDIFF, is as discussed in Section 4. The income differential is squared, reflecting the hypothesis that large differences are proportionally much more important than small ones. This was later tested in piecewise linear forms.

The two racial composition variables reflect the hypothesis that whites and nonwhites perceive the racial composition of a neighborhood quite differently. The coefficient estimates of FBFORW and FBFORB should be negative and positive, respectively.

The density variable is self-explanatory; a negative coefficient would be expected. The DOC dummy variable was defined to correct for the setting of the annual per pupil school expenditure variable to zero in the SCHOOL variable, the coefficient of which should have a positive sign. Note that SCHOOL is defined to be zero for households without children even though DOC is not defined this way. This was done to explore the possibility that the District of Columbia has certain attributes which make it distinct from other locations regardless of whether or not a household has children.

The final variable $\ln N_L$ is the measure of tract size required to correct for the fact that each census tract is, as discussed in Section 2, actually a *group* of housing units.

In order to derive the structure of the utility function for any particular neighborhood/housing/auto ownership/mode to work combination from Table 2, the variables which are set to zero for that alternative can be omitted. For example, if the 25 variables in Table 2 are assigned corresponding parameters denoted as $\beta_1, \beta_2, \ldots, \beta_{25}$, the joint utility of living inside the District in a rented walk-up appartment, owning one auto and using it to commute is as follows: U (live in District of Columbia, rent walk-up apartment, one auto, car to work) $= \beta_2 + \beta_4 + \beta_6 + \beta_7 + \beta_9$ TOTIME $+ \beta_{10}$ OVTT/DIST $+ \beta_{10}$ ln $Z + \beta_{13}$ AALD $+ \beta_{14}$ ILD $+ \beta_{15}$ GPTINV $+ \beta_{16}$ R1 $+ \beta_{19}$ INCDIFF $+ \beta_{20}$ FBFORW $+ \beta_{21}$ FBFORB $+ \beta_{22}$ DENSITY $+ \beta_{24} + \beta_{25}$ ln N_L.

6. ESTIMATION RESULTS

As discussed previously, two different model forms were estimated. The first allowed the coefficient of the variable representing the
size of the group of location and housing alternatives, ln N_L, to attain its
maximum likelihood value. These estimates are the first column of figures in Table 3. The second set of estimates in this table are based on
the constraint that the coefficient of the tract size variable is unity.

For each model, the estimated asymptotic standard errors are given
in parentheses below their corresponding parameter estimates. In addition, six summary statistics are given, defined as follows:

1. $L^*(0)$—the value of the log likelihood function when all param-
    eters are zero (i.e., when every alternative has the same proba-
    bility)
2. $L^*(\hat{\beta})$—the value of the log likelihood function evaluated at its
    maximum
3. χ^2—a statistic equal to $-2(L^*(0) - L^*(\hat{\beta}))$, asymptotically dis-
    tributed as chi square with the number of degrees of freedom
    equal to the number of parameters estimated; this statistic pro-
    vides a test against the null hypothesis that all parameters are
    zero
4. NOBS—the number of households in the sample
5. NCASES—the number of available alternatives (in excess of
    one per household) used in the estimation
6. Percent right—the percentage of households for which the
    alternative with the highest systematic component of utility
    was actually selected. (This value is maximized in Manski's
    (1974) maximum score estimation technique.)

All of the coefficient estimates in both the unconstrained and constrained models for variables about which hypotheses were formulated
have the expected sign. However, the statistical significance of some
coefficients is quite marginal, particularly for the estimate for
OVTT/DIST. This probably results from the very small sample used,
since mode choice models with larger samples of the Washington data
result in estimates significantly different from zero at high levels of
confidence.

Table 3
Parameter Estimates

No.	Variable	Unconstrained Estimates	Constrained Estimates
1	DRENT1	−.361	0.393
		(.350)	(.333)
2	DRENTG	2.31	2.93
		(.805)	(.818)
3	DRENTH	.828	.809
		(.812)	(.831)
4	DAO1	7.86	7.98
		(3.06)	(3.07)
5	DAO2	12.0	12.1
		(4.43)	(4.35)
6	DCAR	.433	.483
		(.866)	(.964)
7	DAPTSTYL	.542	.524
		(.561)	(.565)
8	DSUBSTYL	.336	.261
		(.440)	(.442)
9	TOTIME	−.00831	−.00818
		(.00390)	(.00399)
10	OVTT/DIST	−.0570	−.0526
		(.0724)	(.0743)
11	DCITY	−.437	−.415
		(.469)	(.472)
12	ln Z	1.07	1.20
		(.405)	(.427)
13	AALD	.964	.975
		(.954)	(.956)
14	ILD	−6.57	−6.56
		(3.03)	(3.04)
15	GPTINV	2.92	3.14
		(2.12)	(2.14)
16	R1	−1.35	−1.54
		(1.25)	(1.27)
17	R2	−4.05	−4.11
		(1.35)	(1.36)
18	HHSIZE1	.850	.875
		(.163)	(.170)
19	INCDIFF	−.0123	−.0121
		(.00426)	(.00432)
20	FBFORW	−2.18	−2.21
		(.575)	(.585)
21	FBFORB	1.95	1.85
		(.874)	(.873)
22	DENSITY	−.00557	−.00810
		(.00446)	(.00463)

(*continued*)

Table 3   *(continued)*

No.	Variable	Unconstrained Estimates	Constrained Estimates
23	SCHOOL	.000442	.000342
		(.000645)	(.000654)
24	DOC	−.00993	−.100
		(.00482)	(.490)
25	$\ln N_L$	.492	1
		(.0937)	__[a]
	$L^*(0)$	−824.4	−824.4
	$L^*(\beta)$	−645.9	−658.4
	χ^2	357.0	332.0
	NOBS	177	177
	NCASES	25601	25601
	percent right	8.5%	10.2%

[a] Constraint imposed, hence *t* statistic not relevant.

The constrained estimates are quite similar to the unconstrained ones, with the exception of the coefficient of DRENT1. This suggests the possibility of some measurement error in the number of rented single-family units in a tract. Note that the unconstrained estimate for the parameter of $\ln N_L$ is .492 and that this is statistically different from unity. This strongly indicates that dwelling units in neighborhoods (or as used here, tracts) share some common, unobserved attributes that make the unobserved component of their utilities correlated.

7. PROTOTYPICAL HOUSEHOLD ANALYSIS: THE BASE CASE

The complexity with which the measures described in the previous section interact make a straightforward presentation of the model's implications exceedingly difficult. The form of the utility function for any particular location–housing–automobile ownership–mode to work bundle includes variables that change their value over some of these choices and are constant across others. For example, transportation level of service to work variables are different for the transit and car modes and change value across feasible residential location; however, they are invariant for different housing types and auto ownership levels.

The approach to exploring the implications of the model results adopted in this section is to construct a hypothetical city and examine

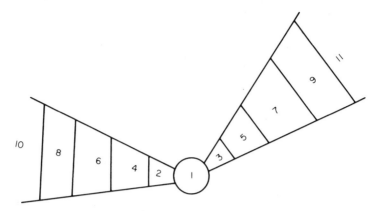

Figure 1. *Zone system for hypothetical city.*

the predicted choice probabilities for a range of "prototypical" households. This method of analysis serves two purposes; it allows for an
intuitive presentation of the behavioral content of the models and provides a preliminary mechanism for predicting the potential impact of
a variety of transportation policies.

   This approach has the unfortunate disadvantage that many of the
conclusions may be highly specific to the particular hypothetical city
constructed. For this reason, an attempt was made to create a simplified
city which has many of the attributes that are typical of older eastern
cities. Much of the hypothetical data was actually selected from the
Washington, D.C., base year data used in the model estimation. However, the reader is cautioned that many of the results may not be
directly extendable to very different circumstances.

   The hypothetical city is a simple two-corridor, eleven-zone city as
depicted in Fig. 1. The central business district (CBD), zone 1, is assumed to be both an employment and residential site. The remaining 10
zones are structured in rings around the core. The rings are symmetric,
and the distances from the zone centroids to the CBD are as follows:

Zone	Distance to CBD (miles)
1	2
2,3	4
4,5	7
6,7	12
8,9	15
10,11	25

The demographic characteristics of these zones are given in Table 4. For simplicity, the shopping generalized prices were assumed to be fixed for a zone rather than a function of the household income as in the model, and it is therefore listed as a zonal attribute. The notation NA appears where the information is not applicable either because the alternative to which it applies is unavailable or, in the case of school expenditures, where the data was simply not needed.[7]

Each zone has attributes which are typical for different areas of existing United States cities. For example, zone 2 might be termed a ghetto, that is, a largely nonwhite residential area characterized by multifamily dwellings and low income. Zone 8 is an outer suburb with predominantly expensive owner-occupied single-family homes, high average income, and is almost entirely white. The fringe zones, 10 and 11, consist entirely of low-density owner-occupied dwellings.

The transportation services in the hypothetical city are provided by conventional highway and bus systems similar to those in Washington in 1968. The highway network is identical in the two corridors, while the transit system is slightly better in the outer areas of the even zones than in their odd counterparts. Transit is assured to be unavailable in zones 9–11.

In the base case, three household parameters were varied: income, race, and driver's license status. All the prototypical households used consist of a CBD worker, a spouse and two school-age children, neither of whom are old enough to have a license. Households without licenses are basically captives to the transit system; zones without transit service are unavailable to them. All the other rules used to define the set of available alternatives in the model estimation were also invoked in the forecasting process.

Five basic impacts will be used to summarize the complete matrix of forecasted choice probabilities. These are as follows:

1. Average distance to the CBD—one way in miles
2. Housing type distribution-marginal choice probabilities for all four housing types
3. Expected auto ownership
4. Transit mode choice probability
5. Total expected daily auto VMT (vehicle miles traveled): for work trips

---

[7] Zones 1, 2, 3 are assumed to be in the District of Columbia, where school expenditures are not used in the model. The remaining zones are assumed to lie in various suburban counties.

Table 4
Attributes of Hypothetical City

Attribute	1	2	3	4	5	6	7	8	9	10	11
Annual per pupil school expenditures	NA	NA	NA	630	630	750	650	890	725	700	700
Average annual income	7500	5000	5000	9000	9000	11000	11000	15000	12000	15000	1400
Fraction nonwhite	.75	.98	.10	.50	.20	.20	.01	.01	.10	.05	.05
Transit shopping generalized price	1.5	1.7	1.7	1.9	1.9	2.2	NA	2.5	NA	NA	NA
Car shopping generalized price	1.5	2.0	2.0	3.0	3.0	3.5	3.5	4.5	4.5	7.0	7.0
Net residential density	200	50	50	25	25	10	10	2	2	.5	.5
Number of owner-occupied single-family dwellings	NA	NA	NA	100	100	400	400	900	900	500	500
Number of rented single-family dwellings	NA	NA	NA	300	300	300	300	100	100	NA	NA
Number of garden-style or walk-up apartments	500	800	800	500	500	100	100	50	50	NA	NA
Number of high-rise apartments	800	500	500	300	300	50	50	NA	NA	NA	NA
Average value of owner-occupied single-family units	NA	NA	NA	2500	2500	3500	30000	40000	30000	30000	30000
Monthly gross rent of rented single-family dwellings	NA	NA	NA	100	100	150	150	175	175	NA	NA
Monthly gross rent of garden-style and high-rise apartments	90	100	100	125	125	175	175	175	175	NA	NA
Monthly gross rent of high-rise apartments	90	80	80	100	100	120	120	NA	NA	NA	NA

The first measure summarizes the compactness of the expected residential pattern and is a useful mechanism for collapsing the entire location distribution to a single index. In addition, it reflects the expected work trip passenger miles traveled (including transit), a measure of the total transportation services which would have to be provided by the area.

The housing type choice probabilities represent the marginal probability distribution which summarizes the housing choices the household would make. The third measure, expected auto ownership, is a significant household characteristic upon which many travel decisions are based, and is, therefore, of particular interest to the transportation planner. Similarly, the transit work mode choice probability is also a basic forecast needed for effective planning. The final measure, total expected work VMT by auto, is a statistic frequently used in assessing the efficacy of various automotive pollution control strategies.

In addition to these fives measures, any special effects which are relevant, such as the choice probabilities for the ghetto area or the relative viability of the CBD as a residential area, will be noted.

Table 5 is an impact summary for the 12 prototypical households in the base case. As might be anticipated, low-income households are completely "priced out" of the owner-occupied single-family housing market. Also, by definition households without licenses choose to own zero autos and take transit to work, so their expected auto ownership, transit mode choice probability and VMT are 0, 1, and 0, respectively.

Average work trip distance increases monotonically with income for all four race and drivers license status groups. Similarly, for households with licenses, increased income results in higher auto VMT. This result corresponds fairly well to the situation in real urban areas, in which the inner rings are for the most part lower income areas, where trips are short and auto usage is low.

The racial composition of the hypothetical city is such that nonwhite areas tend to lie fairly close to the CBD. For this reason, the work trip distances and VMT for black households are substantially smaller than for equivalent white households. This effect is eliminated in the high-income households with drivers licenses, where expected VMT is actually somewhat higher for blacks than for whites.

Black households also tend to have a far lower probability of choosing single-family ownership than do whites. This is partially because they tend to reside with relatively high probability in the ghetto area where there are no owner-occupied dwellings, and because two of the suburban zones, 7 and 8, are 99% white.[8] This effect is somewhat

---

[8] By definition blacks are assigned a zero probability of choosing such zones.

Table 5
Impacts for Base case

Household			Housing Choice Probabilities					Expected Auto Ownership	Transit Probability	Expected Total Daily VMT
Income[a]	Race[b]	License[c]	Work Trip Distance (miles)	Own Single-Family	Rent Single-Family	Rent Garden or Walk-up	Rent High-Rise			
L	W	w/	6.42	0	.094	.764	.143	1.02	.409	8.37
M	W	w/	12.10	.299	.398	.280	.024	1.50	.181	21.00
H	W	w/	16.83	.676	.240	.080	.005	1.69	.084	31.74
L	B	w/	4.56	0	.061	.780	.159	.972	.451	5.17
M	B	w/	7.16	.138	.151	.642	.070	1.17	.296	11.48
H	B	w/	16.77	.692	.130	.163	.015	1.59	.086	32.45
L	W	w/o	6.29	0	.258	.663	.079	0	1.0	0
M	W	w/o	7.64	.141	.309	.504	.045	0	1.0	0
H	W	w/o	11.50	.480	.292	.213	.015	0	1.0	0
L	B	w/o	5.00	0	.152	.749	.099	0	1.0	0
M	B	w/o	5.58	.053	.204	.674	.069	0	1.0	0
H	B	w/o	7.35	.157	.331	.469	.044	0	1.0	0

[a] Income: L = low; M = middle; H = high.
[b] Race: W = white; B = black.
[c] License: w/ = adults have license; w/o = adults lack license.

reversed for high-income blacks with drivers licenses, where the denial of opportunities in some relatively close suburbs (where there is some rental housing) forces them with disproportionate probability to the somewhat more integrated, exclusively owner-occupied fringe housing.

Black households also have lower auto ownership than their white counterparts, primarily because they are attracted to the ghetto which has good transit service. For similar reasons, blacks tend to select transit to work with higher probability than do whites. This effect also diminishes in the highest income group, where the relatively high probability of a black household choosing to live in the fringe area (where transit is unavailable) almost entirely balances the desirability of transit for those living near the CBD.

The group of households without licenses have a much more restricted set of alternatives. By definition, they must use transit to work and cannot own an automobile. Thus, zones 9, 10, and 11 are completely unavailable. Black households in this group must, therefore, live in zones 1–6. For this reason, expected work trip distance within the driverless households is extremely low.

The lack of a license also results in reducing the probability of owning a single-family dwelling, since a large portion of such housing is outside the transit service boundary. A side effect of this is that the spatial distribution of those driverless households who would own their own home would be very limited. For example, white high-income driverless households that did choose to own their home would select zone 8 with probability .70 and equivalent black households would choose zone 6 with probability .63.

The combination of being black, poor, and lacking a license even further restricts available choices. Such households live in a zone which is 50% or more black (zones 1, 2, and 4) with probability 0.71 and have the shortest expected work trip distance. Interestingly, they tend to rent housing in multifamily dwelling units slightly less frequently than low-income white households with licenses, since they have extra income such households might expend on auto ownership available for housing.

Within the city boundary (zones 1, 2, and 3), the expected residential pattern of black and white low-income households is in sharp contrast. The location choice probabilities of zones 1 and 2 combined *conditional* on the city jurisdiction being selected is approximately .86 for low-income black households with and without licenses, whereas it is only about .18 for low-income whites.

8. PROTOTYPICAL HOUSEHOLD ANALYSIS: POLICY SCENARIOS

The base case discussed in the preceding section provides a useful reference point for evaluating the possible impacts of alternative transportation policies. Six such policies, all designed to reduce automobile usage, will be considered. Automobile use reduction strategies were selected for evaluation because they are the major focus of current energy conservation and environmental protection programs.

It should be made clear that the policy evaluation in this section is extremely limited in scope. First, as in the analysis of the base case, it considers only the choice probabilities of individual households, not the aggregate group response. Further, it is only a demand analysis; the supply of housing, its prices, and other possible responses to demand changes are ignored. Finally, it is basically a long run analysis, in which the prototypical households may adjust all their choices rather than simply one or two aspects of it.

For these reasons, the impacts forecasted should be viewed as "demand pressures" rather than as the resolution of a stable market equilibrium. For example, if due to a given policy the expected work trip length decreases, the real-world short run impact may be an increase in housing prices near the CBD and a corresponding reduction near the fringe. In the longer run, new housing construction might be expected close to the center city. These changes will produce shifts in the demographic characteristics in the zone, which in turn will alter household location preferences. In short, the final aggregate response to a policy is determined by a dynamic process which is far more complex than the demand forecasts presented here indicate, and all conclusions drawnfrom the analysis should be viewed as preliminary in nature.

The policies considered are designed to reflect various means of reducing car usage by either decreasing the attractiveness of using and owning automobiles or by improving the quality of transit service, thereby diverting auto users. The basic policies are as follows:

Policy 1: Moderate Auto Use Disincentives
Impose a $1.00 parking charge downtown, increase auto operating costs by 50% via a fuel tax, increase auto out-of-vehicle time by five minutes per trip by regulating on-street parking.

Policy 2: Strong Auto Use Disincentives
Take all actions in Policy 1 as well as a 25% auto ownership tax

($200 per year) and increase car in-vehicle time 25% by banning traffic in certain downtown areas.

Policy 3: Moderate Transit Improvements
   Improve transit routing and scheduling to decrease in-vehicle time by 20% and out-of-vehicle time by 50%; halve all fares.

Policy 4: Major Transit Improvements
   Install a new rapid transit system serving the entire urban area (including fringe) at speeds equal to that of the automobile in non-CBD zones and 2 minutes faster in the CBD. System has wait times 50% less than base case with a 15-minute maximum, and should have fares which are 50% of the base with a 25¢ maximum. Expected nonwork generalized prices for shopping trips should be comparably improved.

Policy 5: Moderate Joint Incentives
   Policies 1 and 3 combined.

Policy 6: Major Joint incentives
   Policies 2 and 4 combined.

   The impact tables for these policies are presented in Tables 6–11. These tables are identical in structure to Table 5 which described the base case forecasts.
   The first two policies which involve only changes to the attributes of the car mode have no effect whatsoever on the choice probabilities of households without drivers licenses, since by definition they are captive to the transit mode. However, these policies do have a substantial impact on the decisions of the prototypical households with licenses. As expected, the transit marginal choice probabilities rise significantly from those in the base case. In absolute terms, this shift is greatest for the low income groups, ranging in policy 1 from .188 to .084 for low- and high-income whites, respectively. However, the greatest percentage shift, 89.4%, is for middle-income blacks. Policy 2 has a similar though obviously greater effect on expected transit usage.
   Policies 1 and 2 have a much more limited impact on automobile ownership. For the high-income households the greatest effect is about .5 and 3% for whites and blacks, respectively, and is never greater than 13% for any household.
   The first two policies have only a marginal impact on the expected spatial distribution of households as measured by the average work trip distance. However, the large changes in transit usage coupled with the small reductions in average trip length result in a substantial reduction in expected auto VMT. This is particularly noticeable in the lowest in-

Table 6
Impacts for Policy 1

| Household | | | | Housing Choice Probabilities | | | | | | |
Income[a]	Race[b]	License[c]	Work Trip Distance (miles)	Own Single-Family	Rent Single-Family	Rent Garden	Rent High-Rise	Expected Auto Ownership	Transit Choice Probability	Expected Total Daily VMT
L	W	w/	6.01	0	.083	.755	.161	.965	.597	.547
M	W	w/	11.54	.245	.421	.308	.026	1.46	.231	18.98
H	W	w/	16.77	.672	.243	.081	.005	1.69	.095	31.36
L	B	w/	4.42	0	.051	.774	.176	.947	.621	3.42
M	B	w/	6.63	.103	.155	.670	.073	1.13	.356	9.83
H	B	w/	16.69	.687	.132	.166	.015	1.58	.098	32.13
L	W	w/o	6.29	0	.258	.663	.079	0	1	0
M	W	w/o	7.64	.141	.309	.504	.045	0	1	0
H	W	w/o	11.50	.480	.292	.213	.015	0	1	0
L	B	w/o	5.00	0	.152	.749	.099	0	1	0
M	B	w/o	5.58	.053	.204	.674	.069	0	1	0
H	B	w/o	7.35	.157	.331	.469	.044	0	1	0

[a] Income: L = low; M = middle; H = high.
[b] Race: W = white; B = black.
[c] License: w/ = adults have license; w/o = adults lack license.

Table 7
Impacts for Policy 2

| Household | | | | Housing Choice Probabilities | | | | | | |
Income[a]	Race[b]	License[c]	Work Trip Distance (miles)	Own Single-Family	Rent Single-Family	Rent Garden	Rent High-Rise	Expected Auto Ownership	Transit Choice Probability	Expected Total Daily VMT
L	W	w/	5.62	0	.081	.738	.006	.892	.687	3.82
M	W	w/	10.76	.179	.443	.348	.031	1.40	.270	16.80
H	W	w/	16.31	.647	.260	.088	.005	1.68	.111	30.08
L	B	w/	4.31	0	.048	.755	.197	.908	.691	2.62
M	B	w/	5.96	.065	.154	.704	.078	1.09	.387	8.20
H	B	w/	16.01	.651	.142	.190	.018	1.54	.117	30.51
L	W	w/o	6.29	0	.258	.663	.079	0	1	0
M	W	w/o	7.64	.141	.309	.504	.045	0	1	0
H	W	w/o	11.50	.480	.292	.213	.015	0	1	0
L	B	w/o	5.00	0	.152	.749	.099	0	1	0
M	B	w/o	5.58	.053	.204	.674	.069	0	1	0
H	B	w/o	7.35	.157	.331	.469	.044	0	1	0

[a] Income: L = low; M = middle; H = high.
[b] Race: W = white; B = black.
[c] License: w/ = adults have license; w/o = adults lack license.

Table 8
Impacts for Policy 3

Household				Housing Choice Probabilities						
Income[a]	Race[b]	License[c]	Work Trip Distance (miles)	Own Single-Family	Rent Single-Family	Rent Garden	Rent High-Rise	Expected Auto Ownership	Transit Choice Probability	Expected Total Daily VMT
L	W	w/	7.06	0	.119	.744	.136	1.00	.501	7.06
M	W	w/	11.94	.291	.403	.282	.024	1.49	.246	19.32
H	W	w/	16.62	.664	.248	.083	.005	1.69	.122	30.42
L	B	w/	4.58	0	.068	.778	.154	.965	.524	4.49
M	B	w/	7.01	.130	.152	.648	.070	1.15	.351	10.58
H	B	w/	16.53	.678	.135	.172	.016	1.57	.110	31.61
L	W	w/o	6.52	0	.280	.645	.076	0	1	0
M	W	w/o	7.91	.157	.317	.483	.043	0	1	0
H	W	w/o	11.70	.496	.289	.201	.014	0	1	0
L	B	w/o	5.11	0	.163	.740	.097	0	1	0
M	B	w/o	5.70	.058	.213	.663	.067	0	1	0
H	B	w/o	7.50	.165	.338	.455	.042	0	1	0

[a] Income: L = low; M = middle; H = high.
[b] Race: W = white; B = black.
[c] License: w/ = adults have license; w/o = adults lack license.

Table 9
Impacts for Policy 4

| Household | | | | Housing Choice Probabilities | | | | | | |
Income[a]	Race[b]	License[c]	Work Trip Distance (miles)	Own Single-Family	Rent Single-Family	Rent Garden	Rent High-Rise	Expected Auto Ownership	Transit Choice Probability	Expected Total Daily VMT
L	W	w/	5.72	0	.137	.733	.130	.925	.562	4.76
M	W	w/	7.90	.128	.307	.517	.049	1.01	.425	8.98
H	W	w/	11.90	.442	.333	.210	.016	.972	.400	14.09
L	B	w/	4.43	0	.070	.775	.156	.951	.544	3.96
M	B	w/	5.13	.035	.147	.737	.082	1.05	.426	5.88
H	B	w/	9.10	.181	.276	.494	.050	1.03	.406	9.10
L	W	w/o	7.39	0	.328	.604	.068	0	1	0
M	W	w/o	10.75	.327	.299	.345	.030	0	1	0
H	W	w/o	15.13	.664	.214	.115	.007	0	1	0
L	B	w/o	5.21	0	.166	.738	.095	0	1	0
M	B	w/o	6.75	.120	.204	.615	.062	0	1	0
H	B	w/o	11.88	.419	.245	.309	.028	0	1	0

[a] Income: L = low; M = middle; H = high.
[b] Race: W = white; B = black.
[c] License: w/ = adults have license; w/o = adults lack license.

Table 10
Impacts for Policy 5

Household			Work Trip Distance (miles)	Housing Choice Probabilities				Expected Auto Ownership	Transit Choice Probability	Expected Total Daily VMT
Income[a]	Race[b]	License[c]		Own Single-Family	Rent Single-Family	Rent Garden	Rent High-Rise			
L	W	w/	6.21	0	.120	.731	.149	.954	.683	4.30
M	W	w/	11.40	.240	.426	.307	.027	1.45	.308	17.08
H	W	w/	16.53	.658	.253	.084	.005	1.68	.138	29.88
L	B	w/	4.48	0	.062	.772	.166	.941	.687	2.83
M	B	w/	6.50	.096	.156	.674	.073	1.12	.415	8.92
H	B	w/	16.41	.670	.138	.176	.016	1.56	.125	31.18
L	W	w/o	6.52	0	.280	.645	.076	0	1	0
M	W	w/o	7.91	.157	.317	.483	.043	0	1	0
H	W	w/o	11.70	.496	.289	.201	.014	0	1	0
L	B	w/o	5.11	0	.163	.740	.097	0	1	0
M	B	w/o	5.70	.058	.213	.663	.067	0	1	0
H	B	w/o	7.50	.165	.338	.455	.042	0	1	0

[a] Income: L = low; M = middle; H = high.
[b] Race: W = white; B = black.
[c] License: w/ = adults have license; w/o = adults lack license.

Table 11
Impacts for Policy 6

Household				Housing Choice Probabilities						
Income[a]	Race[b]	License[c]	Work Trip Distance (miles)	Own Single-Family	Rent Single-Family	Rent Garden	Rent High-Rise	Expected Auto Ownership	Transit Choice Probability	Expected Total Daily VMT
L	W	w/	5.66	0	.119	.724	.157	.875	.788	2.15
M	W	w/	7.78	.114	.307	.528	.051	.991	.504	7.50
H	W	w/	11.84	.435	.336	.214	.016	.959	.463	12.44
L	B	w/	4.37	0	.060	.757	.183	.899	.763	1.92
M	B	w/	5.10	.032	.146	.739	.083	1.04	.498	5.09
H	B	w/	7.05	.178	.277	.495	.050	1.02	.463	8.16
L	W	w/o	7.39	0	.328	.604	.068	0	1	0
M	W	w/o	10.75	.327	.299	.345	.030	0	1	0
H	W	w/o	15.13	.664	.214	.115	.007	0	1	0
L	B	w/o	5.21	0	.166	.738	.095	0	1	0
M	B	w/o	6.75	.120	.204	.615	.062	0	1	0
H	B	w/o	11.88	.419	.245	.309	.028	0	1	0

[a] Income: L = low; M = middle; H = high.
[b] Race: W = white; B = black.
[c] License: w/ = adults have license; w/o = adults lack license.

come households, for whom expected VMT more than halves in Policy 2.

In the first two policies, the biggest shifts in the housing decision are for middle-income households. Increased car costs tend to make home ownership less attractive, both because less income is available for such purposes and because suburban housing is now associated with higher car commuting costs. In a probabilitisic sense, it appears that when faced with higher auto costs, middle-income households shift their housing type far more readily than they alter their level of auto ownership. This effect is minimal for higher income households, and does not exist for low-income households, for whom home ownership is not an available alternative.

Policy 3, which involves moderate transit improvements, in general produces much smaller changes than either policy 1 or 2. However, it does affect both households with and without licenses. The overall impact can be characterized by a reasonably large shift to the transit mode and only very marginal changes in all other impacts. Average trip length for low-income households and those without licenses is slightly increased, while it is decreased for middle and upper income households with licenses. Thus, the moderately improved transit system allows the low-income households and those captive to transit to select further zones with higher probability and provides some moderate incentives for more affluent households to move inward.

The fourth policy represents radical changes in the public transportation system. As one might expect, such changes have very significant impacts on virtually all aspects of the residential decision. The extension of the public transportation system to cover the entire metropolitan area opens new locational opportunities for households without licenses, and the high level of service the system offers coupled with low fares permits low-income groups to move further from the CBD. All these factors are reflected in Table 11.

Some of the effects forecast for policy 4 are not intuitively obvious. First, average work trip distances for households without licenses are actually greater than for corresponding households with licenses. This is primarily caused by a difference in the income allocation of these households; households without licenses by definition do not own cars and therefore allocate more income to the purchase of better housing, which tends to lie in the outer suburban areas of the hypothetical city. This factor is also reflected in the large reduction in the choice probabilities for owner-occupired single-family dwellings for households with licenses, and a corresponding increase for those lacking licenses.

Another interesting effect of policy 4 is the reduction in average automobile ownership for high-income groups. For both black and white households, the expected auto ownership for high-income households is actually less than for the corresponding middle-income households. This results from the interaction between the location and auto ownership decisions. Since high-income households have strong preferences for not residing in lower-income areas, they tend to locate in zones of high average income. In the base case and the previous policies, these zones had poor or nonexistent transit and hence were associated with high auto ownership; however, under policy 4 those zones are extremely well served by public transportation, and the high-income households residing there allocate more of their income to housing and other types of expenditures and less to the purchase of automobiles.

Expected VMT in policy 4 is still a monotonic function of income. However, the expected VMT of low-income households is actually reduced by more than a factor of two from the base case.

Policies 5 and 6, which represent combinations of auto use disincentives and transit improvements at moderate and high levels, respectively, produce impacts which are similar to the previously described policies. The distribution of the impacts of the moderate policy (policy 5) seems to be weighted quite heavily towards low-income households while the major transportation system changes (policy 6) produce strong impacts across all socioeconomic groups.

Of all the policies considered, only policies 4 and 6 produce profound changes in the current location, housing, auto ownership, and mode to work patterns. The remaining policies all result in patterns which are variants of the base case, that is, residential patterns characterized by low-income groups in the inner city with low auto ownership and more affluent residents in the suburbs with high auto ownership. This seems to indicate that while public transportation policy can have significant and widespread effects on locational preferences and is potentially an important policy instrument for altering urban form, major changes rather than incremental ones will be required.

9.   CONCLUSIONS

Transportation policy in urban areas has impacts not only on how residents use the transportation system, but also on the ultimate pattern of neighborhood development. The empirical work presented in this chapter serves to highlight this interaction, and offers useful insights into at least portion of the complex interactions among neighborhood choice, auto ownership, housing, and mode to work.

The study suggests that transportation policy can influence the desirability of different neighborhoods, although other neighborhood attributes such as racial composition, area income, and housing prices appear to have a greater effect. However, these latter neighborhood attributes are often difficult areas for policy intervention, while urban passenger transportation services and infrastructure are generally provided by the public sector. This suggests that the use of transportation facilities as policy instruments to preserve or improve neighborhoods may often prove politically acceptable where other public actions may not. It must be recognized, however, either large shifts in levels of service or smaller shifts accompanied by other supportive public policies, such as housing subsidies or increased school quality, will be required to induce significant changes in residential location demand. For example, VMT does appear to be influenced by transportation changes, particularly if such changes represent very large improvements in transit service or severe restrictions on car use. Accompanying significant transportation changes, area-wide school funding or appropriately targeted housing programs would enhance this VMT reduction.

Unfortunately, transportation planning has generally been done to a great extent independently of other urban policies, and institutional cooperation at federal, state, and local levels between transportation and other urban planning has generally been limited. If the historically large public investments in transportation infrastructure are going to be channeled to achieve desired residential location patterns, mechanisms for coordinating funding planning and implementation of coordinated policies must first be found.

ACKNOWLEDGMENTS

The author wishes to acknowledge the assistance of Moshe Ben-Akiva, Wayne Pecknold, Marvin Manheim, and Gregory Ingram, all of whom contributed their advice in the early phases of this study. In addition, the financial support provided to the author by Motor Vehicle Manufacturers Association is gratefully acknowledged. Subsequent funding was provided under a Research Initiation Grant from the National Science Foundation.

REFERENCES

Ben-Akiva, M. (1973). Structure of passenger travel demand models. Ph.D. dissertation, Department of Civil Engineering, Massachusetts Institute of Technology, Cambridge.

Ben-Akiva, M., and Lerman, S. (1977). Disaggregate travel and mobility choice models and measures of accessibility. *Presented at the Third International Conference on Behav-*

ioral Travel Demand Modelling, Tanunda, Australia, April and to be published in forth-coming proceedings by Croom-Helm, Ltd.

Burns, L., Golob, T., and Nicolaidis, G. (1975). A theory of urban households' automobile ownership behavior. Transportation Research Record 569, Transportation Research Board, Washington, D.C.

Cambridge Systematics, Inc. (1974). *A behavioral model of automobile ownership and mode of travel.* Draft report prepared for the U.S. Department of Transportation, Office of the Secretary and the Federal Highway Administration.

Charles River Associates, Inc. (1972). *A disaggregate behavioral model of urban travel demand.* Federal Highway Administration, U.S. Department of Transportation, Washington, D.C.

Domencich, T., and McFadden, D. (1975). *Urban travel demand: A behavioral analysis.* North Holland Press, Amsterdam.

Ingram, G., Kain, J., and Ginn, R. (1972). The Detroit prototype of the NBER urban simulation model. National Bureau of Economic Research, Cambridge, Massachusetts.

Koppelman, F. (1975). Travel prediction with disaggregate choice models. Ph.D. dissertation, Department of Civil Engineering, Massachusetts Institute of Technology, Cambridge.

Lee, D. (1973). Requiem for large scale models. *Journal of the American Institute of Planners* **39**(3).

Lerman, S. R. (1975). A disaggregate behavioral model of urban mobility decisions. Ph.D. dissertation, Department of Civil Engineering, Massachusetts Institute of Technology, Cambridge.

Lerman, S. R., and Adler, T. J. (1976). Models of destination choice. In *Behavioral travel demand models,* Stopher and Meyberg (eds.). Lexington Books, D. C. Health and Co.

Lerman, S. R., and Ben-Akiva, M. (1975). A disaggreagate behavioral model of auto ownership. Transportation Research Record 569, Transportation Research Board, Washington, D.C.

Manski, C. F. (1974). Maximum score estimation of the stochastic model of choice. Paper in draft.

McFadden, D. (1974). Conditional logit analysis of qualitative choice behavior. In *Frontiers in econometrics,* P. Zarembka (ed.). Academic Press, New York.

McFadden, D. (1977). Quantitative methods for analyzing travel behavior of individuals: Some recent developments. *Presented at the Third International Conference on Behavioral Travel Demand, Tanunda, Australia, April* and to be published in forthcoming proceedings by Pergamon Press.

Nerlove, M., and Press, S. J. (1973). Univariate and multivariate log-linear and logistic models. Prepared for the Economic Development Administration and the National Institutes of Health, The Rand Corporation, R-1306-EDA/NIH.

Oates, W. E. (1969). The effects of property taxes and local public spending on property value: An empirical study of tax capitalization and the Tiebout hypothesis. *Journal of Political Economy* Nov.–Dec.

Richards, M., and Ben-Akiva, M. (1975). *A dissaggregate travel demand model.* Saxon House, Westmead, England.

Wheaton, W. C. (1974). A bid rent approach to housing demand. In mimeograph, Department of Economics, Report Number 135, Massachusetts Institute of Technology, Cambridge.

Williams, H. C. W. L. (1977). On the formation of travel demand models and economic evaluation measures of urban benefit. *Environment and Planning A,* **9**.

III
NEIGHBORHOOD SUPPLY

6

Private Residential Renewal and the Supply of Neighborhoods

CLIFFORD R. KERN

1. ISSUES

In the historical record of the postwar years, there has been little support for the notion that central cities can effectively forestall the loss of middle- and upper-income households to the suburbs. In inner-city areas throughout the country, neighborhood after neighborhood has become impoverished as upper-income residents have left. By the mid-1960s, however, in a reversal of this trend, several downtown neighborhoods in a small number of cities began to experience growth in upper-income demand for residential sites. Although little noticed at first, this reversal has become the urban cliche of the 1970s, with neighborhoods in nearly every city being singled out as ripe for the new found prosperity that has recently transformed, for example, Washington's Capitol Hill and parts of Boston's South End (Rheinhold, 1977).

To assess the plausibility of these expectations, it is necessary to understand first of all what has caused resurgent upper-income demand in some parts of some cities, while the flight to the suburbs continues unabated in others. What do these locations offer that other urban locations do not? What makes their inhabitants reject the dominant pattern

121

of upper-income residence in the suburbs? How large is the population pool from which these residents are drawn, and is it likely to grow or decline in the immediate future?

Since I have examined all of these issues in detail in another paper (Kern, 1977), their treatment here will be relatively brief. Results derived in that paper will be borrowed and explained without complete derivation, for which the reader will be referred to the original source. The principal focus of the present discussion will be on individual neighborhoods and their characteristics. Given a potential demand for inner-city sites by upper-income residents, how do the characteristics of existing city neighborhoods affect its realization? Intuition suggests that neighborhood attributes represent an important consideration in upper-income residential choice and in decisions by private investors to supply upper-income housing. The discussion that follows will specify these relationships formally, test them empirically, and use them to explore how existing neighborhoods affect the spatial pattern of residential renewal and how, in turn, this pattern determines the supply of neighborhoods in the following period.

A second focus of the discussion relates directly to public policy. Municipal officials have been enthusiastic about the prospect of upper-income development in their cities. It can reverse decay in urban housing, revitalize declining shopping areas, contribute to socioeconomic diversity, and enrich the city's tax base. The feasibility and desirability of policies designed to encourage such development will be examined in light of this chapter's other conclusions.

2. THEORETICAL TOOLS

Urban economists have developed a powerful tool for studying residential demand by introducing location into the standard microeconomic model of consumer behavior (see Alonso, 1964; Kain, 1962; Mills, 1967; Muth, 1969). As in the standard consumer model, households in the urban model maximize satisfaction subject to a budget constraint.[1] But in the urban model household satisfaction, household expenditures, or both of these quantities depend not only on the collection of commodities consumed but on residential location as well.

The impact of neighborhood attributes on residential behavior will

[1] The terms "household," "resident," and "consumer" will be used interchangeably. To avoid problems in defining household utility in households with several members, assume that household decisions are made by the household head in accordance with this utility function.

be explored here with a long run equilibrium urban model that embodies the following assumptions. In general, each of these assumptions represents a restriction commonly embodied in urban residential models or an explicit relaxation of one such restriction. Only assumption 7. introduces a restriction not usually found in these models.

    1.   Residential sites are arrayed in a circle around the city's central business district (CBD).

    2.   During any period of time, every household in the metropolitan area makes the same fixed number of worktrips to the CBD.

    3.   Consumption goods include commodities available throughout the metropolitan area, goods and services acquired from the CBD, and residential land. Commodities acquired in the CBD include services such as entertainment and cultural activities and, also, specialized consumer goods.

    4.   Consumption of goods and services supplied in the CBD requires nonwork trips to the center. A fixed quantity of these commodities can be acquired on each trip.[2]

    5.   The out-of-pocket cost of each round trip between home and the CBD increases linearly with residential distance from the city center.[3]

    6.   All residential sites are identical except for their distance from the CBD and for the neighborhood amenities offered to their residents. The amenities offered by any site depend upon the demographic characteristics of neighboring households. Although the spatial distribution of amenities is therefore endogenous for the metropolitan area, it is taken as exogenous by any individual resident. In addition, no necessary relationship is assumed between neighborhood attributes and distance from the CBD. In a newly developed city where there are no existing neighborhoods to affect residential decisions, a regular neighborhood–distance relationship may well emerge, as utility maxi-

---

    [2] The correspondence of this assumption with actual behavior depends upon the characteristics of the goods and services being studied. The correspondence is poor for standardized commodities. Buying more groceries need not require extra trips to the supermarket. It is closer for specialized goods, which require substantial searching before a decision is made. The time required to find a suitable item of clothing, for example, may mean that only a limited quantity can be purchased on any trip. It is closest for entertainment and related services. In general, each movie requires a separate trip to the theater; each meal, a separate trip to the restaurant. Since nonwork trips to the center typically involve specialized goods and entertainment, the assumption is particularly apt for goods and services acquired in the center.

    [3] Time costs of transportation are ignored in this analysis. This specification is analogous to Polinsky and Shavell's (1976, p. 120) assumption that transportation is instantaneous.

mizing residential choice causes demographically different groups to stratify by distance. However, in a city where current residential patterns emerge from historical residential equilibria, neighborhoods inherited from the past are likely to affect residential choices in ways that upset such regularities.

7. Utility functions for all residents are additively separable functions of goods available throughout the metropolitan area, goods acquired from the CBD, residential land, and neighborhood amenities; the marginal utility of each commodity is positive and declines with increased consumption; and all commodities (including neighborhood amenities) are normal goods with positive income elasticities.[4]

Each resident maximizes the utility function

$$U = U(X, Z, Q, A) \tag{1}$$

subject to the budget constraint

$$Y = X + p^z Z + p^Q(A, D)Q + tD\,[W + N], \tag{2}$$

where

X commodities available throughout the metropolitan area (the numeraire with price set equal to 1),
Z commodities acquired in the CBD,
Q residential land,
A neighborhood amenities (a vector with elements $A_1, \ldots, A_i, \ldots, A_n$),
Y income,
D distance from the CBD,
p^z the price of commodities acquired in the CBD,
$P^Q(A, D)$ the rent of residential land,
t round trip transportation cost per mile,
W worktrips to the CBD,
N nonwork trips to the CBD.

Because a fixed quantity of commodities can be acquired on each nonwork trip to the CBD,

$$Z = aN, \tag{3}$$

[4] Because additivity means a utility function in which cross partial derivatives with respect to commodities are equal to zero, an additive function is most appropriate when commodities are large aggregates, each of which serves a distinctly different need, so that goods are interrelated "largely from their competition for the consumer's dollar rather than from any more specific connection [Houthakker, 1960, p. 246]." With additive utility, the assumptions of diminishing marginal utility for all commodities and positive income elasticity for all commodities imply one another. See Green (1961).

where a is the constant of proportionality between consumption and trips. Substitution of Eq. (3) into Eqs. (1) and (2) allows the consumer's objective to be rewritten

Maximize $U(X, aN, Q, A)$
Subject to $Y = X + p^z aN + p^q(A, D)Q + tD[W + N].$ \qquad (4)

Several recent studies (see, e.g., Ellickson, Chapter 12 of this volume; Polinsky and Rubinfeld, 1977; Polinsky and Shavell, 1976; Rosen, 1974) have demonstrated the value of examining residential behavior with an indirect utility function, which assumes that all goods and services other than residential location are chosen to maximize satisfaction and depicts the maximum attainable utility at any location as a function of household income and the prices, trip costs, and amenities prevailing there. For the problem given in Eq. (4), an indirect utility function can be written

$$V = V(Y, P^z, P^q(A, D), tD, A). \qquad (5)$$

If V_j is defined as the partial derivative of V with respect to its jth argument,

$$V_1 > 0,$$
$$V_2, V_3, V_4 < 0,$$
$$V_{4+i} > 0 \qquad (i = 1, \ldots, n).$$

Since V_1 represents the marginal utility of extra income, its positive sign is implied by the earlier assumption of positive marginal utility for all goods and services. Extra income increases utility by making possible increased consumption of commodities yielding positive marginal satisfaction.

The signs and magnitudes of V_2, V_3, and V_4 can be evaluated in terms of V_1 by showing how income would have to change to offset the impact on utility of a change in the price of a commodity or the cost of a trip. Using CBD commodities as an example, we can show from Eq. (5) that a change in their price will leave utility unchanged if accompanied by an increase in income such that

$$V_1 \, dY + V_2 \, dp^z = 0,$$

or

$$V_2 = -V_1(\partial Y / \partial p^z). \qquad (6)$$

Substituting from the budget constraint in Eq. (4),

$$V_2 = -V_1\{aN^*\} - V_1 \left\{ \frac{\partial X^*}{\partial p^z} + [p^z a + tD]\frac{\partial N^*}{\partial p^z} + p^Q(A, D)\frac{\partial Q^*}{\partial p^z} \right\}, \quad (7)$$

where X^*, N^*, and Q^* refer to the utility maximizing quantities assumed in the derivation of the indirect utility function. It is easily shown that if X^*, N^*, and Q^* are chosen to maximize utility and if the changes in Y and p^z just hold utility constant, the quantities in brackets in the second term on the right-hand side of Eq. (7) sum to zero and[5]

$$V_2 = -V_1\{aN^*\} < 0. \quad (8a)$$

Analagous reasoning demonstrates that

$$V_3 = -V_1 Q^* < 0, \quad (8b)$$

$$V_4 = -V_1 [W + N^*] < 0. \quad (8c)$$

Finally, each V_{4+i} is greater than zero because of the initial assumption that amenities are goods with positive marginal utilities.

3. DEMAND: CITY VERSUS SUBURB

Any resident with given income and a given utility function chooses among locations so as to find the combination of prices, trip costs, and amenities that maximizes his satisfaction.[6] Once this maximum (V^*) has been determined, a schedule of rents $\theta = \theta(A, D, V^*, Y, p^z, t)$ can be specified that would leave him equally well off irrespective of his location. Given this schedule of rents, the utility common to all locations is

$$V^* = V(Y, p^z, \theta, tD, A). \quad (9)$$

The maximum utility rent schedule θ can be used to show how dif-

[5] If X^*, Q^*, and N^* are all chosen to maximize satisfaction, prices are proportional to marginal utilities, so the bracketed sum in the second term on the right-hand side of Eq. (7) becomes $k[(\partial U/\partial X^*)(\partial X^*/\partial p^z) + (\partial U/\partial Q^*)(\partial Q^*/\partial p^z) + a(\partial U/\partial Z^*)(\partial N^*/\partial p^z)]$, where k is a contant of proportionality and where $(\partial U/\partial X^*)$ represents the marginal utility of X evaluated at $X = X^*$ and so forth. If utility is held constant, the sum of all terms in the brackets above must be zero and so, therefore, must the bracketed sum in the second term on the right-hand side of Eq. (7).

[6] In a city that is a small component of a system of cities with free migration among them, the maximum attainable utility is exogenous for each city and, for similar households, equal to a common level for all cities. In a closed city, the maximum attainable utility is fixed by land prices that equate supply and demand for urban land (see Polinsky and Shavell, 1976). The mechanism that fixes utility is irrelevant to the issues investigated in this paper.

ferent residents stratify with respect to distance from the CBD. Differentiating Eq. (9) with respect to distance and solving for $(\partial\theta/\partial D)$,

$$(\partial\theta/\partial D) = -(tV_4/V_3). \tag{10}$$

Making use of Eqs. (8b) and (8c), substitute so that

$$\frac{\partial\theta}{\partial D} = -\frac{-tV_1[W + N^*]}{-V_1Q^*} = -\frac{t[W + N^*]}{Q^*}. \tag{11}$$

It is evident from Eq. (11) that a schedule of rents such that all locations yield satisfaction equal to V^* would have to decline with distance from the CBD and would have to decline less rapidly the greater the consumption of residential land. If satisfaction is to remain constant, land prices must decline so that reduced expenditure on land offsets rising expenditure on transportation, but the larger the quantity of land, the smaller the fall in price that is needed to generate the necessary reduction in expenditure.

Land is usually assumed to be a normal good. Therefore, economists have typically concluded that, for a city with two income classes, maximum utility rent schedules, residential location, and the actual rents in the city would be as shown in Fig. 1. The logic behind this conclusion is straightforward. For low-income residents, rents between the CBD and I decline just rapidly enough to hold utility constant at its maximum possible level. Locations beyond I, however, imply reduc-

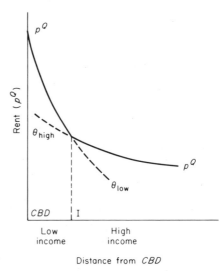

Figure 1. *Income and residential location.*

tions in satisfaction for low-income consumers whose land consumption is small: Low land consumption combined with small declines in the price of land means that reductions in land expenditure are insufficient to offset the increased cost of transportation. Low-income residents, therefore, will cluster near the center. For upper-income residents, high land consumption means that sharply declining rents between the CBD and I generate savings on land that exceed the increased cost of transportation, so that utility increases with distance. At I, maximum satisfaction is attained, and beyond that point rents decline just rapidly enough to maintain it at a constant level. Upper-income residents occupy sites beyond I, among which they are indifferent.

The effects on residential choice of commodities acquired from the CBD are directly opposed to the effects of residential land, as is also evident from Eq. (11). Increased consumption of these commodities implies increased nonwork travel to the CBD, increased travel cost penalties for sites successively farther from the center, and a steeper schedule of rents if maximum utility is to be maintained irrespective of distance. In direct contrast to residential land, consumption of goods from the CBD increases incentives for residential centralization. Taken by itself, therefore, a positive income elasticity for goods acquired in the CBD will produce a residential pattern exactly the reverse of that in Fig. 1, with incentives for the rich to cluster in the city while the poor are dispersed towards the suburbs. Even if residential land and commodities from the CBD are considered together and if both are assumed normal goods, the effects of the latter may still be strong enough to draw the rich more closely to the center than the poor.

Using a form of the utility function that is consistent with assumption 7., I have argued that differences in the relative strength of incentives favoring upper-income dispersal and those favoring upper-income centralization are caused in part by differences in the utility functions of demographically different consumers (Kern, 1977). Two such differences seem partiularly important. First, if income is held constant, tastes that increase the marginal utility of centrally supplied commodities and reduce that of residential land imply increased consumption of the former and reduced consumption of the latter. From Eq. (11), the maximum utility rent gradient becomes steeper, and households with tastes such as these locate closer to the center than others with similar income. Second, if the rate at which marginal utility declines as consumption increases is low for centrally supplied commodities and rapid for residential land, consumption of goods from the CBD will increase rapidly with income while consumption of land grows barely at all. The numerator of Eq. (11) will grow while the denominator remains nearly the same; maximum utility rent gradients will be steepest and incentives for central residence will be strongest for those whose income is highest. Opposite tastes will, in turn produce opposite results.

Since tastes cannot be directly observed, links between utility functions and demographic characteristics can be conjectured but not proved. It is particularly plausible, however, that differences in taste which distinguish childless households from residents with children are similar to those just described. Residents who have not made the commitment to family members implied by a decision to bring up children can be expected to seek more friendships and greater social interaction outside the family than those who have. Entertainment and cultural activities outside the home are a principal means of making and maintaining these friendships, and it is just these services for which the quality and variety advantages of the CBD over other parts of the metropolitan area are most apparent, at least in some cities. The central social role of these activities should ensure a marginal utility that is high and remains high even with frequent use.[7] On the other hand, extra residential land and reductions in residential density to give children places to play and provide parents and children with privacy from one another are irrelevant for childless households. The marginal utility of such surplus space is apt to be low and decline quickly with increased consumption.

In a schematic city with two levels of income—high and low—and two kinds of households—with children and without—that conform to the behavioral assumptions just enumerated, maximum utility gradients, residential choice, and actual rents in the city could be depicted by the solid line in Fig. 2. Evidence for New York City, shown in Table 1, suggests that residential patterns there follow roughly this pattern.[8]

This brief discussion suggests some answers to the first set of questions posed in the introduction. Strong upper-income demand for inner-city sites can be expected in cities rich in entertainment, culture, and other things to do outside the home. Where the city center is weak in these activities, it will also be weak in upper-income residential de-

---

[7] Because one objective of education is to increase appreciation for the kind of cultural activities that are frequently available near the CBD but nowhere else, high levels of education may have similar effects on the marginal utility of centrally supplied services and on incentives for upper-income residence near the CBD. These incentives would exist for families with children as well as for childless households.

[8] A partial exception is evident among the highest income families, which are heavily concentrated in the CBD as well as in the suburbs. A possible explanation is the education effect hypothesized in footnote 7.

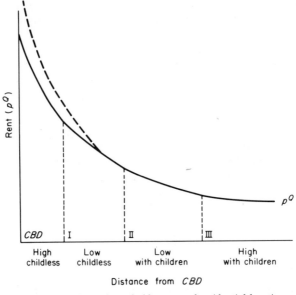

Figure 2. *Income, household type, and residential location.*

Table 1

Spatial Distribution and Median Distance from the CBD, Residents of the New York SMSA, 1970, by Income and Family Type[a]

	Total	Manhattan CBD and Adjacent Areas	Rest of Inner City (Bronx, Brooklyn, Rest of Manhattan)	Outer City (Queens, Staten Island)	Suburbs
Unrelated individuals[b]					
High income[c]	1.00	.61	.13	.09	.16
Upper middle income	1.00	.43	.24	.16	.17
Moderate income	1.00	.31	.37	.17	.14
Low income	1.00	.20	.45	.16	.18
Families					
Low income	1.00	.09	.59	.16	.16
Moderate income	1.00	.06	.40	.23	.31
Upper middle income	1.00	.06	.27	.24	.42
High income	1.00	.17	.17	.16	.50

Sources: U.S. Bureau of the Census (1970; 1972, Table 89).

[a] Italic figure indicates the median distance of each income/family category.

[b] The distinction between families and unrelated individuals is the closest approximation available in census income data to the distinction between households with children and those without.

[c] Definitions of income classes can be found in the text, Section 6.

mand. Although evidence on this issue is sparse, the evidence that exists is consistent with this hypothesis (Kern, 1977; Postlethwaite, 1977). Other causes of upper-income demand for central sites can be advanced, among them a high value for travel time for CBD workers and the presence in the household of several workers with jobs in the center.[9] But none of these effectively explains why different cities, all of which have upper-income workers in the CBD, behave so differently with regard to upper-income residence in the center (see Postlethwaite, 1977).

4. DEMAND: NEIGHBORHOOD AMENITIES

Figure 2 shows income and demographic characteristics to be sharply stratified by distance from the CBD. In fact, such sharp stratification of neighborhood attributes is unlikely. In the center of any city, for example, current residential patterns have emerged from a historical process. Successive spatial patterns of residential demand, which have changed regularly in response to urban growth, migration flows, shifts in job location, and advances in transportation technology, have been confronted by established neighborhoods with socioeconomic characteristics determined by residential demand in past periods. Neighborhood attributes inherited from the past can, in turn, powerfully affect the emerging residential distribution, enabling low-income neighborhoods to persist, for example, on sites that would have been bid away by upper-income residents in a newly developed city.

To examine the effects of neighborhood attributes on residential choice, differentiate Eq. (9) with respect to neighborhood amenities, and solve for $(\partial\theta/\partial A_i)$:

$$(\partial\theta/\partial A_i) = -(V_{4+i}/V_3) = (V_{4+i}/V_1Q^*). \tag{12}$$

To ensure constant utility equal to V^*, rent must increase with the level of neighborhood amenities by an amount just equal to the consumer's willingness to pay for them: any more and the consumer will be made worse off; any less, and the consumer will be better off.

How does the maximum utility rent gradient vary as income increases? In an additive utility function, the marginal utility of any commodity depends only on consumption of that commodity. For any neighborhood, therefore, V_{4+i} is constant and independent of the level of household income or the consumption of other commodities. The ef-

---

[9] Either of these characteristics would increase the maximum utility rent gradient by increasing t in Eq. (11).

fect of income on Eq. (12) depends on its effect on the denominator. If, as assumed, all commodities in the utility function are characterized by diminishing marginal utility and all are normal goods, V_1 must decline and Q^* must increase as income rises, so that the income effect on $(\partial\theta/\partial A_i)$ is ambiguous. This ambiguity implies that willingness to pay higher rent for improvements in neighborhood amenity bears an uncertain relationship to income. An intuitive explanation is immediately apparent from Eq. (12). It is clear from Eq. (12) that $(\partial\theta/\partial A_i)$ rises with income unless the increase in Q^* is large relative to the decrease in V_1. Willingness to bear increased rent in return for neighborhood improvements is an increasing function of income except when the income elasticity of land is especially high. If the rich consume very large quantities of land, even a small increase in its price implies a large expenditure for extra neighborhood amenity. Conversely, if lower-income consumers use very little land, even a large increase in rent means a small expenditure for improved amenities. In these circumstances, even if amenity is a normal good, so that the rich willingly *spend* more than the poor for an identical improvement, they may not willingly pay a larger increase in the price of land than that which the poor will pay.

Implications for residential behavior are evident in Fig. 3, which is drawn for four income classes on the assumption that $(\partial\theta/\partial A_i)$ does increase with income. Higher-income households clearly dwell at higher amenity sites, but this outcome obtains only when high-income residents willingly outbid others for land in high amenity locations. As the immediately preceding discussion makes clear, this behavior cannot be

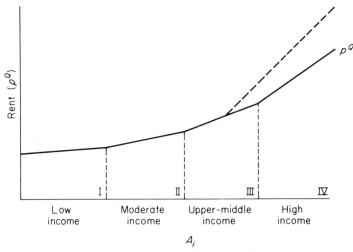

Figure 3. *Neighborhood amenities and residential choice.*

taken for granted, but empirical patterns of residence suggest that it is the rule rather than the exception. If the hypotheses in Section 3 are correct, and residents near the CBD are those for whom land is income inelastic, a positive relationship between income and willingness to bid for high amenity land is particularly likely in inner-city neighborhoods. An assumption that $(\partial\theta/\partial A_i)$ rises with income will govern all subsequent analysis.

To consider a specific example, let A_i in Fig. 3 be a measure of neighborhood income, and let neighborhood income be determined by the incomes of residents at that and nearby locations, weighted by proximity.[10] If, for historical or other reasons, households with different incomes have been stratified into separate neighborhoods at the same distance from the center, so that the range of neighborhood income implied in Fig. 3 actually exists, current residential choices will work to preserve that stratification. As long as $(\partial\theta/\partial A_i)$ rises with income, the segregation of income classes shown in Fig. 3 will be stable, with higher-income classes bidding successfully for higher income neighborhoods.[11]

Although Fig. 3 lacks an explicit spatial dimension, the relationships it depicts can be given a direct spatial interpretation. All sites with neighborhood income between IV and III in Fig. 3 are occupied by households in the highest income class. Of these locations, the highest neighborhood incomes identify sites where high-income residents also occupy immediately adjacent locations and where areas of upper-income residence radiate for some distance in all directions. Midway between IV and III, immediate neighbors still have high incomes but, in at least one direction, those a short distance away are of lower economic status. If these lower incomes are given some weight in determining neighborhood attributes, neighborhood income will be judged lower for these sites than for those where no lower-income residents live nearby. The point III marks the fringe of the upper-income area,

---

[10] A rigorous specification of this idea involves a weighting function to generate an index of neighborhood income as a function of household income at all locations within u miles of the site in question, that is,

$$A_i = \left(\frac{1}{2\pi}\right) \int_0^{2\pi} \left[\int_0^{\bar{u}} w(u)Y(u, \phi)\, du \right] d\phi,$$

where $w(u)$ is a weighting function and $Y(u, \phi)$ is the income of a household at a given location. Other neighborhood attributes, such as race, can be similarly indexed. A similar construct appears in Yinger (1976).

[11] The fact that this relationship need not hold may explain the necessity for upper-income residents to zone high-density, lower-income housing out of their neighborhoods. If the relationship did hold, the lower-income groups would never outbid the rich for these sites.

where even adjacent sites are occupied by lower-income residents. These locations will be judged to have still lower neighborhood income. The point III marks the level of neighborhood amenity at which high-income households are outbid for sites by residents of the next income class and defines the beginning of the residential zone inhabited by this class. Levels of neighborhood income in this and successive residential zones are determined by similar calculations. When neighborhood income for any location is determined by weighting the incomes of nearby residents according to their proximity, even a finite number of income classes yields the continuous distribution of neighborhood income shown in Fig. 3.

Race, which like income is an important determinant of neighborhood attributes, can be examined in like manner. For any site, let A_i be determined by the race of surrounding residents weighted by proximity, and let the resulting weighted ratio of white to total residents be a measure of neighborhood amenity. Assume that whites discriminate but blacks do not, so that racial composition is important for whites and irrelevant for blacks. Then, for blacks $(\partial\theta/\partial A_i) = 0$; for whites $(\partial\theta/\partial A_i) > 0$ and increases with income. These relationships and their implications for residential patterns are illustrated in Fig. 4. The segregation of whites and blacks is stable, since whites outbid blacks for sites in predominantly white neighborhoods.[12] Among whites, income levels vary directly with the predominance of whites in neighborhood racial composition.

5. NEIGHBORHOOD AMENITIES: SUPPLY

Some insight into neighborhood supply arises as a by-product of the demand analysis, which identifies a stable configuration of socioeconomically and racially differentiated neighborhoods. The demand analysis therefore implies an equilibrium supply of neighborhoods that can be expected to persist in the absence of exogenous disturbance.

To explore supply more fully, consider an exogenous disturbance: a growth in upper income demand for central locations. How does the

[12] Assuming that blacks are indifferent to integration, rather than preferring it, eliminates the possibility that upper-income blacks may bid integrated sites from moderate-income whites. In addition, by considering each neighborhood attribute in isolation from the others, I ignore more complex residential patterns that can result from combinations of neighborhood characteristics. For example, since most black neighborhoods are poor, it is likely that upper-income blacks will bid for sites in white neighborhoods because of their socioeconomic, if not their racial, characteristics. In general, the issues considered in this chapter do not require the introduction of these complexities.

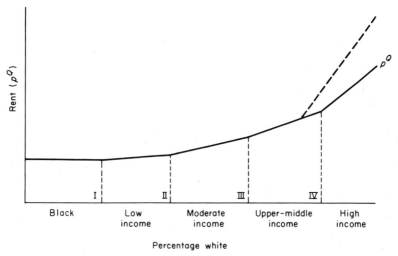

Figure 4. *Race and residential choice.*

growth in demand interact with housing investment to change the supply of neighborhoods?

In the simplified long-run equilibrium model used throughout this chapter, the growth in demand can be portrayed as an upward shift in the rent gradient on the extreme left in Fig. 2 and on the extreme right in Figs. 3 and 4. Increased demand drives up the price of sites in established areas of upper-income residence. Residential behavior responds in two ways. First, in these neighborhoods, rising prices cause residents to economize on land and live at higher density, so that some of the increased demand is accommodated within their boundaries. In addition, upper-income households bid away sites formerly occupied by others and, in the process, change the demography of these locations to conform more closely with upper-income preferences. In this way, the supply of neighborhoods adjusts to the demand for them.

This bidding process takes place in strictly limited areas with characteristics that are readily identified from the diagrams. As is evident from Fig. 2, expansion away from the CBD will take place first in areas only marginally more remote from the center than existing areas of upper-income residence. It is clear from Figs. 3 and 4 that areas with neighborhood income and racial composition most like those in established upper-income settlements will be bid away before those with lower income and higher concentration of blacks. Both the benefits and the dislocation attendant on neighborhood change are most likely in new neighborhoods that differ little from the old.

This discussion of neighborhood change in the context of long-run equilibrium has no explicit reference to housing suppliers. Housing is implicitly lumped together with the other goods available at fixed price throughout the metropolitan area. Once land consumption (density) has been chosen, the household can acquire its desired dwelling unit (size and quality) at a given price irrespective of location.

The separate consideration of land and structure and the assumption of invariant structure price may be defensible when considering the supply of housing on vacant land. For the inner-city locations of interest in this analysis, however, this assumption is particularly inappropriate. Most land there has already been covered by structures built in the past. Providing dwellings in this market is not simply a matter of arranging them at the appropriate density on previously unoccupied sites. It requires either new construction on land cleared by demolition or transformation of existing structures by renovation. Because the nature of pre-existing structures determines the cost of each of these alternatives, the supply price of newly provided dwellings can vary greatly from site to site.

Assume that high-income residents demand housing quality commensurate with their incomes. A market for high-quality housing in a neighborhood with no vacant land is depicted in Fig. 5. Panel (a) shows demand for newly supplied units, which is equal to the difference between the existing stock (H_0) and the number of units demanded at the currently prevailing price (H^d). This demand is met both by new construction on land cleared of existing structures (H^c) and by renovation of existing housing (H^r), as shown in panel (b). Both supply curves slope upward. The production of renovated units becomes progressively more expensive as easily acquired and easily transformed struc-

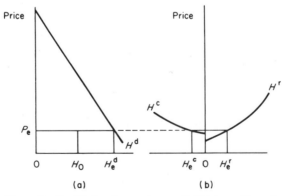

Figure 5. *Equilibrium for newly supplied high-quality units.*

tures are used up, and remaining housing requires ever more extensive investment to reach the appropriate level of quality. The cost of newly constructed units is inflated when the exhaustion of easily and cheaply assembled sites drives up the cost of site acquisition. Equilibrium requires a price such that

$$H^d - H_0 = H^c + H^r. \tag{13}$$

Growing upper-income demand can be represented for any neighborhood by an outward shift in H^d in Fig. 5. The importance of neighborhood expansion in meeting this demand depends on the shape of supply curves in existing upper-income settlements and in other areas. If supply in established settlements is inelastic, steeply rising prices there will cause demand to spill over into other neighborhoods. If they rise far enough, even neighborhoods where initial attributes differ substantially from existing upper-income settlements may experience neighborhood change. On the other hand, inelastic supply outside existing settlements will impede the spread of upper-income areas by limiting the amount of attractive housing available in other places.

There are at least two plausible reasons to expect high-quality housing to be inelastically supplied in existing upper-income settlements. Nearly all sites in these neighborhoods are already covered by high-quality dwellings. As a result, there is little opportunity for higher prices to stimulate renovation from other uses, and their power to stimulate construction is weakened because they raise the cost of construction sites as well as the gross receipts from newly built units.

Outside these neighborhoods, high-quality housing may be inelastically supplied for either physical or behavioral reasons. The physical characteristics of existing structures may, for example, preclude their transformation into high-quality structures or make the transformation very costly. Even where physical impediments to supply are absent, housing investors may fail to perceive the emergence of demand for quality where it had never existed before. Alternatively, they may regard it as so uncertain that investments in housing improvements are unacceptably risky.[13] Even if such perceptions are not universal among investors, they may dominate the thinking of financial institutions, whose importance as sources of investment funds gives them veto power over real estate development decisions. Indeed, accusations that redlining by banks hastens decline and forestalls reinvestment in urban

---

[13] This is not equivalent to the prisoner's dilemma, where unwillingness to invest stems from neighborhood effects. Here I am arguing that an investment in housing quality is profitable given the current neighborhood characteristics, but inaccurate perceptions make it appear unprofitable.

neighborhoods reflects a widespread belief that such behavior is common.

This discussion of neighborhood supply suggests two testable hypotheses:

1.   Does neighborhood matter? When upper-income residents and upper-income neighborhoods increase in number, is the spatial allocation of the increase affected by the attributes of existing neighborhoods in ways consistent with the analysis presented here?

2.   Do, deviations from the pattern suggested by the long-run equilibrium model confirm the importance of certain inelasticities of supply?

6.   EVIDENCE

Recent demographic trends make possible a direct test of these hypotheses. As has been widely reported, there has been rapid growth in the number of childless households in the United States in the years since 1960 (see Alonso, 1977). Partly, this growth has been caused by the coming of age of the babies of the post-war baby boom, greatly enlarging the cohort of young adults who have yet to start their families. Partly, it results from changes in lifestyle—decisions to remain single, later marriages, greater incidence of divorce, and decisions to postpone or forego having children. Whatever its causes, the increased number of childless households should, if the preceding analysis is correct, cause substantial growth in upper-income demand for sites near the nonwork activities of the CBD and with the neighborhood attributes identified in the theory, while other city neighborhoods continue to suffer the losses of upper-income residents to the suburbs that have characterized American cities throughout the twentieth century. This behavior should be especially evident in cities especially rich in entertainment, cultural, and other nonwork activities in the CBD. For this reason, census data for inner-city locations in New York City will be used for empirical analysis of relationships among growth in upper-income population, neighborhood characteristics, neighborhood change, and neighborhood supply in the 1960s.

As a first step, a measure of neighborhod change must be specified. Such a measure requires knowledge of the number of 1970 residents, their incomes, and estimates of what the size and income of the population would have been had their number and socioeconomic characteristics remained unchanged since 1960. Even in neighborhoods where the number of residents and their socioeconomic attributes had remained unchanged, measured income levels would have risen over the decade, reflecting the normal effects of inflation and growth in real income. These effects must be isolated before neighborhood change can be identified.

For neighborhoods that are congruent with census tracts, the actual numbers and incomes of 1970 residents are available directly from the census. For families, let 1970 income of $0–6999 define low income; $7000–14999, moderate income; $15000–24999, upper-middle income; and $25000 and more, high income. For unrelated individuals, fix the levels of income that divide the classes one-third lower. To estimate what population and incomes would have been had no neighborhood change occurred, assume that the number of families and unrelated individuals in areas with no neighborhood change would have remained the same over the decade and so would their places in the metropolitan income distribution. Then, translate the income classes just defined into percentiles of the 1970 metropolitan distribution, and define 1960 classes that mark off identical percentiles of the 1960 distribution. For New York City families, the appropriate 1960 classes are low income, $0–4594; moderate, $4595–8840; upper-middle, $8841–14,913; and high, over $14,913. Then, for any neighborhood, an identical number of residents in each class in both years would be evidence that no neighborhood change had occurred. Any differences between 1970 and 1960 would be measures of change, either because the neighborhood had shared in metropolitan growth or because it had gained residents from or lost them to other parts of the metropolitan region.

Since the focus of this analysis is residential behavior in neighborhoods near the CBD, the sample is limited to Bronx, Brooklyn, and Manhattan neighborhoods enclosed by a circle with its center at the center of the CBD and a radius of 8 miles. This area comprises the oldest, most central, most densely developed parts of the city. Within the sample, Manhattan neighborhoods within or immediately adjacent to the CBD have been designated the city center, distinguished from other places by especially convenient access to centrally located activities. The boundaries of the center are 110th Street on the north and the southern tip of the island, enclosing an area 8 miles long and 2.5 miles wide. Each neighborhood is an aggregate of several census tracts, and there are 157 neighborhoods in the entire sample.

Neighborhoods have been stratified by their 1960 income and racial composition, as shown in Table 2. Neighborhood income is measured by the median income of families in the neighborhood. As with individual families, a neighborhood can be classified as low, moderate, upper-middle, or high income, according to the class into which its

Table 2
Number of Neighborhoods in Each Location, Income, Race Class, 1960[a]

	Race			
Income	Black	Mixed	Mostly White	White
City center				
Low	4	11	2	0
	(1)	(5)	(1)	(0)
Moderate	0	4	14	7
	(0)	(2)	(5)	(0)
Upper middle	0	0	1	3
	(0)	(0)	(0)	(1)
High	0	0	0	3
	(0)	(0)	(0)	(0)
Rest of sample				
Low	20	18	0	0
	(0)	(3)	(0)	(0)
Moderate	7	15	23	25
	(0)	(0)	(1)	(0)
Upper middle	0	0	0	0
	(0)	(0)	(0)	(0)
High	0	0	0	0
	(0)	(0)	(0)	(0)

Source: U.S. Bureau of the Census (1960).
[a] First figure represents total number of neighborhoods; figure in parentheses shows number with active urban renewal projects during the 1960s.

median income falls. Racial stratification, according to the white pro-portion of the total population, is as follows: black, 0–30% white; mixed, 30–75% white; mostly white, 75–95% white; and white, greater than 95% white. Neighborhood residents of Puerto Rican birth or par-entage are classified with blacks for this analysis. Finally, since urban renewal projects are often designed to foster neighborhood change through large-scale, coordinated changes in neighborhood attributes, neighborhoods where urban renewal was active during the 1960s have been separately identified.

This stratification is used to explain variation among neighbor-hoods in the growth of upper-income households, the component of neighborhood change of principal interest in this study. Upper-income growth is measured by the change from 1960 to 1970 in the total number of upper-middle and high-income families and unrelated individuals. For any neighborhood,

$$\Delta U = \alpha + \sum_{k=2}^{23} \beta_k X_k + \varepsilon, \tag{14}$$

where

ΔU the growth in upper-income households,

X_k dummy neighborhood variables that take the value 1 when the observation describes a neighborhood in the corresponding class and 0 otherwise,

α, β_k parameters,

ε a random normal error.

Estimating Eq. (14) by ordinary least squares for the sample of New York neighborhoods yields the results shown in Table 3. For the absolute change, the dependent variable is simply the change in upper-

Table 3
Growth of Upper-Income Households, 1960–1970

	Absolute Change		Change per 1000 1960 Households	
	Number	t-Ratio	Number	t-Ratio
City center—no urban renewal				
1. Low income black	−40	−.15	−3	−.10
2. Low income mixed	68	.36	11	.54
3. Low income mostly white	84	.18	10	.20
4. Moderate income mixed	−249	−.77	−16	−.45
5. Moderate income mostly white	−268	−1.75	−16	−.95
6. Moderate income white	1713	9.89	187	9.99
7. Upper-middle income mostly white	−97	−.21	−11	−.23
8. Upper-middle income white	1893	5.84	145	4.13
9. High income white	65	.25	5	.19
City center—urban renewal				
10. Low income black	386	.84	52	1.06
11. Low income mixed	367	1.79	38	1.74
12. Low income mostly white	1968	4.29	276	5.56
13. Moderate income mixed	1341	4.14	169	4.81
14. Moderate income mostly white	378	1.84	59	2.64
15. Upper-middle income white	1261	2.75	76	1.53
Rest of sample—no urban renewal				
16. Low income black	−132	−1.29	−19	−1.70
17. Low income mixed	−190	−1.60	−30	−2.33
18. Moderate income black	−227	−1.31	−30	−1.58
19. Moderate income mixed	−358	−3.03	−44	−3.45
20. Moderate income mostly white	−435	−3.64	−58	−5.51
21. Moderate income white	−315	−3.44	−39	−3.94
Rest of sample—urban renewal				
22. Low income mixed	−233	−.88	−34	−1.18
23. Moderate income mostly white	−126	−.27	−9	−.18
Adjusted R^2	.57		.59	

income households, as defined above. For the change per 1000 1960 households, the dependent variable is the change in upper-income households divided by a measure of the total number of 1960 households, to adjust for variations in upper-income growth that result solely from differences in neighborhood size.[14] The numbers and t-ratios reported in Table 3 do not refer directly to the estimated coefficients of Eq. (14) but, rather, to tests of the hypothesis that upper-income growth in each neighborhood category is significantly different from zero. In terms of Eq. (14), the numbers and tests of significance in Table 3 represent for each neighborhood group (k) the quantity $(\alpha + \beta_k)$.

The findings in Table 3 are almost fully consistent with the equilibrium model of neighborhood choice and neighborhood supply. First, irrespective of neighborhood attributes, upper-income growth occurred only in the city center, those locations for which proximity to the CBD creates especially convenient access to centrally located activities. Other neighborhoods in the sample suffered consistent losses of upper-income residents, even those with neighborhood characteristics that led to upper-income growth in their city center counterparts. Within the center, neighborhood characteristics strongly affected the spatial pattern of neighborhood change. In the absence of urban renewal, significant gains in upper-income residents took place only in neighborhoods with at least moderate income and only in those that were essentially all white. The expectation that upper-income demand spills over into neighborhoods much like established upper-income settlements was borne out, especially with regard to race.[15]

The only unexpected result was the lack of upper-income growth in high-income white locations. This lack is presumably the result of a lack of renovation opportunities and a high cost for new construction sites, as discussed in Section 5 in connection with supply elasticities.

Changes in neighborhood supply, as shown in Table 4, are consistent both with a priori hypotheses and with the results in Table 3. In the city center, there is a striking increase in white neighborhoods at the

---

[14] The total number of 1960 households has been defined as the sum of all families and 80% of the unrelated individuals in the neighborhood. The 80% figure is derived from census data on the average ratio of primary individuals (household heads) to total unrelated individuals in Bronx, Brooklyn, and Manhattan.

[15] This correspondence between equilibrium theory and empirical results does not rule out the possibility of supply inelasticities caused by investor misperception or redlining by banks. The fact that upper-income growth was not confined to existing upper-income settlements suggests that such inelasticity is far from absolute. Still, it may have contributed to observed development patterns, such as the absence of upper-income growth in racially mixed areas. Because this kind of supply behavior is not necessary to explain the observed results, the data cannot confirm its existence, however.

Table 4

Changes in Neighborhood Supply, 1960–1970

	Number of neighborhoods	
	(1960)	(1970)
City center		
Low income black	4	5
Low income mixed	11	5
Low income mostly white	2	2
Moderate income mixed	4	5
Moderate income mostly white	14	19
Moderate income white	7	2
Upper-middle income mostly white	1	1
Upper-middle income white	3	8
High income white	3	2
Rest of sample		
Low income black	20	46
Low income mixed	18	11
Moderate income black	7	8
Moderate income mixed	15	16
Moderate income mostly white	23	16
Moderate income white	25	11

Sources: U.S. Bureau of the Census (1960, 1970).

upper end of the income scale and a corresponding decline in white neighborhoods with moderate income, reflecting the transformation of latter into the former. Outside the city center, there is marked shift in neighborhood composition from moderate to low income and from white to black, reflecting continued white flight to the suburbs from these areas.

The power of urban renewal to affect residential choice is also evident in the empirical results. In the center, urban renewal projects produced strong upper-income gains in neighborhoods that otherwise would have had none. Except for low-income black locations, where urban renewal was probably not designed to attract upper-income residents, upper-income growth was significant at the .10 level or better in almost all neighborhoods in which renewal was active.[16] Similarly, in sample locations outside the center, renewal appears to have halted white flight from mostly white neighborhoods with moderate income,

[16] The reduction in low-income mixed neighborhoods and the increase in moderate-income mixed and mostly white neighborhoods in the center, as shown in Table 4, reflect the impact on neighborhood averages of upper-income urban renewal in part of a neighborhood, while the rest of the neighborhood remained essentially unchanged.

where otherwise it was strong. Much of renewal's power to affect residential choice may, of course, be the result of the subsidies it entails as well as the changes it makes in neighborhood characteristics.

7. IMPLICATIONS FOR POLICY

1. Cities like New York, where upper-income growth in central locations has been strong in recent years, have welcomed it for the vitality, financial and otherwise, that it has brought to the inner city. Yet this silver lining is not without its cloud. Consistent with the foregoing analysis, increased supply of upper-income neighborhoods has implied displacement of existing residents from the most stable and most attractive of center's other neighborhoods—first from ethnic enclaves of working-class whites; then from moderate-income interracial areas. This displacement can disrupt strong neighborhood ties and impose moving costs, search costs, and the possibility of inferior housing opportunities on those affected by it. If they are homeowners who sell willingly in return for capital gains, there is no cause for concern, since the willingness to sell implies adequate compensation. If they are driven to leave by rising rents, rising taxes, or landlord decisions, compensation will be inadequate, and the process of neighborhood change will inevitably generate welfare losses and bitterness among the displaced.

2. Given the costs of displacement, two alternative patterns of upper-income development seem potentially more desirable than that which has emerged. First, perhaps it could be diverted to moderate-income neighborhoods just outside the center, where white flight to the suburbs suggests that involuntary displacement may not be a serious issue. Unfortunately, evidence suggests that these neighborhoods are too far from the center to be compatible with frequent nonwork trips to the CBD. And once trips become infrequent, there is little reason for the upper-income resident to forego the still more attractive neighborhoods at more suburban locations. A second alternative is to use urban renewal or similar land clearance mechanisms to transform neighborhoods that are now extremely deteriorated, unstable, and often largely abandoned. The displacement costs of such upper-income development would presumably be less than those that are currently imposed. But the complete replacement of existing residents, such as would be necessary to create a neighborhood environment acceptable to upper-income households, would render such projects vulnerable to attack for being antipoor and antiblack, as were the large-scale urban renewal projects of the 1950s and 1960s.

3. Years of white flight have left many American cities with nothing but relatively poor, relatively black neighborhoods near the CBD, except, perhaps, for an isolated urban renewal project here and there. In these cities, the assumption that neighborhood amenities are uncorrelated with distance from the CBD is best replaced by an assumption of positive correlation between the two. Then, the maximum utility gradient is written

$$\frac{\partial \theta}{\partial D} = - \frac{t[W + N^*]}{Q^*} + \frac{\partial \theta}{\partial A_i} \frac{\partial A_i}{\partial D}. \tag{15}$$

Making use of previous assuptions on the behavior of childless households, the first term on the right of Eq. (15) is negative and becomes more steeply negative with increased income; the second is positive and becomes more steeply positive as income rises. If the second income effect dominates the first, neighborhood attributes will draw even childless households farther from the center the higher their income. If there are, in addition, no nonwork attractions in the core, so that $N^* = 0$ and there is nothing to create incentives for upper-income residence near the CBD, this possibility becomes a certainty. Therefore, in cities where the downtown has become largely lower-class and largely devoid of unique nonwork activities, the likelihood of substantial upper-income development in the private market is small. Even with publicly supported and publicly coordinated redevelopment, the scale of activity required for success and the risks involved weigh heavily against such development.

4. As noted in conjunction with the empirical analysis, growth in upper-income demand for inner-city living appears to stem largely from a vast increase in childless households in recent years. Some of this increase, in turn, has been caused by the coming of age of the children of the post-war baby boom. These young adults have swelled the ranks of 20–35 year olds, for whom living in childless households is common. When this group grows older, begins to raise children in greater numbers, and is replaced by the much smaller cohort that follows it, upper-income demand for central sites may well weaken, even in cities where it is now strong.

REFERENCES

Alonso, W. (1964). *Location and land use.* Harvard University Press, Cambridge, Massachusetts.

Alonso, W. (1977). The population factor and urban structure. Working Paper 102, Harvard Center for Population studies, August 1977.

Green, H. A. J. (1961). Direct additivity and consumers' behavior. *Oxford Economic Papers* **13**, 132–136.

Houthakker, H. S. (1960). Additive preferences. *Econometrica* **28**, 244–257.

Kain, J. F. (1962). The journey-to-work as a determinant of residential location. *Papers and Proceedings of the Regional Science Association* **9**, 137–160.

Kern, C. R. (1977). High income neighborhoods in the city: Will the new demography guarantee their future? Paper presented at the annual meetings of the Regional Science Assoc., Philadelphia.

Mills, E. S. (1967). An aggregative model of resource allocation in a metropolitan area. *American Economic Review* **57**, Papers and Proceedings of the American Economic Association, 197–211.

Muth, R. F. (1969). *Cities and housing.* University of Chicago Press, Chicago.

Polinsky, A. M., and Rubinfeld, D. (1977). Property values and the benefits of environmental improvements: Theory and measurement. In *Public economics and the quality of life*, L. Wingo and A. Evans (eds.). Johns Hopkins University Press, Baltimore. Pp. 154–180.

Polinsky, A. M., and Shavell, S. (1976). Amenities and property values in a model of an urban area. *Journal of Public Economics* **5**, 119–130.

Postlethwaite, A. J. (1977). The return of upper income persons to the city center: Fact or fantasy? Senior honors thesis, Harvard University, Cambridge, Massachusetts.

Rheinhold, R. (1977). Middle-class return displaces some urban poor. *New York Times* **126**, 1 (June 5).

Rosen, S. (1974). Hedonic prices and implicit markets: Product differentiation in pure competition. *Journal of Political Economy* **82**, 34–53.

U.S. Bureau of the Census, (1962). U.S. census of population: 1960, general social and economic characteristics, final report PC(1)-34C, New York. Government Printing Office, Washington, D.C.

U.S. Bureau of the Census, (1962). U.S. census of population: 1960, detailed characteristics, final report PC(1)-34D, New York. Government Printing Ofice.

U.S. Bureau of the Census, (1960). U.S. censuses of population and housing: 1960, special unpublished health area tabulation for the Department of City Planning, City of New York.

U.S. Bureau of the Census, (1972). Census of population: 1970, general social and economic characteristics, final report PC(1)-C34, New York. Government Printing Office, Washington, D.C.

U.S. Bureau of the Census, (1970). Census of population and housing: 1970, special unpublished health area tabulation for the Department of City Planning, City of New York.

Yinger, J. (1976). Racial prejudice and racial residential structure in an urban model. *Journal Urban Economics* **3**, 383–396.

7

The Role of Governments as Suppliers of Neighborhoods

LESLEY DANIELS

What constitutes a neighborhood differs from individual to individual, and from function to function. In the case of individuals, boundaries often are established on the basis of maximal homogeneity within and maximal heterogeneity between geographical groupings of people. The shared characteristics may be ethnicity, race, socioeconomic status, and age cohorts. Alternatively, one could employ a definition based on locational proximity to goods shared by a neighborhood. This functional description could be represented as a vector of collective goods geographically specific to an area (e.g., schools, parks and recreation centers, shopping districts, district representatives, etc.).

This chapter is concerned with the supply of the latter. Usually in the literature the supply mechanism of these collective goods is subsumed under median voter outcomes or as exogenously given implicit qualities of the housing stock. Offering "types" of neighborhoods to the market is thus viewed as decentralized or as determined in equilibrium by adoption (see Tiebout, 1956). However, the supply of local public goods to neighborhoods incorporated under one centralized authority is not necessarily a duplication of decentralized market outcomes when each neighborhood is self-incorporated. In the former case there is but one decision maker, the centralized government, and many possible partitions of aggregate supply that determine the types of functional neighborhoods available to consumers. And there is no reason to suppose that the array of types of public goods supplied under a central authority duplicates that offered to consumers if the jurisdictions were to become independent.

The conjecture of this chapter is that the spread of public good (neighborhood) types will be less complete than the one assumed by Tiebout at the outset of the consumer adoption process. Furthermore, it will be shown that the institutional structure on the supply side of the local public goods market determines the degree to which the spread is less complete than that necessary for full consumer sovereignty.

Why is this important? To the extent that there is a narrowing of the spectrum of available public goods, there is a loss in consumer welfare. If the "narrowness" of the neighborhood array differs depending on the centrality of decision making, then there will be a difference in the degree of loss of consumer welfare, given alternative jurisdictional structures. Therefore the optimum of the consumer can be only *locally* optimal *given* the organizational form assumed on the supply side, but will not be *globally* optimal in general. In short, consumer sovereignty will be constrained with an imperfect supply side.

The analysis that follows is partial equilibrium. It deals with interrelated markets in the sense that neighborhoods (more precisely, those public goods characterizing each zone) are substitutes, but only imperfect ones given an individual's preferences. Questions of existence and uniqueness of equilibria in these markets reach beyond the interests of this chapter; only issues of bias in the types of public services provided under centralized and decentralized authorities will be considered.

1. THE GEOGRAPHY

In the model the urban area L is viewed as divided into a finite number of zones, $j = 1, \ldots , z$, $\cup_j = L$, $j_1, \ldots , j_z$ disjoint. The shape of these zones is not critical as long as they are dense and nonoverlapping—squares, hexagonal and triangular configurations are examples.

Each zone is characterized by a locationally specific public good P_j

that is provided only at predetermined fixed points.[1] Each P_j in turn defines the zone around it. The boundaries of each zone may be determined through legal sharing rules; alternatively there may be some physical constraint, such as distance traveled or time spent procurring the public good, that may generate a de facto sharing rule. For example, using a Lancastrian household production function of the type

$$G_j = G_j[P_j, \, 24\text{-}H(d(x[P_j], y)^\alpha)],$$

where G_j is output of a public good activity for the household, P_j is the public good input into household production, 24-H is the number of leisure hours spent traveling to the good, $d(x[P_j], y)$ is the Euclidian distance defined over the two-dimensional jth zone between the site $x(P_j)$ of the public good and the household's location at y, and α is the measure of congestion, $\alpha > 1$, will define a "technological" boundary to each zone and each type of public good given the relevant cost parameters. It is assumed that the boundaries are given exogenously and are optimal with respect to distance, the type of public good, and the congestion exponent (usually written in the literature as a function of the density of population).

2. THE GOVERNMENT SECTOR

Concerning the supply of public goods, it is assumed that both the quantity supplied in each zone and types of goods (zones) supplied is determined by the criterion of fiscal profitability. In this case, the objective function of the government authority is to maximize land value net of the cost of providing the public goods. The justification for selecting this objective function is twofold: given a constant output level of the local public good in a zone, if land values increase this amounts to a reduction in the tax burden of residents in that neighborhood. Having elected this administrator once, the rational voter would obviously choose to reelect this person, if the above occurs, ceteris paribus. Because of this, selecting net land value maximization as an objective function satisfies the need for reelection in the political market. Moreover, by holding the tax rate constant, in the face increasing land values, the administrator is able to expand production (whether internal to the bureaucracy or through increasing output of the public good) due to higher revenues. Thus maximizing land values net of cost meets reelec-

---

[1] The necessity of such an assumption to avoid considering a class of economies with nonexistent equilibria in a world where all agents and goods are freely mobile has been shown by Starrett (1976).

tion and expansion criteria, yet avoids the problems inherent in median voter schemes of assuming unidimensionality of the preference space or symmetry of voters' maxima around the mean. [See Niskanen (1971) for a fuller description of the role of reelection constraints and expansion goals in determining the actions of a political administrator.]

The cost function associated with each zone's type of public good P_j will be the simple functional form

$$c_j(P_j) + F_j \qquad c_j, F_j > 0, \; \forall j, \qquad (1)$$

where $c_j(P_j)$ are continuous variable costs, and F_j is the fixed cost associated with each zone's type of public good. It is assumed further that the social optimization problem as to selection of the boundary, or

such that
$$\min_{l_j} C^j[P_j, \; 24 - H(d(x[P_j], \; y)^\alpha)]$$
$$C^j = C^j(c_j P_j; \; F_j; \; w)$$
$$P_j > 0,$$

where l_j is total land area and w is the wage rate, has been solved for the optimal size l_j of each zone j for a given number of people.

What then is the value of land? Its sole determinant of value is the social overhead capital provided by the local government. In other words, land that is devoid of a local public good has no use in consumption or household production. Therefore it can be written as

$$l_j = l_j(P_j) \qquad (\partial l_j)/(\partial P_j) > 0, \qquad (2)$$

where l_j is monotonic transformation:

$$l_j(P_j) > l_k(P_k) \qquad \text{for} \quad P_j > P_k$$
$$l_j(P_j) = l_k(P_k) \qquad \text{for} \quad P_j = P_k.$$

If public overhead is land's sole value, then the aggregate valuation of land in each zone must be the consumers' willingness to pay for the public good characterizing that neighborhood. Total land value in each zone, therefore, is each individual's willingness to pay times the amount of public good provided, summed over all individuals living in that zone.

It is further assumed that there are no externalities between zones and that public services are not jointly produced.[2]

[2] It may be asked why, if goods are not jointly produced and if boundaries are selected optimally, would one have a centralized government? The answer does not rest on assuming the existence of governmental functions with large economies of scale in some other services not considered here; for neighborhoods may be incorporated under a central authority, but independent jurisdictions usually belong to a county organization. Rather, the allocation mechanism may be centralized in one, and decentralized in the other without a corresponding loss in technical efficiency, a priori.

3. THE CONSUMER

There are n consumers in the urban area. Each consumer i, $i = 1, \ldots , n$ is further described by j, indicating in which zone the consumer lives. In order that the benefits to the individual living in neighborhood j can be written as the benefit function

$$u_{ij}(l_j) \tag{3}$$

and that the aggregate benefits of all residents living in j be described as

$$\sum_i u_{ij}(l_j) \qquad \forall i \in j, \tag{4}$$

some restrictive assumptions on utility functions must be made.

It is assumed that utility functions generating the benefit function[3] $u_{ij}(l_j)$ are homothetic with respect to the origin, that is, they are monotonically increasing transforms of a homogeneous function,[4] and are twice differentiable. Given the assumption of homotheticity, consumer surplus benefit functions are then simply the corresponding indirect utility functions. In using a consumer surplus measure of benefits in the analysis, income effects are assumed away. That is, it is assumed that the marginal utility of income is equal to a constant; or for the indirect utility function associated with the utility function generating $u_{ij}(l_j)$

$$V_{ij} = V_{ij}(t_j, I), \tag{5}$$

where t_j is the (tax) price of living in zone j, and I is income, that

$$\lambda_{ij}(t_j, I)$$
$$\lambda_{ij} = (\partial V_{ij})/(\partial I)$$

is independent of I, or equal to a constant. Also, it is assumed that $\lambda_{ij}(t_j, I)$ is independent of j[5] so that $\lambda_{ij} = a > 0$ is invariant with respect to zone (see Chipman and Moore, 1977). The reason for this is that a total measurement of benefits to the urban area, or

$$\sum_{j=1}^{z} \sum_i u_{ij}(l_j) \tag{6}$$

must be independent of income effects.

[3] The benefit function is a monotonic transform (1:1 correspondence) of the direct utility function with direct preferences.

[4] Given utility functions $U_0, U_1, F(U)$ is a monotonic transformation if $F(U_1) > F(U_0)$ wherever $U_1 > U_0$.

[5] In general, the fact that people live in only one zone or neighborhood implies non-convexities in the consumption or household production set (see Pines and Weiss 1976). As such, P_j represents a singleton in the indirect utility function, or $U_{ij}(l_j)$ is defined only for the zone l_j, $u_{ij}(l_k) = 0$ for $k \neq j$.

This way of representing aggregate benefits can be shown to be consistent with an Eisenberg social welfare function (Eisenberg, 1961). The functional form of an Eisenberg social welfare function is

$$SW = \Pi U_{ij}{}^{\alpha_i}(l_j),\tag{6'}$$

where

$$\alpha_i = \left(m_{ij} \Big/ \sum_j \sum_i m_{ij} \right),$$

m_{ij} is the income of individual i and Π the product over each i's utility. Taking the log of (6') yields

$$\log SW = \sum_{j=1}^{z} \sum_i \alpha_i \log U_{ij}(l_j).\tag{6''}$$

Equation (6'') is a monotonic transform of Eq. (6)

$$\sum_{j=1}^{z} \sum_i U_{ij}(l_j),$$

and is therefore representable by Eq. (6), with the exception of the income weights α_i.

However, by assuming that the initial distribution of income is optimal in a first-best sense,

$$\alpha_i = \beta \frac{1}{\lambda_{ij}} \; \forall_{i,j}.\tag{6'''}$$

In making this assumption, Eq. (6'') is then a simple monotonic transform of Eq. (6) except for a constant of proportionality β and therefore represents an Eisenberg social utility function. (For a further discussion see Rader, 1976.)

There are three properties of the benefit function that should be mentioned due to their centrality in the analysis. The first is the concavity of the benefit function $u_{ij}(l_j)$. This is necessary to insure downward sloping demand curves for land in neighborhood j. The second is that the derivative of the benefit function with respect to land in the jth zone is the inverse demand function for land in that zone, given that residents face a spectrum of (tax) prices of land (public good) over the zones:

$$\partial u_{ij}(l_j)/\partial l_j = t_j.\tag{7}$$

Third, it is assumed that

$$\partial u_{ij}(lj)/(\partial l_i \partial l_j) < 0.\tag{8}$$

The implication is that neighborhood characteristics are pairwise substitutes (albeit imperfectly) in the individuals' benefit function. However, the fact that the goods are pairwise substitutes in terms of preference does not rule out corner solutions of consuming only one zone's public good (or having residency in only one jurisdiction). This will be due to either the presence of de jure sharing rules or by the use of a distance function in the household production function; either way the effect is the same—a law of inclusion (exclusion) with respect to residency or proximity.

4. BENEFIT FROM INCREASING THE PUBLIC GOOD SPECTRUM

Given the independence of the marginal utility of income from the zone of residence, the aggregate benefits from urban incorporation for a given number of zones z is

$$\sum_{j=1}^{z} \sum_{i} u_{ij}(l_j). \tag{9}$$

Each zone is represented by a different type of public good[6]: households locate in the zone approximating most closely their optimum type of service given that convex combinations of types across zones is ruled out by sharing rules.

The gross benefits from the zth zone added to the urban area can be measured as

$$\sum_{j=1}^{z} \sum_{i} u_{ij}(l_j) - \sum_{j=1}^{z-1} \sum_{i} u_{ij}(l_j). \tag{10}$$

Net benefits from the addition of a zone on the margin are

$$u_z = \sum_{j=1}^{z} \sum_{i} u_{ij}(l_j) - \sum_{j=1}^{z-1} \sum_{i} u_{ij}(l_j) - [c_z(P_z) + F_z]. \tag{11}$$

The first term in Eq. (10) represents aggregate benefits from the spread of neighborhood types when the "type" of neighborhoods has been increased by one. The second term in Eq. (10) represents aggregate benefits prior to the change. As an example, consider ten school districts, all but one with similar general-education high schools, and

---

[6] It is convenient to think of each zone as characterized by one specific type of good, $l_j = l_j(P_j)$; but P_j may also be thought of as representing a vector in production space of different types or combinations of public goods $s = 1, \ldots, n$ (e.g., type of school, garbage pickup frequency, water clarity). Then if p represents the product space, $P \subset R_+^s$ for $P_j \in P$, $P_j = (p_1, \ldots, p_n)|p_s \geq 0$, $s = 1, 2, \ldots, n$; $P_j \neq P_k \Longrightarrow (P_{1j}, \ldots, p_{nj}) \neq (p_{1k}, \ldots, p_{nk})$ for at least 1s.

one with a technical orientation. Equation (10) captures the benefits with this given differentiation of one of the high schools.

It is possible to expand upon the two terms in (10) to make clearer the nature of benefits from substitutions of a neighborhood that is a closer approximation to a set of consumers' true preferences:

$$\sum_{j=1}^{z} \sum_{i} u_{ij}(l_j) - \sum_{j=1}^{z-1} \sum_{i} u_{ij}(l_j)$$

$$= \sum_{i} u_{iz}(l_z) - \sum_{j=1}^{z-1} \sum_{i \in z} u_{ij}(l_j). \qquad (12)$$

The first term in Eq. (12) is the total benefits from those individuals now residing in the (differentiated) zone z and is positive; given that they have relocated, or transferred consumer loyalty, they must be receiving a higher utility level than when located in $j = 1, \ldots, z - 1$ zones (i.e., the new P_z more closely resembles their optimum). The second term represents the corresponding decrease in benefits, aggregated over all other zones, due to the transference of some proportion of surplus from the $j = 1, \ldots, z - 1$ zones to the zth zone. It is a pairwise comparison and it is negative since the residents in z were receiving some benefits from prior consumption of $(P_1, \ldots, P_{z-1})$, and these must be subtracted from aggregate benefits received in z in order to not overstate the incremental benefits from "adding" z.

It is assumed that the first term of Eq. (12) is concave and the second term of Eq. (12) is convex in order to insure downward sloping demand curves.[7] Since the first term represents the willingness to pay schedule of those located in the new neighborhood, and the second term is the degree to which substitution of the new zone for the old zones has taken place, Eq. (12) can be put in a more general functional form:

$$\sum_{i} \phi_{iz}(l_z) - \sum_{j=1}^{z-1} \eta_{jz}(l_j). \qquad (13)$$

Net benefits from adding an additional neighborhood of type z to the urban area become

$$u_z = \sum_{i} \phi_{iz}(l_z) - \sum_{j=1}^{z-1} \eta_{iz}(l_j) - c_z(P_z) - F_z. \qquad (14)$$

[7] It is true that neither term is continuous since people migrate in only discrete jumps, but each can be approximated by a continuous curve.

5. BIASES NOT DUE TO INSTITUTIONAL FORM

In this section the problem of "narrowness" of the neighborhood spectrum will be explored without regard to the institutional framework. The question to be answered here is in a Tiebout selection process to what extent at any point in time is there a full range of neighborhoods, or jurisdictions, over which choices of residence can be exercised? If there are biases against provision of particular types of local public goods then the exercise of consumer sovereignty is constrained to those types of neighborhoods (or zones) consistent with land value maximization objectives.

From Eq. (13), gross incremental benefits from expanding the types of neighborhoods by one is

$$\sum_i \phi_{iz}(l_z) - \sum_{j=1}^{z-1} \eta_{jz}(l_j).$$

The inverse demand for land in the zth zone, and therefore the P_z public good type characterizing this zth neighborhood [since $l_z = l_z(P_z)$], is the derivative of Eq. (13) with respect to l_z,

$$\sum_i \phi'_{iz}(l_z) - \sum_{j=1}^{z-1} \eta'_{jz}(l_j), \tag{15}$$

where prime denotes the derivative. Net land value associated with the zth zone is the inverse demand for P_z times the amount of improved land in this zone:

$$\sum_i \phi'_{iz}(l_z)l_z - \sum_{j=1}^{z-1} \eta'_{jz}(l_j)l_z - c_z P_z - F_z. \tag{16}$$

The decision rule for providing the zth type of neighborhood is

$$\sum_i \phi'_{iz}(l_z)l_z \geq \sum_{j=1}^{z-1} \eta'_{jz}(l_j)l_z + c_z P_z + F_z, \tag{17}$$

or that the total land value evaluated at the marginal willingness to pay for each resident must at least equal the corresponding loss in land value in the preexisting zones and cover fixed costs if it is to be provided. If the right-hand side of Eq. (17) is less than the left-hand side then the zth neighborhood type will fail to be provided in the market.

By inspection of Eq. (16), it is obvious that the greater F_z is relative to $\sum \phi'_{iz}(l_z)l_z$ (expropriated surplus) ceteris paribus, the more likely the spectrum of public good neighborhoods will not encompass this type of zone.[8,9]

6. BIASES INDUCED BY INSTITUTIONAL STRUCTURE

As shown in the preceding section, the neighborhood spectrum in no sense will be complete, and will be biased against those public goods for which (a) the number of people and the amount they are willing to pay is small relative to costs; and (b) those public goods for which fixed costs are high. In this section the argument is considered that the degree to which the neighborhood spectrum is narrowed depends upon the decentralized versus centralized institutional framework of the Tiebout market.

For the centralized case, the abstraction is easily accomplished. One need only consider the local government as owning all the land in the urban area, and then deciding how many neighborhoods of different types should be provided to capture the maximal amount of consumers' willingness to pay, consistent with meeting costs. However, in the case of a decentralized market, the problem is not that of a centralized monopolist deciding to what extent to segment the market given that net population changes are equal to zero.[10] The problem is more akin to that of monopolistic competition.

This was suggested by Thompson (1968),

Local governments compete for residents, even though the inconvenience of moving one's household may make it a sluggish market. The analogy between differentiated products in the market place and differential political subdivisions suggests the applicability of the concepts of monopolistic competition to the large metropolitan area [pp. 258–259].

[8] This result on market failure is well known; see Spence (1975).

[9] This may also explain why large physical structures that are locationally specific public goods and involve high plant costs (e.g., museums, concert halls, zoos) are not provided by general revenues from the local fisc, but by private benefactors and/or the federal government.

[10] The analogy can be made to zero versus nonzero sum games. For the centralized producer in a closed system such as the one in this chapter, there is no net change in population due to change in number of types of neighborhoods. Thus the problem discussed in Starrett (1976b) disappears. However, with decentralized competitors for population, one zone's gain is another's loss. For each zone, therefore, the game is nonzero sum, and reaction functions must be specified.

The problem confronting the centralized authority is to

$$\max_{P_j} \sum_{j=1} \sum_{i} \left[\phi'_{ij}(l_j)l_j - \sum_{k \neq j} \eta'_{kj}(l_k)l_j - c_j P_j - F_j \right] \qquad (18)$$

for all feasible $P_j \in P$, which is aggregate net land value expressed for all possible types of neighborhoods in the set P.

Given the inclusion of the j as a decision variable, the centralized authority will seek to minimize the term $\Sigma_k \eta'_{kj}(l_k)l_j$. In general it will be true that minimizing this term implies *not* producing close substitutes in the set $P_j \in P$. A large product spectrum will be covered to minimize the subtracted loss in land value from people leaving the old zones, relative to the gain in land value from being able to extract higher land value (willingness to pay) from the specialized set of residents now located in the new zone.[11]

For decentralized governments, the equation corresponding to Eq. (18) is

$$\max_{P_z} l_z \left[\sum_{i} \phi'_{iz}(l_z) - \sum_{j \neq z} \eta'_{jz}(l_j)l_z \right] - c_z P_z - F_z. \qquad (19)$$

What type of P_z should be selected? Unlike the centralized authority to whom neighborhood specialization yields the maximal land value, the decentralized administration has no control over the selection of $l_j = l_j(P_j)$ made by the $z - 1$ firms. There will be a different net land value in the zth zone depending on the types of local public goods provided by its rivals. Thus net land value in z is a function of the "type of jurisdiction" decisions taken in other autonomous zones j, $j \neq z$, as well as its own.

Consider the representative municipality. Given that this government can provide any type of local public good it wants, it would select that type that minimizes the ratio of average land value to marginal land value. Since people are taxed at the marginal willingness-to-pay land value under fiscal profitability criteria, without perfect discrimination, minimizing this ratio with respect to selection of P_z will yield the maximal capture of sonsumer surplus. Average land value for type of public good P_z is

$$\sum_{i} \phi'_{iz}(l_z) - \sum_{j \neq z} \eta'_{zj}(l_j)l_z. \qquad (20)$$

---

[11] However, since fixed costs must be covered, the spectrum is still reduced relative to the optimum; furthermore, not all surplus is appropriated since $\phi'_{ij}(l_j)l_j < \phi_{ij}(l_j)$ due to concavity of ϕ.

Land value evaluated at the marginal willingness-to-pay point is

$$\sum_i [\phi_{iz}'(l_z) + l_z\phi_{iz}''] - \sum_{j\neq z} [\eta_{zj}'l_j + \eta''l_jl_z]. \tag{21}$$

The ratio of average land value to marginal land value is

$$\frac{\Sigma_i \, \phi_{iz}'(l_z) - \Sigma_{j\neq z} \, \eta_{zj}'l_j}{\Sigma_i \, [\phi_{iz}'(l_z) + l_z\phi_{iz}''] - \Sigma_{j\neq z} \, [\eta_{zj}'l_j + \eta_{jz}''l_jl_z]} = A. \tag{22}$$

A is minimized when B is maximized:

$$\sum_i l_z\phi_{iz}'' - \sum_j \eta_{jz}''l_jl_z = B. \tag{23}$$

B is large when the inverse demand curves are relatively flat, or when the type of good has a high elasticity of demand. The sort of neighborhood local public good with this characteristic is that which appeals to a wide spectrum of tastes, and not the type that attracts only those with "extreme" or pronouncedly different preferences. Thus the optimal strategy for autonomous decentralized jurisdictions is to offer those types of public goods most likely to attract the maximal number of people from other jurisdictions, and not to specialize in offering a good for which minimal total willingness-to-pay can be captured in land values.

The difference between centralized and decentralized provision now becomes apparent, given that land value maximization is the objective function in both cases. A centralized authority will accentuate the differences between neighborhoods, though not to a socially optimal degree, because substitutability effects can be controlled. The decentralization of such a system would lead to competitive or comparable types of jurisdictions, thus narrowing the spectrum of public good neighborhood types available in a Tiebout market. With measure of welfare in terms of consumer surplus, the effect of altering market structure on incentives to provide diversified public services (or, for that matter, any good) becomes obvious; the degree to which transference of surplus is internalized in a given market structure has a direct effect on the resulting broadness of the choice spectrum.

There are two conclusions reached in this chapter.

1. It is impossible to have a full spectrum of neighborhood types available for a Tiebout residence selection process. This is because some types of neighborhoods or locationally specific public goods, while valued by a small subset of consumers, do not permit coverage of fixed costs when the goods are financed by a land value tax. This may be exacerbated by the fact that residents' benefits from living in a zone

with the special public good cannot be fully taxed away; only the marginal valuation of sites in that zone is actually taxed.

2. Given that jurisdictions seek to maximize land value net of the costs of providing the social overhead capital, large cities with central planning will provide a larger spectrum of neighborhood public good types than would be available with autonomous neighborhoods. This result does not rest on technical efficiency grounds, but rather on ability to control for substitutability of sites in one case as opposed to the other.

There are several policy recommendations that can be made in light of these results. Most obvious is the need for subsidization in those cases where incremental land value tax revenues are insufficient to cover the fixed costs of large capital construction. The market cost–benefit test may be an underestimation of true benefits relative to costs in urban areas dependent on land value taxes, so that intervention by higher levels of government may be socially beneficial.

The basis of economic theory and welfare analysis is the exercise of consumer sovereignty. To the extent that such exercise is constrained by institutional structures causing a reduction in public good differentiation, central planning becomes necessary. Maximal consumer sovereignty with land value taxation is achieved through centralized decision making; as such, the role of providing diversity within the urban area should be stressed as a function of metro-wide political organizations.

Third, the past few years have seen a return of middle-income younger people to the larger cities. One of the reasons for this may be the greater diversity of large city neighborhoods and the feelings of vitality generated by their variety. This variety need not be of major proportions—examples may be different types of street lamps, parks provided, specialized services, or the uniqueness of the neighborhood school. No doubt this inmigration will have healthy effects on the urban tax base. If their demand is due to diversity within big cities, then in this age of urban fiscal plight it should be encouraged by providing maximal heterogeneity of services in the cities.

A caveat is in order. Even though the context in this chapter has been that of locationally specific public goods and the neighborhoods that form around them, public service differentials do not account for most of the distinctiveness between neighborhoods. The type of architecture, socioeconomic status of residents, and age of housing stock contribute a great deal to the vector of neighborhood characteristics. In any effort to revitalize neighborhoods in large urban areas, the composite package of housing must be taken into account in planning particulars of policy recommendations.

REFERENCES

Chipman, J., and Moore, J. (1977). The scope of consumer's surplus arguments. In *Evolution, welfare, and time in economics,* Anthony M. Tang *et al.* (eds.). D. C. Heath and Company, Lexington, Massachusetts.

Eisenberg, E. (1961). Aggregation of Utility functions. *Management Science* **7,** 337–350.

Niskanen, W. (1971). *Bureaucracy and representative government.* Aldine, Chicago.

Pines, D., and Weiss, Y. (1976). Land improvement projects and land values. *Journal of Urban Economics* **3,** 1–13.

Rader, T. (1976). Equivalence of consumer surplus, the divisia index of output, and Eisenberg's addilog social utility. *Journal of Economic Theory* **131,** 58–66.

Sonstelie, J., and Portney, P. (1976). Profit maximizing communities and the theory of local public expenditure. Unpublished paper, Resources for the Future. Forthcoming in the *Journal of Urban Economics.*

Spence, M. (1975). Product selection, fixed costs, and monopolistic competition. Technical Report No. 157, Economics Series, Institute for Mathematical Studies in the Social Sciences, Stanford University.

Starrett, D. (1976a). Market allocations of location choice in a model with free mobility. Technical Report No. 200, Economics Series, Institute for Mathematical Studies in the Social Sciences, Stanford University.

Starrett, D. (1976b). Welfare measurement for local public finance. Technical Report No. 228, Economics Series, Institute for Mathematical Studies in the Social Sciences, Stanford University.

Tiebout, C. (1956). A pure theory of local expenditure. *Journal of Political Economy* **64,** 416–424.

Thompson, W. (1968). *A preface to urban economics.* Johns Hopkins Press, Baltimore.

8

Modeling Neighborhood Change

JOHN F. KAIN
WILLIAM C. APGAR, JR.

1. INTRODUCTION

The NBER (National Bureau of Economic Research) Urban Simulation Model is primarily a model of the urban housing market.[1] Although it represents other phenomena such as industrial location, transportation systems, and changes in the demographic structure of the population, the behavior of housing consumers, suppliers, and the housing "market" is its central focus. The Demand Sector of the model represents changes in the level and mix of employment at each of several workplaces; decisions of individual sample households to move; their choices of housing bundles and residence locations; and decisions to own or rent their housing. The several supply submodels simulate the production of housing services by individual property owners and owner–occupants; changes in the amounts of maintenance and structure capital embodied in existing structures; alterations in the size and configuration of individual structures through additions or subdivisions; and the construction of new structures on vacant land. The

[1] A detailed description of the NBER Urban Simulation Model and the Pittsburgh and Chicago simulations is contained in Kain et al. (1977) and Kain and Apgar (1977).

THE ECONOMICS OF NEIGHBORHOOD

Market Sector assigns households with specific workplace locations to available units in specific residence zones; calculates the market rents for each housing bundle type in each residence zone; and determines the quantities of structure services consumed by each household and the rents paid for them. In general, housing prices are represented by monthly market rents in the case of rental units, and imputed monthly rents for owner-occupied units.

Of the existing operational models of urban housing markets, the NBER model provides the most explicit representation of how neighborhood characteristics influence the behavior of housing consumers and suppliers, and how their decisions in turn affect neighborhood quality. The NBER model, calibrated to Pittsburgh and Chicago, has been used to carry out baseline and policy simulations for the period 1960–1970. In these simulations, we annually consider between 72,000 and 84,000 sample households and dwelling units. These households are a 1-in-10 random sample of Pittsburgh households and a 1-in-25 sample of Chicago households. The large samples are dictated by the highly detailed and disaggregated descriptions of households, dwelling units, structures, and neighborhoods represented in the model. In our judgment, the analysis of neighborhood change and other aspects of housing market dynamics requires this extensive detail and high level of disaggregation.

Current period neighborhood characteristics and expectations about neighborhood change influence all aspects of the model. In this chapter we examine selected results from the Pittsburgh and Chicago simulations which illustrate the importance of neighborhood change in housing market dynamics. We then discuss how neighborhood characteristics and expectations about neighborhood change are represented in the NBER model.

2. SIMULATIONS OF NEIGHBORHOOD CHANGE

The current version of the NBER model distinguishes 50 types of housing bundles defined by structure type, number of rooms, and neighborhood quality. Displayed in Table 1 are statistics on the simulated numbers of dwelling units in Pittsburgh and Chicago summarized by the 10 structure types and 5 neighborhood types that combine to create the 50 housing bundles included in the analysis. These data reveal similarities in the pattern of housing stock changes in the two cities, but also important differences.

Table 1

Number of Units by Structure Type and Neighborhood in 1960, 1965, and 1970:
Pittsburgh and Chicago Baseline Simulations

Structure Type	Pittsburgh			Chicago		
	1960	1965	1970	1960	1965	1970
Small-lot single-family						
0–2 bedrooms	213,940	210,100	222,550	385,000	393,950	389,425
3 bedrooms	124,700	135,570	149,810	184,325	210,925	234,225
4 or more bedrooms	65,870	63,600	61,980	111,675	114,725	117,225
Large-lot single-family						
0–2 bedrooms	62,680	67,620	74,590	95,075	124,525	161,975
3 bedrooms	50,430	50,620	50,740	56,375	72,050	88,275
4 or more bedrooms	34,600	34,020	33,360	60,075	59,850	57,925
Small multifamily						
0–1 bedroom	80,790	83,760	98,790	242,550	251,250	279,150
2 or more bedrooms	36,570	34,080	34,170	297,600	343,500	405,300
Large multifamily						
0–1 bedroom	45,680	45,680	47,840	406,800	389,800	397,400
2 or more bedrooms	9,840	9,120	9,760	102,800	104,800	111,800
Neighborhood type						
I worst	270,970	274,260	220,970	454,325	512,975	568,275
II	202,960	140,370	145,110	384,250	326,050	236,175
III	139,660	123,150	92,260	395,125	264,600	192,200
IV	77,370	121,320	159,660	267,975	313,800	234,325
V best	34,140	75,070	165,590	440,600	647,950	1,011,725
All	725,100	734,170	783,590	1,942,275	2,065,375	2,242,700

In the Pittsburgh baseline simulations, the number of dwelling units increased over the decade for 6 of the 10 structure type categories and 2 of the 5 neighborhood types. Structure types with the highest growth rates are small multiple structures with zero or one bedrooms (22%); small-lot single-family units with three bedrooms (20%); and large-lot single-family units with zero or one bedrooms (19%). In contrast, the four structure types demonstrating decreases are those with the most bedrooms: single-family homes with four or more bedrooms are 94 and 96% of their 1960 levels by the end of the decade; and units with two or more bedrooms in both small and large multifamily structures, 93 and 99%. These simulated changes in Pittsburgh's housing stock apparently result from a shift in demand toward smaller units over the decade.

The three lowest quality neighborhoods in Pittsburgh have simulated losses over the decade so that the numbers of units in 1970 are only 82, 71, and 66% of 1960 levels. At the same time, the number of units in the best and second-best neighborhoods experienced growth rates of 385 and 106%, respectively. These increases refer to a relatively small base, however, since the highest quality neighborhoods contained only 34,140 structures in 1960 and the second best, only 77,370.

In the Chicago baseline simulations, eight structure type categories gained units over the decade, reflecting that city's higher overall growth rate. The two exceptions are large-lot single-family units with four or more bedrooms and zero or one bedroom units in large apartment structures. The structure types exhibiting the most rapid growth rates are large-lot single-family units with zero to two bedrooms (70%), and with three bedrooms (56%); and units in small apartment buildings with two or more bedrooms (36%). The number of small-lot single-family units with three bedrooms also increased by 27%. In Chicago, then, the simulated growth in dwelling units is concentrated in single-family homes and larger apartment units, that is, those with two or more bedrooms. Such changes in the housing stock suggest a different market response than Pittsburgh's and apparently reflect differences in the rates of income or population growth.

The pattern of changes in Chicago's housing stock by neighborhood type also differs somewhat from Pittsburgh's. During the period 1960–1965, the number of dwelling units located in Chicago's worst, best, and second-best neighborhoods increased, with the largest percentage growth occurring in the best neighborhoods. In the second half of the decade, however, the number of units in the second best neighborhood category declined to only 87% of the number existing in 1960; the number of units located in the best neighborhoods increased by 130%; and the number in the worst neighborhood category increased by 25%.

Simulated changes in dwelling units reflect the combined effects of new construction, demolitions, conversions, and neighborhood transition. Shown in Table 2 are the components of inventory change for each of the 10 structure types included in the model. For Pittsburgh, approximately two-thirds of the simulated new construction activity between 1960 and 1970 consists of single-family units. The Chicago baseline simulations, in contrast, indicate that 54% of new construction consists of apartment buildings, particularly those containing zero or one bedroom units. Chicago's single-family completions are also more heavily concentrated in large lot units than Pittsburgh's.

The Chicago and Pittsburgh baseline simulations demonstrate that emphasis of most housing market analyses on new construction is somewhat misplaced since neighborhood change has a far more important influence on housing stock characteristics. As Table 3 illustrates,

Table 2
Simulated Stock Changes for the Decade 1960–1970 by Structure Type: Pittsburgh and Chicago Baseline Simulations

Stucture Type	Pittsburgh				Chicago			
	New Construction	Losses		Total Change	New Construction	Losses		Total Change
		Demolition	Conversion			Demolition	Conversion	
Small-lot single-family								
0–2 bedrooms	36,190	27,220	−360	8,610	22,225	−15,200	−2,600	4,425
3 bedrooms	31,310	6,200	0	25,110	54,700	−3,650	−1,150	49,900
4 or more bedrooms	1,300	5,190	0	−3,890	9,400	−3,850	0	5,550
Large-lot single-family								
0–2 bedrooms	17,850	5,620	−320	11,910	70,175	−2,900	−375	66,900
3 bedrooms	3,250	2,670	−270	310	33,125	−1,025	−200	31,900
4 or more bedrooms	1,130	2,370	0	−1,240	975	−2,925	−200	−2,150
Small multifamily								
0–1 bedroom	30,000	12,000	0	18,000	64,125	−27,225	−300	36,600
2 or more bedrooms	3,210	5,610	0	2,400	124,200	−16,500	0	107,700
Large multifamily								
0–1 bedroom	8,800	6,640	0	2,160	51,200	−59,600	−1,000	−9,400
2 or more bedrooms	2,320	2,400	0	−80	22,200	−13,200	0	9,000
Total	135,360	−75,920	−950	58,490	452,325	−146,075	−5,825	300,425

Table 3
Simulated Stock Changes for the Decade 1960–1970 by Type of Neighborhood: Pittsburgh and Chicago Baseline Simulations

Neighborhood Type	New Construction	Losses		Neighborhood Change	Total Change
		Demolitions	Conversions		
Pittsburgh					
I Worst	20,830	−49,960	−290	−20,580	−50,000
II	33,890	−13,540	−530	−77,670	−57,850
III	25,710	−6,030	−90	−66,990	−37,400
IV	28,670	−4,610	−40	58,270	82,290
V Best	26,260	−1,780	0	106,970	131,450
All	135,360	−75,920	−950	0	58,490
Chicago					
I Worst	87,600	−95,225	−3,750	98,675	87,300
II	79,025	−18,500	−1,350	−180,600	−121,425
III	72,250	−10,775	−325	−310,675	−249,525
IV	67,175	−10,175	−275	−83,050	−26,325
V Best	146,275	−11,400	−125	475,650	610,400
All	452,325	−146,075	−5,825	0	300,425

81% of the 131,450 simulated increase in dwelling units in Pittsburgh's best neighborhoods is due to neighborhood upgrading, compared to a 20% increase, or 26,260 units, resulting from new construction. For Chicago, the simulated 610,400 unit increase for neighborhood type V represents the combined impacts of 146,275 units added by new construction, 11,525 units lost through demolition or conversion, and a 475,650 unit increase from neighborhood upgrading.

The current version of the NBER model is unique in its attempt to represent explicitly the process of neighborhood change as well as the relationship between neighborhood change and other aspects of urban housing markets. Current and anticipated neighborhood quality strongly influence the types of housing bundles and the quantities of structure services that households demand and housing suppliers provide. Moreover, changes in the spatial distribution of neighborhood types have important implications for the location of new construction and other supply activities.

The Pittsburgh and Chicago simulations employ a single index of neighborhood quality, defined by the average quantity of structure services provided by dwelling units located in each residence zone. For use in the housing demand equations and many of the supply activities represented in the model, the continuous neighborhood quality variable is divided into five levels. Although the classification of residence zones into only five neighborhood types provides a rather crude description of a highly complex process, the simulation results identify several distinct patterns of neighborhood change.

Shown in Table 4 is the distribution of Pittsburgh's 191 residence zones by initial neighborhood type and the extent of neighborhood change over the decade. In 1960, 73 residence zones were classified as type I (the worst), while only four were classified as type V (the best). Of the zones originally assigned to neighborhood type I, 53 remained unchanged throughout the simulated 10-year period; 15 improved by one neighborhood type; and 2 improved by two or more quality levels. Three neighborhoods improved from type I at the beginning of the simulation period to some higher quality, only to deteriorate to the worst neighborhood type at the end of the decade. A total of 27 residence zones oscillated between neighborhood types, showing no clear trend over the 10 years.

As in Pittsburgh, nearly half of the Chicago residence zones retained their initial neighborhood classification throughout the decade. In addition, relatively large numbers of residence zones improved by one category and only 3 improved by two categories or more. Similarly, 9 residence zones in Pittsburgh and 12 in Chicago declined by one

Table 4
*Number of Pittsburgh and Chicago Residence Zones by 1960–1970 Changes
in Neighborhood Type*

Neighborhood Change	Initial Neighborhood Type					Total
	I Worst	II	III	IV	V Best	
Pittsburgh						
No change	53	16	3	3	3	78
Improvement by:						
1 quality level	15	15	17	8	0	55
2 quality levels	1	9	9	0	0	19
3 or more levels	1	2	0	0	0	3
Decline by:						
1 quality level	0	8	1	0	0	9
2 or more levels	0	0	0	0	0	0
Oscillated	3	16	4	3	1	27
Total	73	66	34	14	4	191
Chicago						
No change	35	7	4	1	34	81
Improvement by:						
1 quality level	7	5	9	21	0	42
2 quality levels	4	5	14	0	0	23
3 or more levels	1	2	0	0	0	3
Decline by:						
1 quality level	0	9	0	3	0	12
2 or more levels	0	0	0	0	0	0
Oscillated	3	5	5	5	3	21
Total	50	33	32	30	37	182

neighborhood category, but none in either city declined by two or more categories. The declines that did occur were limited to zones that were either neighborhood type II or III at the beginning of the period.

Comparison of simulated and actual neighborhood changes for the decade 1960–1970, presented in Table 5, indicates that the current version of the NBER model has reasonable success in representing the dynamics of neighborhood transition. Neighborhood change in this case refers to the movement of a residence zone from one neighborhood type at the beginning of the decade to a different type at the end of the period. In Chicago, 56 residence zones improved by at least one category between 1960 and 1970. The model simulated improvement in 26 zones, declines in 5 zones, and no change in 25 zones. For neighborhoods that experienced no change in quality level, the simulation results were more precise: 52 of the 103 neighborhoods that remained in the same quality category between 1960 and 1970 were correctly classi-

Table 5

Comparison of Actual and Simulated Changes in Neighborhood Quality for Pittsburgh and Chicago

Actual Changes	Simulated Changes			
	Improvement	No Change	Decline	Total
Pittsburgh				
Improvement	81	51	9	141
No change	11	34	5	50
Decline	0	0	0	0
Total	92	85	14	191
Chicago				
Improvement	26	25	5	56
No change	45	52	6	103
Decline	7	16	0	23
Total	78	93	11	182

fied. The most frequent simulation error is the upgrading of Chicago neighborhoods that actually remained unchanged, an error that reflects the general tendency of the Chicago baselines to overstate the extent of neighborhood improvement during the decade.

Comparisons presented in Table 5 for Pittsburgh indicate that the model correctly predicts the direction of neighborhood change for 115 of the 191 residence zones. Like the Chicago results, the Pittsburgh baseline simulations demonstrate that the current representation of neighborhood change in the NBER model can grossly replicate what actually occurred. Even so, it clearly requires improvement. In particular, it will be necessary to analyze the mechanisms responsible for simulating neighborhood declines in 9 Pittsburgh residence zones that actually improved significantly over the decade.

3. THE ROLE OF NEIGHBORHOODS

Although our representation of neighborhood change and its role in housing market dynamics is still quite primitive and tentative, our results illustrate the ways in which past and anticipated changes in neighborhood quality affect nearly all aspects of the model simulations. Households demand neighborhood quality as part of the specific bundle of housing services they consume, that is, one of 50 types of housing bundles located in approximately 200 geographically distinct residence zones. Although we concentrate here on its role in the supply sector, neighborhood quality also affects household demand and the selling prices and rents for particular types of housing units in particular residence zones, as well as property owners' investment decisions. Roberton Williams (Chapter 2, this volume) deals more fully with the way the demand for neighborhood quality is treated in the NBER model.

The NBER model represents housing services as a bundle of heterogeneous attributes that must be consumed jointly. The current version of the model explicitly recognizes four distinct types of housing bundle attributes: neighborhood quality, accessibility, structure type, and the quantity of structure services provided.[2] Neighborhood quality, a characteristic of the residence zone in which a particular structure is located, is a composite of such factors as the socioeconomic and demographic characteristics of neighborhood residents, the condition and quality of the structures, and the level of local public services. The Pittsburgh and Chicago simulations employ a single index of neighborhood quality, defined by the average quantity of structure services provided by dwelling units located in each residence zone. Existing empirical knowledge about consumer preferences is insufficient to support a more sophisticated index.

The NBER model assumes that individual property owners have no discernible influence on overall neighborhood quality, or at least behave as though this were true. Instead, neighborhood quality depends on the aggregate effects of decisions made by hundreds or even thousands of individual housing suppliers; on the aggregate effects of location decisions made by an even larger number of individual households; and on the types and levels of local public services.

The second dimension of housing bundles, accessibility to workplaces and other desirable destinations, depends solely on the parcel's location. Accessibility can be viewed in two ways. First, particular locations are more or less accessible to the destinations demanded by specific households; this aspect is represented in the model by gross price and it influences individual household demand for specific housing bundles and residence locations.[3] Second, particular sites may be characterized by their overall accessibility to destinations demanded by households in general; this aspect of accessibility is reflected in the

[2] A more extensive discussion of these concepts is presented in Ingram and Kain (1973) and in Kain and Quigley (1975). See also Ingram and Oron (forthcoming), Ingram et al. (1977).

[3] A housing bundle's gross price is its monthly rent plus the household's monthly travel costs, including the value of time spent in commuting. In the current version of the NBER model, travel costs vary principally with the workplace location of the household's primary worker and with household income.

market rents for particular housing bundles at particular locations. Once a particular structure has been built, its accessibility and structural attributes are inextricably linked since structures are seldom moved from one location to another.

The remaining two dimensions of the housing bundle are structure type and the quantity of structure services supplied. Unlike neighborhood quality and accessibility, individual property owners can alter the physical characteristics of their buildings and the level of structure services they provide. Structure services are unobserved flows of services produced by combining structure and maintenance capital and operating inputs.

4. PROJECTIONS OF NEIGHBORHOOD QUALITY

As we have observed previously, expectations about neighborhood change play a central and crucial role in the NBER model's simulations of housing market dynamics and behavior. In the current version of the model, projected changes in neighborhood quality for each of the nearly 200 residence zones (neighborhoods) identified in the Pittsburgh and Chicago simulations are obtained from a simple extrapolation of trends for the previous 4 years, as depicted in Fig. 1 for 3 hypothetical residence zones. Each zone in the example is assumed to have an average of 288 units of neighborhood quality in 1960 and thus belong in neighborhood type II. Extrapolation of the 1956–1959 experience for these zones, however, yields markedly different projections of average quality in 1965: while residence zone C continues at level II, residence zone B reaches level III, and residence zone A reaches level IV by the end of the 5-year planning period assumed for the Pittsburgh and Chicago simulations. The projected quality levels in 1965 are 348 for residence zone A; 318 for residence zone B; and 294 for residence zone C.

Projected neighborhood quality for each zone determines the assignment of investor types to each structure. Each property owner is assigned to one of two investor classes in the initial year: investor type I are those property owners who expect the residence zone to remain at the same neighborhood quality level; investor type II are those who expect their residence zone to improve or deteriorate by one neighborhood quality level. This feature of the NBER model is calibrated so that the proportion of property owners in each residence zone assigned to each investor type depends on how far the projection of average dwelling unit quality is from the boundary of the initial quality class. For ex-

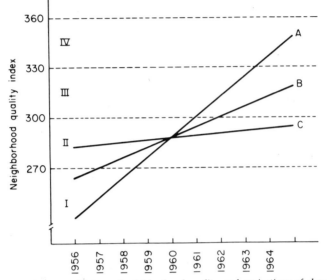

Figure 1. *Four-year history of neighborhood quality and projections of change over the planning period for three hypothetical residence zones in 1960.*

ample, residence zone A in Fig. 1 has a projected quality level of 348 in 1965, or well beyond the boundary of neighborhood quality level II. Indeed, its projected quality actually falls in the interval for level IV. The level of neighborhood quality projected for zone B in 1965 is also well within the interval for level III. In contrast, the projected level of quality for zone C has not yet reached level III. The model, therefore, assigns a larger fraction of zone B than C property owners to investor type II, and a still larger fraction of zone A property owners.

The specific proportion of property owners in each residence zone assigned to each investor class depends on how much the projected level exceeds the value which defines the boundary of the next quality level. Thus, for zone B the projected neighborhood quality level of 318 is 18 units above the upper boundary of neighborhood type II. This distance is divided by the width of the interval for quality level III (330–300) and the resulting ratio is compared to the function shown in Fig. 2 to determine the proportion of property owners that expect neighborhood quality to change. As Fig. 2 indicates, the ratio for zone B (18/30 = .6) determines that 56% of the property owners should be assigned to investor type II. Similar calculations for zone A and C result in the assignment of 92 and 18%, respectively, of property owners to investor type II. The remaining property owners in each zone are assigned to investor type I.

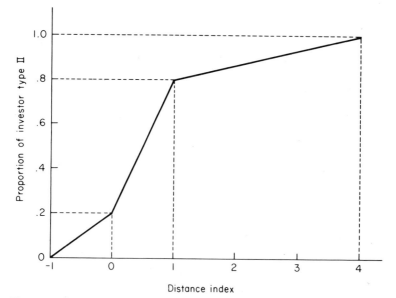

Figure 2. *Proportion of property owners who expect a change in neighborhood quality level. Proportion of investor type II is the proportion of property owners who expect the residence zone to change one neighborhood quality level. Distance index is the distance of the projected neighborhood type divided by the width of the interval of the projected neighborhood type.*

It should be emphasized that while the examples depicted in Figs. 1 and 2 relate to improving neighborhoods, the model projects neighborhood deterioration as well, although the findings described previously indicate that instances of both actual and simulated neighborhood decline over the decade are not very numerous. In cases of decline, all calculations refer to the lower boundary of the neighborhood quality level.

After the model projects neighborhood quality levels and assigns investor types to each sample structure, it estimates future rents for each housing bundle in each residence zone. The rent projections used in the Chicago and Pittsburgh simulations are based on simple extrapolations of 4-year rent trends, with the constraint that rents at the end of the planning period cannot exceed 130% of the long-run supply price for a particular housing bundle type at a particular location. Assuming that neighborhood quality remains unchanged, the naive straightline projections shown in Fig. 3 indicate that 1960 rents for a particular housing bundle will be $102 in residence zone A and $140 in zone B. In the investment calculations, however, the rent at the end of the planning period is assumed to be $125, or 130% of the long-run supply cost.

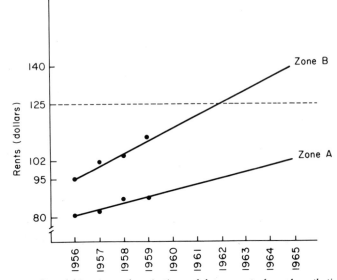

Figure 3. *Rental histories and projections of future rents for a hypothetical housing bundle and residence zone.*

For the several investment analyses carried out by the model's supply sector, we assume that landlords base their decisions on simple trend projections such as those depicted in Fig. 3 and that they expect rents projected for the end of the planning period to persist forever. These rents are converted to an annual net rental stream using Eq. (1):

$$NET(K, I, T) = ERENT(K, I, T) - OCOST(K, I, T),\qquad (1)$$

where

$NET(K, I, T)$ = net rent received for housing bundle K in zone I and time period T;

$ERENT(K, I, T)$ = expected rent for housing bundle K in residence zone I and time period T;

$OCOST(K, I, T)$ = operating cost for housing bundle K in residence zone I and time period T.

Given the assumption that rents are expected to change during the planning period to some new level that will then persist forever, the calculation of the present value of the net rental stream can be divided into two portions as indicated in Eq. (2):

$$PVNETR(K, I) = \sum_{T=1}^{5} \frac{NET(K, I, T)}{(1 + i)^T} + \frac{NET(K, I, T = 6)}{i * (1 + i)^6},\qquad (2)$$

where

$\qquad$ PVNETR(K, I) = present value of the net rental stream for housing bundle K in residence zone I;

$\qquad\qquad$ i = rate of time discount, set to .03 for the Pittsburgh and Chicago simulations;

$\qquad$ NET(K, I, T) = as defined in Eq. (1).

$\qquad$ Property owners who expect neighborhood quality to remain at the same level will use the simple extrapolation of future rents and income depicted by Eq. (1) in making their investment decisions. In contrast, property owners who expect a change in neighborhood quality will instead consider the rents of comparable structures in other residence zones which exhibit the projected neighborhood quality and have equal accessibility.

$\qquad$ The simple extrapolation of rents for each zone expected to change in quality, shown in Fig. 3, combines the quasi-rents associated with each particular type of structure, neighborhood quality, and accessibility level. Since neighborhoods of various quality levels are typically distributed unevenly across the metropolitan area, location must be taken into account. As Eq. (3) indicates, the NBER model makes these adjustments by subtracting an estimated locational premium from the composite rent projected for each unit:

$$\text{SRENT}(K, I, T) = \text{ERENT}(K, I, T) - \text{LRENT}(K, I), \qquad (3)$$

where

$\qquad$ SRENT(K, I, T) = bundle type K, structure rent for residence zone I, and time period T;

$\qquad$ LRENT(K, I) = location rent for bundle type K in residence zone I in the current period.

$\qquad$ Then, as expressed in Eq. (4), the model classifies each zone by its current neighborhood type (N = I, II, III, IV, V) and calculates a stock weighted average of structure prices for the residence zones belonging to each of the five neighborhood quality levels:

$$\text{NRENT}(K, I, T) = \sum_I \frac{\text{SRENT}(K, I, T) * \text{STOCK}(K, I)}{\Sigma_I \, \text{STOCK}(K, I)}, \qquad (4)$$

where

$\qquad$ STOCK(K, I) = number of dwelling units of type K in residence zone I in the current period.

The estimated average rent for each structure type in each type of neighborhood provides an estimate of the expected rental premium applicable to each structure type if a neighborhood changes in quality.

The composite projections of rents for each residence zone and housing bundle at the end of the planning period, shown in Eq. (5), then combine the location premium for each residence zone and structure type with the average rent for each neighborhood and structure type:

$$FRENT(K, I, T) = LRENT(K, I) + NRENT(K, T), \qquad (5)$$

where

FRENT(K, I, T) = projection of rents during the planning period for bundle type K in each residence zone I, for neighborhoods that are projected to change to quality level N by the end of the planning period.

If property owners expect a change in neighborhood quality, they will use Eq. (6) to calculate their expected net revenue rather than Eq. (1). The only difference in the two equations is that FRENT(K, I, T) is used instead of ERENT($K, I, T = 5$) as the estimate of net rents during the planning period:

$$ENET(K, I, T) = FRENT(K, I, T) - OCOST(K, I, T), \qquad (6)$$

where

ENET(K, I, T) = the expected net rent received for housing bundle K, residence zone I, and time period T.

5. NEIGHBORHOOD CHANGE, MAINTENANCE, AND IMPROVEMENTS

Current neighborhood quality and expectations about neighborhood change affect the location of new construction and structure conversions in several ways, but principally through their impact on vacant land costs and on future rental income.[4] Expectations about neighborhood change have an even greater influence on investment and maintenance decisions for existing structures. Since the NBER model's treatment of these decisions is unusually detailed and realistic, it warrants brief exposition.

Neighborhood quality is defined as the average level of structure services provided by dwelling units in each residence zone. The way the model simulates the quantity of structure services provided by indi-

---

[4] For a discussion of the way neighborhood quality affects these aspects of housing market behavior, see Kain et al. (1977, Chapters 6 and 7).

vidual units is therefore of central importance to the discussion of neighborhood change. Housing suppliers are assumed to produce structure services by combining current operating inputs and the quantities of maintenance and structure capital embodied in their structures at the start of the simulation period. Capital outlays this period that increase a building's maintenance or structure capital reduce the amount of operating inputs required to produce a given quantity of structure services during subsequent periods, but have no effect on this period's production. Even so, property owners can increase structure services during the current period by using more operating inputs, although at an ever-increasing unit cost. Because no long-term commitment is involved, the quantity of structure services supplied depends solely on current period rents and the demand of each unit's occupants.

Operating inputs, maintenance capital, and structure capital are categories of hundreds or even thousands of heterogeneous inputs: operating inputs include labor, fuel, utilities, and other nondurable inputs expended during the year to produce structure services; maintenance capital consists of a variety of capital goods with relatively short service lives; and structure capital includes capital goods with longer service lives. For obvious reasons, quantities of these inputs are composite indexes measured in terms of dollars. The Pittsburgh and Chicago simulations assume that one unit of maintenance capital and of operating inputs can be purchased for $1.00 and all calculations are done in 1970 dollars. The cost of maintenance capital is converted to an annual opportunity cost by multiplying the price of capital times the rate of depreciation plus the normal rate of return. Should future empirical work identify important changes in the relative price of capital and operating inputs, these changes can be easily accommodated in the model. In addition, the model could also be used to evaluate the effects of neighborhood differentials in factor prices, if such differences could be documented.[5]

Structure capital has two dimensions. Structure type represents the initial quantity of structure capital required to provide each type of structure at the minimum quality level allowed or demanded. Construction type, in contrast, represents differences in the quality of original construction and obsolescence. The current model includes three construction types which correspond to different quantities of structure capital for each type of structure: construction type 1 has 125% as much structure capital as construction type 2, and 150% as much as construction

[5] Fragmentary evidence of such differentials is presented in a study by Schafer *et al.* (1975).

type 3. Since 1% of structure capital depreciation cannot be offset by annual investment expenditures, a structure which was originally construction type 1 will depreciate to construction type 2 in 25 years, even if the property owner pursues a good-as-new investment policy. In another 25 years it will further depreciate to construction type 3. Of course, if no investment in structure capital is made, the building will depreciate at four times the rate. A building that depreciates to construction type 2 or 3 can be upgraded to construction type 1 only at a significantly higher cost than the original difference in construction cost between the two types.

Structure services are supplied according to a production function embodying operating inputs, maintenance capital, and structure capital. The Pittsburgh and Chicago simulations use the same production function parameters for rental units, owner-occupied multifamily structures, and owner-occupied single-family homes, a feature that could easily be modified if subsequent research justifies the change. We assume that a minimum quantity of structure capital is required to produce structure services, and that the level produced each period depends on the amount of maintenance capital embodied in the building at the start of the period, the amount of operating inputs used, and the building's construction type. Units of a better construction type, that is, containing more structure capital, can produce a given level of structure services with fewer operating inputs than structures of a worse construction type. A decline from construction type 1 to 3 increases the quantities of maintenance capital and operating inputs required to produce a given quantity of structure services by 33%.

The structure services production functions used for the Pittsburgh and Chicago simulations are Cobb–Douglas and assume constant returns to scale.[6] To produce a new level of structure services at minimum cost requires changes in the levels of both operating and capital inputs. Since provision of maintenance capital takes time and commits property owners for several years, structures will often possess either more or less than the optimum quantity. Moreover, property owners will not attempt to adjust their structure capital stocks to the level required to produce current period structure services unless they expect to supply at least as many structure services for the foreseeable future. In deciding

---

[6] One of the properties of the Cobb–Douglas production function employed in the Pittsburgh and Chicago simulations is that the relative expenditures for each input are not affected by changes in their relative prices. With constant returns to scale, the ratio $(B/1 - B)$ is equal to the ratio of the cost of capital to the costs of operating inputs when factors are paid their marginal products and production occurs at the most efficient point.

whether to add maintenance and structure capital, property owners therefore consider both current occupants' and probable future demand for structure services; projections of future demand, in turn, depend largely on expectations about neighborhood change.

The simulated quantity of structure services actually provided by each unit during each year depends on the occupant's demand curve and the unit's supply curve. This supply curve is based on the marginal cost curve for each dwelling unit which, of course, defines the quantities of structure services a profit-maximizing property owner would be willing to supply at each rental level, where rent is defined in terms of the cost per unit of structure services. The NBER model determines the quantity and price of structure services supplied annually by each sample structure by comparing the unit's supply curve and the demand for structure services for each occupant. The model is calibrated so that increases in the rent per unit of structure services, decreases in household income, or a change in tenure status from owner to renter, cause decreases in household demand for structure services.

The structure services demand functions thus assume that the income elasticity of demand is .6 for renters and .8 for owners. The constant price elasticity of demand for structure services, which is -1 for both owner–occupants and renters, implies that increases or decreases in the price of structure services will be exactly offset by proportional and opposite changes in the quantities of structure services consumed. Consequently, a household's expenditures for structure services will remain constant at all rent levels.

In the current version of the NBER model, households with an annual income of $3000 are used as reference households and the long-run marginal cost of producing one unit of structure services is made equal to $1.00. The demand function is calibrated so that both owners and renters with an annual income of $3000 demand 150 units of structure services at a unit price of $1.00; this results in an annual payment of $150 or a monthly payment of $12.50 for structure services. If the unit price is $1.00 and household income is $7000, however, owner–occupants will demand 295 units of structure services, while renters will demand 250 units.

Shown in Fig. 4 are the short-run marginal cost curves for hypothetical housing suppliers and the demand curve for households assigned to each unit. The curve labeled LRMC is the long-run average and marginal cost of producing structure services using the optimal quantity of maintenance capital for a unit of construction type 2. The simulated quantity of structure services supplied this period for each

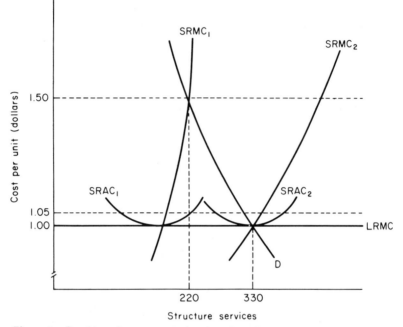

Figure 4. *Provision of structure services for a hypothetical owner–occupant.*

unit is determined by the intersection of the marginal cost and demand curves.[7] In the example depicted in Fig. 4, the landlord's profit-maximizing production level occurs at a price of $1.50 and a quantity of 220 units. At this level of structure services, the cost per unit is $1.05, a figure determined by the short-run average cost curve.

The demand relationship and the marginal cost curve shown in Fig. 4 are used to determine the quantity of structure services provided by each dwelling unit and define an optimum quantity of maintenance capital to produce this quantity. Comparison of this optimum quantity of maintenance capital and the unit's current quantity in turn defines a target level of investment for each property. For multifamily structures, these calculations employ the average quantity of structure services per unit. All units in the same building are assumed to possess identical quantities of maintenance and structure capital.

The preceding discussion makes no distinction between owner-

---

[7] The production function parameters used in the Pittsburgh and Chicago simulations imply a nonlinear marginal cost curve. Since the β parameter has been set to .667, the marginal costs increase with the square of the quantity of structure services produced. This reflects the fact that with a fixed quantity of maintenance capital, larger quantities of operating inputs become increasingly less efficient in the production of structure services.

occupied units and renter-occupied units except to note that owner–occupants are assumed to have higher income elasticities of demand for structure services. The current version of the NBER model, however, uses somewhat different approaches in simulating the investment and production decisions of owner–occupants and profit-maximizing land-lords. First, in the case of owner–occupants we adjust the quantities of structure services supplied, the quantities of maintenance capital, and construction type only every fourth year or when a new owner moves into the unit. At that time, the model provides owner-occupied units with the optimum quantities of structure services and optimum addi-tions to maintenance capital. Since the real rate of depreciation of main-tenance capital may not exceed 9% per year, however, owner-occupied units may still have more than the optimum quantity of maintenance capital required to produce the current quantity of structure services.

Owner–occupants' annual expenditures for structure capital may vary from 0–3%, depending on both current and projected levels of neighborhood quality. The schedule of allowable rates is shown in Table 6. Structure capital depreciates at 4% a year in the current version of the NBER model, and no more than three-quarters of this annual de-preciation can be offset by annual maintenance expenditures. If the expenditures required for maintenance and structure capital are not made during the year, this neglect cannot be made up during subse-quent periods.

The structure capital that a dwelling unit possesses affects the quantity of structure services it can provide in two ways. First, dwelling units with less than half as much structure capital as new units are de-molished. Second, the quantity of structure capital determines a build-ing's construction type. As structure capital depreciates, properties de-cline to a worse construction type, thus increasing the quantities of

Table 6
Allowable Rate of Investment of Structure Capital by Initial and Expected Neighborhood Type

Expected Neighborhood Type	Initial Neighborhood Type				
	I Worst	II	III	IV	V Best
I Worst	3.0[a]	1.5	0.8	0.0	0.0
II	3.0	3.0	1.5	0.8	0.0
III	3.0	3.0	3.0	1.5	0.8
IV	3.0	3.0	3.0	3.0	1.5
V Best	3.0	3.0	3.0	3.0	3.0

[a] In percentages.

operating inputs and maintenance capital required to produce a given quantity of structure services. The quantity of structure services demanded by owner–occupants and the relationship between construction type and the quantities of operating inputs and maintenance capital required to produce this desired level of structure services is the basis for owner–occupants' decisions to upgrade construction type. Actual decisions to upgrade a unit's structure type again depend on both the initial level and anticipated changes in neighborhood quality.

Decisions to upgrade a building's construction type are simulated using the probabilities shown in Table 7. In calibrating this portion of the model, we assume that owner–occupants will be reluctant to make major capital improvements in declining neighborhoods, even if they are currently consuming relatively large quantities of structure services. Construction type for owner-occupied units is therefore never upgraded in declining neighborhoods. Moreover, as Table 7 indicates, only 10% of those who reside in neighborhood type I and expect their neighborhood to remain the same are permitted to upgrade the construction type of their units.

A more elaborate procedure is used to simulate the quantities of structure services supplied by owners of rental properties, the quantities consumed by tenants, and the competition among landlords to obtain tenants. To determine rents and quantities for renter–occupants, the demand and supply curves for individual units must be aggregated to obtain market demand and supply curves for each type of structure in each zone. The market supply curve would be the envelope of the marginal cost curves of the individual suppliers. Determination of market rents and quantities for each housing bundle could then be simulated as a bidding process among households for available units. We considered using a miniature linear programming model to simulate the determination of rents for structure services, but concluded that it

Table 7

Probability of Upgrading Construction Type by Initial and Expected Neighborhood Type

Expected Neighborhood Type	Initial Neighborhood Type				
	I Worst	II	III	IV	V Best
I Worst	.1	.0	.0	.0	.0
II	.1	.2	.0	.0	.0
III	.2	.2	.3	.0	.0
IV	.3	.3	.3	.3	.0
V Best	.4	.4	.4	.4	.4

would be impractical to obtain market demand and supply curves for each residence zone, particularly since the demand for structure services supplied by a particular housing bundle in a particular residence zone depends on the price of structure services provided by competing structures in nearby residence zones.

The NBER model uses a simpler algorithm that exploits more general information about the likely characteristics of the market supply and demand curves for structure services in each residence zone. First, the structure services demand function is solved for each sample household using last period's market price for structure services for its assigned bundle type and residence zone. Then households are ordered by their expected demand for structure services and assigned to the available unit that is the most efficient producer of that particular quantity of structure services. The ranking of units by production efficiency depends on construction type and the amount of embodied maintenance capital; units of the best construction type and those having the most maintenance capital are the most efficient producers of the largest quantities of structure services.

The ranking algorithm used to assign households to specific units within a bundle type and residence zone is depicted by Fig. 5, which illustrates the assignment of three hypothetical households to dwelling units. The intersection of the demand and marginal cost curves for the

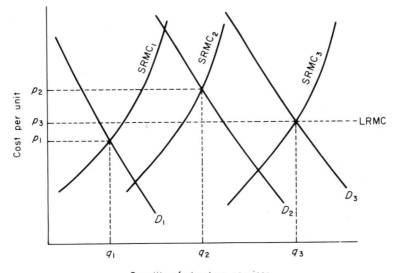

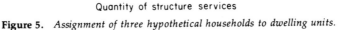

Figure 5. *Assignment of three hypothetical households to dwelling units.*

first dwelling unit/household indicates a quantity of structure services q_1, and a price p_1, which is below the long-run marginal and average costs of producing structure services. This property owner will be earning less than a competitive return on his capital and will therefore allow some depreciation of maintenance capital to occur. In the second case, the occupant's demand curve intersects the unit's marginal cost curve at a price well above the long-run marginal cost curve; this property owner will find it profitable to increase his stock of maintenance capital. In the third situation, the occupant's demand curve intersects the unit's marginal cost curve at the point where it is equal to the long-run marginal cost; the quantity of maintenance capital embodied in this unit is exactly equal to the optimal amount.

Intersection of the tenant's demand curve and the unit's short-run marginal cost curve defines the quantity of structure services provided this year. For this quantity the model calculates an optimum, that is, least-cost, capital stock for each unit, which is compared to this person's quantity of maintenance capital. If the optimum quantity of maintenance capital is less than the quantity supplied at the start of the period, the excess maintenance capital is allowed to depreciate up to a maximum rate of 9% a year. If the optimum level of maintenance capital is more than the amount at the start of the period, the landlord must consider whether current and anticipated levels of neighborhood quality justify additions to the stock of maintenance capital.

Since we assume that landlords are risk-averse, the model provides only a fraction of the difference between current and optimum levels of maintenance capital. Proportions of the target level of net maintenance which will actually be made this period are shown in Table 8 by current and expected neighborhood quality. For stable or improving neighborhoods, the model permits investments in maintenance capital at a rate

Table 8

Actual Net Investment in Maintenance Capital as a Proportion of the Target Level of Net Maintenance by Initial and Expected Neighborhood Type

Expected Neighborhood Type	Initial Neighborhood Type				
	I Worst	II	III	IV	V Best
I Worst	.25	.13	.06	.00	.00
II	.25	.25	.13	.06	.00
III	.25	.25	.25	.13	.06
IV	.25	.25	.25	.25	.13
V Best	.25	.25	.25	.25	.25

equal to 25% of the target level. If the landlord expects the neighborhood to decline, however, net maintenance investment is set to zero
and the landlord only invests at a level which would offset the rate of
depreciation. The maintenance rules employed in the NBER model
therefore attempt to represent how a landlord's decisions are influenced
by both current production of structure services and expectations about
future demand, as indicated by projections of neighborhood change.

If a building passes the tests outlined above, it is further subject to
a cash flow constraint to determine if its current rental income is sufficient to pay for existing fixed obligations, current operating expenses,
and for improvements. For the cash flow calculation, the model begins
with this period's rent for the building and makes a number of subtrac-
tions to obtain the amounts available to pay for the maintenance
outlays. The calculation first subtracts the annual operating outlays;
then an amount to pay the carrying costs on the capital value of the unit;
then an amount equal to 3% of the structure capital stock to maintain
the structure. If the residual cash flow is large enough to pay for the investments in maintenance capital, the improvements are made. Investments in structure capital are also subject to a cash flow constraint. Because depreciation of structure capital is irreversible except by the upgrading of construction type, however, structure capital investments
take precedence over investments in maintenance capital.

Finally, owners of rental properties can change their buildings'
construction type. Since upgrading construction type requires large
investments and cannot be done incrementally, these decisions are particularly sensitive to expectations about neighborhood change. To de-
cide whether a particular unit should be upgraded, the model first determines the most efficient construction type for producing the current
level of structure services. If this comparison indicates an upgrading of
construction type would result in discounted savings in maintenance
capital and operating outlays sufficient to justify the investment, the
model applies the probabilities shown in Table 7. Since the owners of
rental properties located in the same neighborhood may have been assigned different investor types, different probabilities from Table 7 may
be used for property owners within the same neighborhood.

6. CONCLUDING OBSERVATIONS

Existing econometric analyses of the linkage between housing
supply activities and neighborhood change are quite meager. This reflects the poor quality of spatially detailed information on the invest-

ment activities of individual property owners and builder/developers. The investment rules represented in the NBER model are based less on existing econometric knowledge of specific parameters than on subjective guesstimates of the response of property owners to past, present, and projected neighborhood quality levels. Thus, while the simulation results presented in the first section of this chapter strongly support the role of neighborhood quality, additional analysis of model output and further simulations will be required before we can claim a very precise understanding of the way in which neighborhood change affects housing market behavior and dynamics. Fortunately, the numerous investment rules used in the Pittsburgh and Chicago simulations could be changed easily if further research indicates that such changes would be appropriate. Changes in particular values, for example, the 9% depreciation rate of maintenance capital and the income elasticity of demand for structure services, require no reprogramming and can thus be easily subjected to sensitivity testing. Changes in some of the remaining rules require reprogramming, but may also be easily accomplished.

While we cannot claim that the representation of neighborhood quality described in this chapter is completely accurate, the NBER model has simulated a pattern of neighborhood change that conforms broadly to what actually occurred in the Pittsburgh and Chicago metropolitan areas from 1960 to 1970. In our work to date, we have used the model primarily to analyze the market effects of housing allowance programs. We include neighborhood quality, neighborhood change, and expectations about neighborhood change because these aspects of market behavior are essential to understanding housing market behavior and the impact of urban housing policy. Our exploratory simulations and analyses have strengthened this belief.

REFERENCES

Ingram, G. K., and Kain, J. F. (1973). A simple model of housing production and the abandonment problem. *American Real Estate and Urban Economics Association Journal* **1**, 79–105.

Ingram, G. K., and Oron, Y. (1974). A stand-alone supply model for dwelling unit quality. In *Progress report on the development of the NBER Urban Simulation Model and interim analyses of housing allowance programs*, J. F. Kain (ed.), Report prepared for the U.S. Department of Housing and Urban Development, Sec. IV, pp. 296–324.

Ingram, G. K., and Oron, Y. (Forthcoming). The production of housing services from existing dwelling units. In *The economics of residential location and urban housing markets*, G. K. Ingram (ed.). National Bureau of Economic Research, New York.

Ingram, G. K., Leonard, H., and Schafer, R. (1977). Simulation of the market effects of housing allowances, Vol. III: Development of the supply sector of the NBER Urban

Simulation Model. City and Regional Planning Research Report R77-4, Harvard University, Cambridge, Massachusetts.

Kain, J. F., and Quigley, J. M. (1975). *Housing markets and racial discrimination: A microeconomic analysis.* National Bureau of Economic Research, New York.

Kain, J. F., and Apgar, W. C. (1977). Simulation of the market effects of housing allowances, Vol. II: Baseline and policy simulations for Pittsburgh and Chicago. City and Regional Planning Research Report R77-3, Harvard University, Cambridge, Massachusetts.

Kain, J. F., Apgar, W. C., and Ginn, J. R. (1977). Simulation of the market effects of housing allowances, Vol. I: Description of the NBER Urban Simulation Model. City and Regional Planning Research Report R77-2, Harvard University, Cambridge, Massachusetts.

Schafer, R. *et al.* (1975). Spatial variations in the operating costs of rental housing. City and Regional Planning Discussion Paper D75-4, Harvard University, Cambridge, Massachusetts.

IV

EQUILIBRIUM
APPROACHES TO
NEIGHBORHOOD

9

The Hedonic Price Approach to Measuring Demand for Neighborhood Characteristics

A. MYRICK FREEMAN, III

There has been considerable interest among economists in the possibility of using land rent or land value information for residential properties to measure the benefits to households due to changes in environmental amenities such as air quality. Ridker (1967) was the first economist to attempt to use residential property value data as the basis for estimating the benefits of changes in air pollution. He reasoned as follows (see also Ridker and Henning, 1967):

> If the land market were to work perfectly, the price of a plot of land would equal the sum of the present discounted streams of benefits and costs derivable from it. If some of its costs rise, (e.g., if additional maintenance and cleaning costs are required) or if some of its benefits fall (e.g., if one cannot see the mountains from the terrace) the property will be discounted in the market to reflect people's evaluation of these changes. Since air pollution is specific to locations and the supply of locations is fixed, there is less likelihood that the negative effects of pollution can be significantly shifted on to other markets. We should therefore expect to find the majority of effects reflected in this market, and we can measure them by observing associated changes in property values [p. 25].

Ridker employed both time-series and cross-sectional data in his efforts to measure the influence of air pollution on residential property

191

values. Since Ridker's work, time-series studies have not been common because of the difficulties in controlling for other influences on property values over time. But there have been many cross-section studies relating the variation in property values across an urban area at a point in time to differences in air pollution levels and other explanatory variables.

An extensive literature has developed on the proper interpretation of these studies. Many authors have followed Ridker's initial insight by examining how and under what circumstances observed *changes* in property values could be interpreted as benefits. A related question is whether regression equations from cross-section data can be the basis for making ex ante predictions about changes in property values to be expected when air quality changes. [See Lind (1973), Polinsky and Shavell (1975, 1976), Polinsky and Rubinfeld (1977). This literature is reviewed and summarized in Freeman (1979).] More recently several researchers have designed their empirical studies as applications of the hedonic price technique for estimating the implicit prices of attributes such as air quality from cross-sectional data. By this approach benefit measures are based on property value *differences* at a point in time (see Nelson, 1978a; Harrison and Rubinfeld, 1978). It has been shown that hedonic price relationships can be used directly to compute the marginal benefit of improved air quality, that is, the benefit associated with marginal improvements in air quality over all parts of the urban area (see Freeman, 1974). It has also been shown that hedonic price data can be used as an input into a second stage of analysis to estimate individual inverse demand or marginal willingness to pay functions for air quality (see Freeman, 1974; Rosen, 1974; Nelson, 1978b; Harrison and Rubinfeld, 1978).

The local air quality is just one of many distinguishing characteristics of housing sites. The hedonic technique is potentially applicable to any attribute which differentiates houses in the eyes of potential occupants. These attributes include the physical characteristics of the structure itself and its site, the location of the site (e.g., relative to employment centers), and the physical, social, and economic characteristics of the local environment or neighborhood. These could include the social, economic, and ethnic characteristics of the local population, the presence of amenities such as pleasant views or parks, and the types and qualities of locally provided public services such as education and fire protection. If these things matter to people (i.e., they are arguments in utility functions) and their levels vary across the array of available housing, then the interaction of available supply and individual preferences can affect the pattern of housing prices. This chapter is about how to use the information imbedded in housing prices to estimate the demand for a variety of characteristics of housing and neighborhood.

In the next section of this chapter, the hedonic price approach as a technique for measuring the implicit prices of goods that are not themselves explicitly traded in markets but which are characteristics of traded goods is reviewed. Following that, the identification of the demand functions for characteristics as functions of their implicit prices is discussed. In the fourth section several problems in the empirical application of the hedonic technique to housing price data are reviewed. A review of the treatment of neighborhood characteristics in studies of the air pollution–property value relationship concludes the chapter.

1. HEDONIC PRICES AND THE DEMAND FOR NEIGHBORHOOD

Estimating the demand for a characteristic of housing, for example, its neighborhood setting, involves a two-step procedure in which first the implicit price of the characteristic is estimated by the application of the hedonic price technique, and then the implicit price is regressed against observed quantities to estimate the demand function itself.

The hedonic technique is a method for estimating the implicit prices of the characteristics which differentiate closely related products in a product class.[1] For example, houses constitute a product class differentiated by characteristics such as number of rooms and size of lot. In principle, if there are enough models with different combinations of rooms and lot size, it is possible to estimate an implicit price relationship which gives the price of any model as a function of the quantities of its various characteristics. The derivatives of this function with respect to the characteristics give the implicit prices. For example, the difference in price between two models with different numbers of rooms but identical in all other respects is interpreted as the implicit price of additional rooms.

There are several assumptions which must be satisfied in order to apply the hedonic technique to estimating the demand for neighbor-

---

[1] The hedonic price technique was developed by Griliches and others initially for the purpose of estimating the value of quality change in consumer goods. See Griliches (1971). Rosen (1974) has used the hedonic price concept to analyze the supply and demand of the characteristics which differentiate products in competitive markets. For discussion of the application of the concept to measuring the demand for environmental quality characteristics, see Anderson and Crocker (1972), Bishop and Cicchetti (1975), and Freeman (1974).

hood characteristics. First any large area has in it a wide variety of sizes and types of housing with different locational, neighborhood, and environmental characteristics. An important assumption of the hedonic technique is that the urban area as a whole can be treated as a single market for housing services. Individuals must have information on all alternatives and must be free to choose a housing location anywhere in the urban market. It is as if the urban area were one huge supermarket offering a wide selection of varieties. Of course, households cannot move their shopping cart through the supermarket. Rather their selection of a residential location fixes for them the whole bundle of housing services. It is much as if shoppers were forced to make their choice from an array of already filled shopping carts. Households can alter the level of any characteristic by finding an alternative location alike in every respect but offering more of the desired characteristic. It must be assumed that the housing market is an equilibrium, that is, that all households have made their utility maximizing residential choice given the prices of alternative housing locations, and that these prices just clear the market given the existing stock of housing and its characteristics.

Given these assumptions, the price of a house can be taken to be a function of its structural, neighborhood, and environmental characteristics. More formally, let H represent the product or commodity class—housing. Any unit of H, say h_i, can be completely described by a vector of its characteristics, including locational, neighborhood, and environmental characteristics. If S_j, N_k, and Q_m indicate the vectors of site, neighborhood, and environmental variables, respectively, then the price of h_i is a function of the levels of these characteristics:

$$P_{hi} = P_h(S_{i1}, \ldots, S_{ij}, N_{i1}, \ldots, N_{ik}, Q_{i1}, \ldots, Q_{im}). \qquad (1)$$

The function P_h is the hedonic or implicit price function for H. If P_h can be estimated from observations of the prices and characteristics of different models, the price of any possible model can be calculated from knowledge of its characteristics.

The implicit price of a characteristic can be found by differentiating the implicit price function with respect to that characteristic. That is

$$\partial P_h / \partial N_k = P_{N_k}(N_k). \qquad (2)$$

This gives the increase in expenditure on H that is required to obtain a house with one more unit of N_k, ceteris paribus.

If Eq. (1) is linear in the characteristics, then the implicit prices are constants for individuals. But if Eq. (1) is nonlinear, then the implicit price of an additional unit of a characteristic depends on the quantity of the characteristic being purchased. Equation (1) need not be linear. Linearity will occur only if consumers can "arbitrage" activities by untieing and repackaging bundles of attributes (Rosen, 1974, pp. 37–38). For example if individuals are indifferent between owning two 6-foot-long cars and one 12-foot car, ceteris paribus, they can create equivalents of 12-foot cars by repackaging smaller units. If both sizes exist on the market, the larger size must sell at twice the price of the smaller one and the implicit price function will be linear in length. The example suggests that nonlinearity will not be uncommon.

Assume that Eq. (1) has been estimated for an urban area. If it is nonlinear, the marginal implicit prices of characteristics are not constant, but depend on their levels and perhaps the levels of other characteristics as well. If the household is assumed to be a price taker in the housing market, it can be viewed as facing an array of implicit marginal price schedules for various characteristics. A household maximizes its utility by simultaneously moving along each marginal price schedule until it reaches a point where its marginal willingness to pay for an additional unit of each characteristic just equals the marginal implicit price of that characteristic. If a household is in equilibrium, the marginal implicit prices associated with the housing bundle actually chosen must be equal to the corresponding marginal willingnesses to pay for those characteristics.

Now let us consider only the implicit price of N_k. Figure 1a shows the partial relationship between P_h and N_k as estimated from (1), that is, holding all other characteristics constant. Figure 1b shows the marginal implicit price of N_k, $P_{N_k}(N_k)$. It also shows the inverse demand or marginal willingness to pay curves for two households $w_i(N_k)$ and $w_j(N_k)$, and the equilibrium positions for these two households. Each household chooses a location where its marginal willingness to pay for N_k is equated with the marginal implicit price of N_k. Thus the implicit price function is a locus of individual equilibrium marginal willingnesses to pay.

The first stage just described develops a measure of the price of N_k but does not directly reveal or identify the inverse demand function for N_k. The second stage of the hedonic technique is to combine the quantity and implicit price information in an effort to identify this inverse demand function. It is hypothesized that the household's demand price or willingness to pay for N_k is a function of its level, income, and other household variables which influence tastes and preferences. In other words

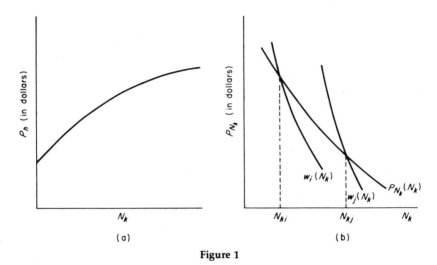

Figure 1

$$w_i = w(N_{ki}, M_i, \ldots).$$

Each household's observed P_N (N_{ki}) is taken to be a measure of w_i. Can this demand function be identified with the information at hand?

There are two special cases. First, if the hedonic price function is linear in N_k, identification of the inverse demand function is not possible. This is because the implicit marginal price is constant. With no variation in price across the data set, nothing is revealed about the relationship between implicit price and the quantity of the characteristics. However even in this case the income elasticity of demand can be estimated.

The second special case arises when all households have identical incomes and utility functions. In this case Eq. (1) is itself the inverse demand function. Recall that the marginal implicit price curve is a locus of points on households' marginal willingness to pay curves. With identical incomes and utility functions, these points all fall on the same marginal willingness to pay curve.

If neither special case applies then the supply side of the implicit market for the characteristic must be examined. There are three possibilities. First, if the supply of houses with given bundles of characteristics is perfectly elastic at the observed prices, then the implicit price function of a characteristic can be taken as exogenous to individuals. A regression of observed levels of the characteristic against the observed implicit prices as defined by Eq. (2), incomes, and other socioeconomic characteristics of individuals should identify the demand function. In other words, estimate

$$N_{ki} = N_{ki}(P_{N_{ki}}, M_i, \ldots).$$

Second, if the available quantity of each model is fixed, individuals can be viewed as bidding for fixed quantities of models with desired bundles of characteristics. A regression of each individual's implicit price against the quantity of the characteristic actually taken, incomes and other variables should identify an inverse demand function. In this case, estimate

$$w_i = w(N_{ki}, M_i, \ldots),$$

where $P_{N_{ki}}$ is taken as an observation on w_i.

Finally if both the quantities demanded and quantities supplied of characteristics are functions of prices, a simultaneous equation approach can be used. (For further discussion of this case, see Rosen, 1974, pp. 48–51.)

In summary, in this section we have outlined the hedonic theory of implicit price estimation as applied to urban residential housing markets. We have shown that the implicit prices of nonmarketed attributes can be derived from the hedonic price function. Furthermore with reasonable assumptions, it is possible to use implicit price and quantity information to identify the inverse demand functions.

Once the household marginal willingness to pay function has been identified, it is possible to estimate the benefits of changes in the levels of neighborhood characteristics, local public goods, or environmental amenities. For example, if air quality improves over the urban area, the household's benefit is the integral of the marginal willingness to pay function between the old and new levels of Q at that site. To find aggregate benefits, sum over all households. Since the willingness to pay curves are not compensated to a constant utility level, this does not give a precise compensating or equivalent variation measure, but only an approximation.

This form of benefit measure is appropriate provided that the prices of other characteristics do not change at the same time. Individuals may alter the quantities purchased of other attributes, and demand curves for other attributes may shift back and forth because of complementary and substitute relationships among housing attributes. But all this is irrelevant for benefit estimation provided that the prices of other attributes do not change. If the implicit prices of other attributes do change, than we have the well-known problem of evaluating welfare gains with multiple price changes. And we need to know the new hedonic price function to know how the marginal implicit prices of other attributes have changed.

2.   THE IDENTIFICATION PROBLEM

The steps necessary to identify properly the demand function for a characteristic depend on the assumptions made about the supply side of the implicit market. There have been two studies of the air pollution–property value relationship in which the authors attempted to identify the demand function for clean air. They approached the identification problem quite differently. Harrison and Rubinfeld (1978) assume that the supply of air quality is perfectly inelastic with respect to price or willingness to pay at each residential location. In other words at a given location, air quality is independent of households' willingness to pay. Thus they argue that a fully identified inverse demand curve would be estimated by regressing equilibrium marginal prices on quantities, incomes, and other variables.

Nelson (1978b) has taken a different view. He argues that there is a supply side effect on the implicit price of air quality.

> Taking the total supply of land for all uses in a metropolitan area as fixed at a point in time, the supply of land to the residential housing industry is simply this fixed amount less the effective demand for land for all other uses. . . . Ceteris paribus, suppliers of residential housing will have higher bid prices [to bid land away from nonresidential uses] for a given unit of land and improvements the higher the associated level of environmental quality [p. 365].

Thus offer prices for residential land will be higher the higher the air quality. Nelson specifies a two-equation model. The demand side equation is similar to Harrison and Rubinfeld's. The supply side equation is

$$O_i = O(Q_i, \text{Density}, d),$$

where O_1 is the offer price and d the distance from the central business district (CBD). Nelson argues that the two-stage least squares estimation of this system identifies both bid (demand) and offer (supply) functions for air quality.

Neither paper has clearly and correctly stated the case for their position. The issue is one of short run versus long run equilibrium in the market for housing. But neither paper provides a fully satisfactory treatment of what adjustments are assumed to take place in response to market forces. Harrison and Rubinfeld assume that air quality at given locations is unresponsive to the implicit price of air quality. This would be true in both the short run and long run. But the relevant supply variable is not air quality; it is the number of houses with a given air quality. For example, the larger the number of clean air houses, the lower their price relative to other types of houses, ceteris paribus, and the lower the marginal implicit price of clean air derived from the hedonic price equation. The number of houses of a given air quality can be increased either by an improvement in air quality over the urban area, or by increasing the number of houses available in the region of given air quality.[2] With present institutional arrangements, the former can be assumed to be unresponsive to price; but the latter is likely to be somewhat price elastic. This is the type of adjustment mechanism hypothesized by Nelson. However he focused on switching land between industrial and residential land use rather than on changes in residential density.

The question of which assumption, exogenous or endogenous supply, is more appropriate boils down to the speed of the supply side adjustment to price changes relative to the speed at which housing prices adjust to changes in supply. In order to use the hedonic price approach at all, it is necessary to assume that the observed housing prices approximate equilibrium prices, that is, those prices which just make everyone willing to hold the existing stock of houses. In other words the assumption of rapid price adjustment is basic to the technique. On the other hand since supply adjustments typically require changes in land use patterns including replacing old structures and adding to overhead capital, they are likely to proceed slowly—at speeds measured in years. This is an argument for treating the supply side as exogenous. But it is recognized that the question is an empirical one. And there may be instances, for example in rapidly growing regions, where the short run assumption would be inappropriate.

Turning to other types of neighborhood characteristics, even if it is reasonable to assume that the changes in quantities of housing embodying environmental and amenity characteristics can be ignored in the short run, the assumption may be inappropriate for other characteristics. For example some studies have used percentage of substandard or dilapidated units as a measure of neighborhood quality. The quantities of housing units in neighborhoods with low proportions of dilapidated units could change quickly in response to prices. And this supply response would have to be taken into account in estimating demand functions for these characteristics.

Finally, changes in the socioeconomic characteristics of neighborhoods need not require major changes in the housing stock. Rather they can occur relatively quickly and in response to prices. The exo-

---

[2] Unless there is vacant land, it is not possible to expand the supply of houses alike in all respects including lot size. Rather residential density must increase, lots will be smaller, etc.

genous supply assumption would be particularly inappropriate here. (See Schnare, 1976, for some discussion of how changes in racial composition can occur in response to implicit prices for this dimension of neighborhood.)

3. EMPIRICAL PROBLEMS IN APPLYING THE HEDONIC TECHNIQUE

3.1. Land Value or Property Value

One question is whether the dependent variable to be explained should be pure land rent (site value) or the price of housing. The latter is a measure of total expenditure on the site and its improvements. Since neighborhood quality is a characteristic of the site rather than its structural improvements, the former measure seems desirable on a priori grounds. Researchers have used ingenious approaches to construct measures of site value from available data on housing expenditures (Wieand, 1973; Steele, 1972; and Smith, 1978). However, this effort may not have been necessary.

The importance of the choice between site value and expenditure depends upon the model chosen as the basis for the estimating technique. One of the virtues of the hedonic price technique is that the problem can be handled through the choice of variables included in the hedonic price function. This function seeks to explain the price or expenditure on a unit of housing as a function of the size and characteristics of housing structure and other improvements to the site, the size of the site, and various locational characteristics. If all of these variables are properly controlled for, the coefficient on the neighborhood variable measures the implicit price of that characteristic independently of other attributes such as lot size, housing structure, etc. No special effort is required to construct or measure a separate land value variable.

3.2. Measuring Property Value

Another question is the source of data on housing expenditures and values. Most preferable are data on actual market transactions. For rental housing there is a regular monthly "market transaction" and fairly accurate data could be gathered on housing rents. However, the majority of residential housing is owner occupied. And only a very small percentage of the total owner occupied housing stock is exchanged through the market each year. Collecting an adequate sample of market transactions for an urban area is a major task.

A second-best source of property value data would be professional appraisals of individual properties for taxation or other purposes. Some jurisdictions have developed computer based systems of appraisals and assessments which include data not only on appraised values but also on a variety of structural and site characteristics. As these systems are developed and extended, they can provide a valuable data source for further property value studies. However, the appraisals must be used with caution. At least in some jurisdictions they may be systematically biased for political or other reasons (see Berry and Bednarz, 1975).

The most commonly used source of data in property value–air pollution studies is the U.S. Census of Population and Housing. The census asks each owner to estimate the value of his property. The census also gathers other data on structural characteristics as well as socioeconomic data on occupants. These data are aggregated by census tracts and reported as means or medians. Although the census tract observations represent a convenient source of data for property value studies, they present two kinds of problems.[3]

The first concerns the degree of accuracy of individual owner estimates of values. Nelson (1978a) was able to compare median owner estimates with median professional assessments by census tracts for Washington, D.C. He found that owner estimates were systematically higher by between 3 and 6% while zero order correlation coefficients were approximately .9 or better. He concluded that as long as errors in owners estimates are random, statistical estimates of price functions will be unbiased.

The second problem is the loss of detail and reduced ability to control for relevant housing and location characteristics, both because of the limited number of variables reported and because of aggregation of individual data by census tract. Census tract boundaries are chosen in an effort to construct relatively homogeneous units in terms of housing and socioeconomic characteristics. If within-tract variation is relatively small compared to the variation among tracts, than relatively little is lost by aggregating a given set of observations to census tract units before undertaking the statistical analysis. But even within generally homogeneous communities there may be substantial variation in relevant characteristics such as number of rooms. The effect of these variables on individual property values would be masked by aggregation.

---

[3] There is a third type of problem specific to the estimation of the demand for certain types of neighborhood characteristics. This problem is discussed in the next section.

3.3. *Income as an Explanatory Variable*

As with other questions, the answer to whether income should be
included as an explanatory variable in the equation explaining property
values depends on the model from which the equation is derived.
Polinsky and Rubinfeld (1977) have developed a general model in
which income net of transportation cost is an argument in the rent
function which is derived mathematically from the model. If estimation
is based on models of this general class, then income logically should
be included as a variable.

The hedonic price technique seeks to explain price or expenditures
on housing in terms of its own characteristics. Since income is a characteristic of households rather than of housing, the logic of the technique
dictates that income of the purchaser not be included in the regression
equation. However there is a rationale for using an income aggregate
such as census tract median income. Median income of a census tract
could be taken as a proxy for socioeconomic dimensions of neighborhood quality. The inclusion of census tract income could be justified on
this basis either where the unit of observation were the census tract or
individual properties.

3.4. *Functional Form*

The choice of the functional form for the hedonic price function is
not simply a matter of econometric convenience. There are interesting
economic implications of alternative functional forms. Of course the
first concern is with the sign and magnitude of the first derivative, the
marginal implicit price. Is it significantly different from zero? And does
it have the expected sign—positive for desirable characteristics and
negative for disamenities such as pollution? Beyond this, most researchers have considered the choice of functional form to be primarily
a matter of obtaining the best fit and have tried few alternatives, typically only the linear, log, and semilog forms. But there are two additional questions about the properties of this function which have economic implications.

The first is whether the marginal implicit price of a characteristic
is independent of the levels of other housing attributes. Table 1 shows
eight functional forms which have been tried, or at least discussed, in
the literature. Of these only the log and the Box–Cox transformation
make the implicit price of a characteristic depend on the levels of other
characteristics. The others all imply independence. The second question is whether the marginal implicit price varies with the level of the

Table 1
Some Alternative Functional Forms

Hedonic Price Function	Second Derivative	Sign of Second Derivative	
		For "goods" with $b > 0$	For "bads" with $b < 0$
Linear			
$P_h = a + bN_k$	0	Zero	Zero
Quadratic			
$P_h = a + bN_k + cN_k^2$	$2c$	Positive for $c > 0$	Positive for $c > 0$
		Zero for $c = 0$	Zero for $c = 0$
		Negative for $c < 0$	Negative for $c < 0$
Log			
$P_h = aN_k^b$	$(b - 1)b\dfrac{P_h}{N_k^2}$	Positive for $b > 1$	Positive
		Negative for $b < 1$	
Semilog			
$\log P_h = a + bN_k$	$b^2 N_k$	Positive	Positive
Inverse semilog			
$P_h = \log a + b \log N_k$	$-b/N_k^2$	Negative	Positive
Exponential			
$P_h = a + bN_k^c,$	$(c - 1)cbN_k^{c-2}$	Positive for $c > 1$	Positive for $c < 1$
		Zero for $c = 1$	Zero for $c = 1$
		Negative for $c < 1$	Negative for $c > 1$
where c (>0) is an unknown parameter			
Semilog exponential			
$\log P_h = a + bN_k^c,$	$2be^{a+bN_k^c}[1 + 2bN_k^c]$	Positive	Negative if $2bN_k^c > -1$
where c (>0) is an unknown parameter			
Box–Cox transformation			
$(P_h^c - 1)/c = a + bN_k,$	$(1 - c)b^2 P_h^{(1-2c)}$	Positive	Positive for $c < 1$
where c is an unknown parameter			Zero for $c = 1$
			Negative for $c > 1$

characteristics, and if so, in what way. Specifically the question concerns the sign of the second derivative of the hedonic price function. This function could be convex from below, linear, or concave, with the signs of the second derivative being positive, zero, and negative, respectively. As already noted, if the hedonic price function is linear, the implicit marginal prices of characteristics are constants, and estimation of demand curves for characteristics is not possible. However most researchers have found nonlinear functional forms to give better fits.

Figure 1 showed an hedonic price function which was increasing in the characteristic, but concave from below, indicating a decreasing marginal implicit price. This means that those households that have chosen a high level of this characteristic have high total willingnesses to pay (areas under their inverse demand functions) but low *marginal* willingnesses to pay for additional units of the characteristic. If the hedonic price function is concave upward, those with the most of the characteristic would also have the highest marginal willingnesses to pay for more. Which patterns would emerge in the housing market depend on the determinants of demand, especially the income elasticity of demand for the characteristic, as well as the relative quantities of housing with various levels of the characteristic. A similar argument can be made for a negative characteristic such as pollution, P. If the hedonic price function is convex from below as shown in Fig. 2a, the implicit (negative) price of pollution is an increasing function of P. This is shown in the lower quadrant of Fig. 2a. In economic terms, this means that the marginal damage due to pollution is a decreasing function of pollution levels; and the marginal willingness to pay to avoid pollution is greater the lower the level of pollution. If, on the other hand, the hedonic price function is concave from below as shown in Fig. 2b marginal damages are highest (i.e., the implicit price is a large negative number) at high pollution levels.

As the last two columns of Table 1 show, some functional forms impose restrictions on the relationship between marginal implicit price and quantity, but almost no attention has been given to the appro-

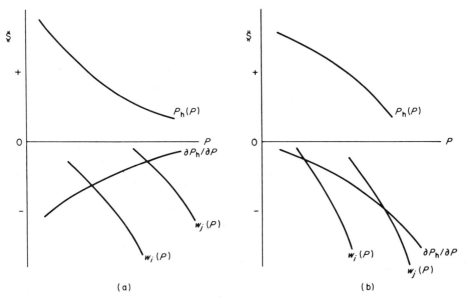

Figure 2

priateness of these restrictions. There is a case to be made for choosing functional forms such as the exponential (and semilog exponential and Box–Cox transformation for negative characteristics) which allow for a test of the sign of the second derivative as part of the estimating procedure.

3.5. Market Segmentation

Straszheim (1974) was the first to raise the question of market segmentation in the context of estimating hedonic price functions for housing. He argued that the urban housing market really consisted of a series of separate, compartmentalized markets with different hedonic price functions in each. As evidence in support of the segmentation hypothesis, Straszheim showed that estimating separate hedonic price functions for different geographic areas of the San Francisco Bay area reduced the sum of squared errors for the sample as a whole.

For different hedonic price functions to exist in an urban area two conditions must be met. First, purchasers in one market stratum must not participate significantly in other market strata. In other words, there must be some barrier to mobility of buyers among market strata. These barriers could be due to geography, discrimination, lack of information, or a desire for ethnically homogeneous neighborhoods, for example. The second condition is that either the structure of demand, the structure of supply, or both must be different across regions. Either buyers in separate submarkets must have different structures of demands, or the structure of characteristics of the housing stocks must be different. Even with buyer immobility, if demand and supply structures are the same, they will produce similar structures of hedonic prices. And perfect mobility and information on the part of buyers will eliminate differences in the implicit prices for any characteristic across market strata.

If market segmentation does exist, the hedonic price function estimated for the urban area as a whole will provide faulty estimates of the implicit prices facing subsets of buyers in different market segments. Thus estimates of benefits and estimates of demand functions based on faulty price data will also be faulty. If market segmentation does exist, separate hedonic price functions must be estimated for each segment; and benefit and demand functions must be separately estimated for each segment with a different set of implicit prices.

It is not clear how significant the problem of market segmentation is at the empirical level for air pollution–property value studies. Only two studies of the property value–air pollution relationship have tested their data for market segmentation. Harrison and Rubinfeld (1978) stratified their Boston data on the basis of income, accessability to employment, and household social status. They did not report the effects of stratification on the implicit price function. But they did report that estimates of benefits calculated from the implicit price function were reduced by up to 41%, depending upon the basis for market stratification. Thus there apparently was a significant effect on the implicit price function. On the other hand, Nelson (1978a) stratified his Washington, D.C., sample according to urban versus suburban census tracts. A Chow (F) test could not reject the hypothesis that the hedonic price functions were the same in the two submarkets. In a study which did not include air pollution, Schnare and Struyk (1976) stratified their sample of individual sales transactions from the Boston Standard Metropolitan Statistical Area (SMSA) on the basis of median income of the census tract in which the housing unit was located, number of rooms in the housing unit, a measure of the accessability of the housing unit, and by political jurisdiction. Their tests indicated different hedonic price functions for submarkets stratified by these characteristics.

4.   NEIGHBORHOOD VARIABLES IN AIR POLLUTION–PROPERTY VALUE STUDIES

I am aware of 15 different studies covering 11 cities in the United States and Canada which have been based implicitly or explicitly on the hedonic price approach. All of these studies have used cross-section data within a city to test for a relationship between air pollution and property values. In one case, St. Louis, there are four separate studies examining basically the same set of data. For Boston there are three studies; and for Chicago and Washington, D.C., there are two studies all using different sets of data. Some of the key features of these studies are summarized in Table 2.

All but two of these studies had as their primary purpose the measurement of the air pollution–property value relationship. Thus the inclusion of neighborhood variables was incidental and meant to improve the explanatory power of the equations. However, Schnare (1976) was interested in the role of ethnic and racial patterns of residential choice in explaining housing differentials. Hence a larger number of racial, ethnic, and other socioeconomic variables were included in her data base. Sonstelie and Portney (1977) were investigating the Tiebout hypothesis. Thus they included several public service variables.

Conceptually it is possible to distinguish between site or property

Table 2
Key Features of Air Pollution–Property Value Studies

City; Author	Base Year; Dependent Variables	Pollutants; Measures	Other Independent Variables	Functional Form	Results
I. St. Louis					
A. Ridker-Henning (1967)	1960 Property value: census tract median, owner occupied	Sulfation: annual geometric mean by lead candle (1963)	Property: 3 variables Neighborhood: 8 variables Income: as poxy for neighborhood	Linear	In best equations, the linear coefficient indicates that median property values fall by $186.50–245.00 per .25 μm/100 cm^2/day increase in sulfation
B. Wieand (1973)	1960 Housing expenditures per acre by census tract (a proxy for land value	Sulfation: annual geometric mean by lead candle (1963) Particulates: Annual mean. Measures of temporal variation were also tried but did not improve the fit (1963)	Property: 3 variables Neighborhood: 7 variables Income: as proxy for neighborhood	Linear	Neither pollution variable was significant

(*continued*)

Table 2 (continued)

City; Author	Base Year; Dependent Variables	Pollutants; Measures	Other Independent Variables	Functional Form	Results
C. Anderson-Cocker (1971)	1960 Property value: census tract median, separate equation for owner and rental	Sulfation: annual arithmetic mean by lead candle (1963) Particulates: annual arithmetic mean (1963)	Property: 3 variables Neighborhood: 2 variables Income: on basis that each census tract is a sub-market in equilibrium	Log-linear	Sulfation and particulates both included. Best results with owner occupied property value; coefficients on: $\log S = -.102$, $\log P = -.119$. They imply a "composite elasticity" of $.1-.2$. At the mean an additional $10 \ \mu g/m^3$ of particulates *plus* $.1 \ \mu g/100 \ cm^2$/day of sulfation reduces value of mean property by $300–700
D. Polinsky-Rubinfeld (1977)	1960 Property value: census tract median, separate equations for owner and rental	Sulfation: annual arithmetic mean by lead candle (1963) Particulates: annual arithmetic mean (1963)	Property: 2 variables Neighborhood: 2 variables Income: from deriva-tion of open city model	Log-linear	Sulfation and particulates both included. Owner equation coefficients on: $\log S = -.063$* $\log P = -.132$** Rental equation coefficients on: $\log S = -.006$ $\log P = -.137$** * significant at 10% level ** significant at 5% level They imply a "composite elasticity" of about .2

208

Study	Data	Pollution measure	Variables	Functional form	Results
II. Chicago A. Crocker (1970)	1964–1967 Property value: individual transactions	Sulfation: annual arithmetic means by lead candle (1964–1967) Particulates: Annual arithmetic means (1964–1967)	Property: 6 variables Neighborhood: 4 variables Income: based on interpretation of housing price equation as a bid function	Log-linear	Many equations with different specifications When SO_2 and particulates both included, coefficient on particulates usually negative and significant in range .2–.5; SO_2 often positive and usually not significant. When only one pollution variable included—it was always negative and significant Elasticities imply at the mean an additional 10 $\mu g/m^3$ of particulates plus 1 PPB of SO_2 reduces value of mean property by \$350–600
B. Smith (1978)	1971 Site value premium from individual transactions in new houses	Particulates: computed from dispersion model	Neighborhood: 6 variables Property: 2 variables	Linear	Individual site values fall by \$430–500 per 10 $\mu g/m^3$ increase in particulates
III. Washington, D.C. A. Anderson-Crocker (1971)	1960 Same as I.C	Same as I.C	Same as I.C	Log-linear	Sulfation and particulates both included two equations for owner and two for renter. One pollutant variable significant at .01 level in each equation. Coefficients ranged from .07–.17. (Also see I.C)

(continued)

Table 2 (*continued*)

City; Author	Base Year; Dependent Variables	Pollutants; Measures	Other Independent Variables	Functional Form	Results
B. Nelson (1978a)	1970 Property value: census tract median, owner occupied	Particulates: monthly geometric mean. Feb.–July 1967 Sulfation: monthly arithmetic mean. Feb.–July 1967 Oxidants: arithmetic average of daily means—May–September 1968	Property: 5 variables Neighborhood: 6 variables	Linear, semilog inverse semilog, and log-linear form were tested. Semilog and log-linear forms gave best resutls. Only the latter were reported	Sulfation variable significant only when particulate variable not present. Particulate coefficient always significant in range .048–.116. Oxidant significant in range .007–.019. At the mean an additional 10 $\mu g/m^3$ of particulates reduces value of mean property by $576–693. At the mean an additional .01 ppm of oxidants reduces value of mean property by $141–152
IV. Boston A. Harrison-Rubinfeld (1978)	1970 Property value: census tract median value of owner occupied housing	Mean concentration of nitrogen oxide and particulates calculated from dispersion model	Property: 2 variables Neighborhood: 10 variables	Exponential semilog: $\log MV = a_0 + a_1 NO_x^c \cdots$, where c is an unspecified parameter. Best results obtained with $c = 2$	Separate equations run for each pollutant. Each pollutant significant at .01 level. Many alternative specifications employed. Authors conclude that pollution coefficient is quite sensitive to the specification of the hedonic housing value equation

	Year	Dependent variable	Pollution data	Independent variables	Functional form	Results
B. Goodwin (1977)	1970	Monthly rent: census tract median value	Towns and Boston subdivision classified as "Little," "Moderate," or "High." Pollutants and averaging times not specified	Property: 3 variables Neighborhood: 23 socioeconomic variables Location: 21 accessibility and transportation variables	Linear	Pollution index variable negative and significant
C. Schnare (1976)	1970	Property value: owner estimate Gross rent	Particulates: year and averaging period not stated	Property: 7 variables Neighborhood: 11 variables Income as proxy for neighborhood	Semilog	Particulates negative and significant
V. Miscellaneous A. Kansas City: Anderson-Crocker (1971)	1960	Same as I.C	Same as I.C	Same as I.C	Log-linear	Sulfation and particulates both included. At least one pollution variable significant at the .05 level in each equation (also see I.C and III.A)
B. Toronto–Hamilton: Zerbe (1969)	1961	Property value: census tract median—owner occupied	Sulfation: annual average by lead candle—median of averages 1961–1967 Dustfall (Toronto only): annual average—median of averages 1961–1967	Property: 5 variables Neighborhood: 8 variables Income: as a proxy for neighborhood characteristics	Both linear and log-linear	Sulfation—linear form coefficients range from $200–450 per .25 μg/100 cm²/day; log linear coefficients .061–.121 for Toronto. For Hamilton the linear coefficient ranged from $580 to $882; and the log linear estimate was .081

(*continued*)

Table 2 (*continued*)

City; Author	Base Year; Dependent Variables	Pollutants; Measures	Other Independent Variables	Functional Form	Results
C. Philadelphia: Peckham (1970)	1960 Property value: census tract median—owner occupied	Sulfation: 1 month average by lead candle for January 1969 Particulates: arithmetic mean, averaging period not stated, 1969	Property: 3 variables Neighborhood: 3 variables Income: as proxy for neighborhood characteristics	Linear and log-linear	Sulfation—in linear form, the coefficient was $298 per .25 μg/100 cm² /day. The log linear coefficient was .096 Particulates was significant only in the log form with a coefficient of .116
D. Charleston, South Carolina: Steele (1972)	1970 Census enumeration district—mean per room of owner occupied housing	SO_2 and Particulates: Averaging period is not stated	Neighborhood: 14 variables Income: As a proxy for other neighborhood characteristics	Linear	Pollution variables had expected signs but were not significant at .05 level
E. Pittsburgh: Spore (1972)	1970 Property value: census tract mean values of owner occupied housing and mean values of contract rent for renter occupied housing	Sulfation: annual geometric mean and maximum monthly value by lead candle (1967) Dustfall: annual geometric mean and maximum monthly value (1969)	Property: 3 variables Neighborhood: 12 variables Income: As a determinant of demand	Log-linear	Many alternative specifications with sulfation and dustfall both entering. Annual mean or maximum dustfall almost always significant as .05 level Dustfall coefficients (elasticities) generally in range .092–.149

F. Los Angeles: Harrison-MacDonald (1974)	1970	Property value: census tract median value of owner occupied housing	Mean concentration of hydrocarbons, nitrogen oxide and oxidant index calculated from dispersion model	Property: 3 variables Neighborhood: 4 variables	Linear and semilog	Separate equations run for each pollutant. Each pollutant significant at .05 level. Coefficients substantially different from similar analysis of Boston also reported. A more detailed analysis of the Boston area is presented above
G. San Mateo County, California: Sonstelie and Portney (1977)	1970	Imputed gross rent calculated from individual sales data	Number of days per year photo-chemical oxidant reading exceeded .10 ppm	Property: 10 variables Neighborhood: 9 variables	Box–Cox transformation	Pollution variable negative and significant

characteristics and neighborhood characteristics as explanatory variables. But in many of these studies the distinction is blurred because of
the source and nature of the data. Four of the studies summarized here
used data based on individual sales or self-reported estimates of value
or rent along with data describing the characteristics of each property.
When data measuring various aspects of average housing quality by
census tract or other jurisdictions are added, they clearly measure the
separate effect of the quality of the physical environment of the neighborhood. Thus it is possible to separate the effects of, for example, the
age of a house from the age of the neighborhood as determinants of
the values of specific houses.

For the majority of the studies summarized here, the dependent
variable was the median or mean value of housing by census tract.
Explanatory variables included measures of average housing quality by
census tract. In these cases the distinction between property and neighborhood variables is not meaningful. Average age can be interpreted
both as a property specific characteristic of the "average house" whose
value is to be explained, and as a characteristic of the neighborhood
in which the house is found.

Within the general class of neighborhood characteristics, the variables used in the studies summarized here can be grouped into five
categories.

1. *Environmental quality*   All of the studies included one or more
measures of air quality. In addition the Boston studies included proximity to the Charles River; and Crocker (1970) used various measures
of proximity to Lake Michigan in his study of Chicago.

2. *Accessibility*   The effects of accessibility to the central business
district or centers of employment could be confounded with the effects
of air pollution (which is often worse closer to the CBD). It is important
to control for accessibility and the value of reduced travel time by including some accessibility variable in the property value equation. All
but one of the studies used distance to the CBD or some other locational measure such as travel time to control for accessibility. The exception is the Harrison–MacDonald (1974) study of Los Angeles where
it is difficult to identify a single center to use as a point of reference.
Instead Harrison and MacDonald used a variable which reflected accessibility to major freeways.

3. *Public services*   The most commonly used public service variable has been some measure of the quality of local schools. But the
variables chosen reflect the difficulty in identifying an unambiguous

measure of quality. In addition to school expenditures investigators have used indicators such as pupil–teacher ratios, success in college admissions, and improved reading scores. While these variables have been useful in explaining property value differentials, their relationship to school quality is unclear.

Sonstelie and Portney (1977) have investigated other public services, specifically road and street expenditures, quality of fire protection, and local recreation expenditures. All were significant, but recreation unexpectedly had a negative sign.

4. *Socioeconomic characteristics* The most commonly used socioeconomic characteristic has been some measure of the racial composition of the neighborhood, for example percent black, or percent nonwhite. Zerbe (1969) and Schnare (1976) have also used other ethnic groupings for example, Italian, Jewish, Polish, and Puerto Rican. Median family income is the second most commonly used socioeconomic characteristic. However, not all of the authors have agreed on the rationale for including income. Anderson and Crocker (1972) argued that their regression equations were bid functions, and that income was properly a determinant of demand (see also Crocker, 1970).

Seven studies have used neighborhood crime rates of some form as negative social indicators. Finally, four studies have used some measure of occupational status.

5. *Physical characteristics* Those studies using census tract average housing values or rents as dependent variables have had to rely for the most part on census tract aggregates for measures of physical quality. As discussed above, this does not make it possible to distinguish between site characteristics and neighborhood characteristics as determinants of housing prices. In addition to aggregated data on the characteristics of the housing stock, some of these studies have included some measure of land use such as percent industrial or percent commercial.

Those studies utilizing data on individual sites have had an opportunity for more detailed analysis of the physical neighborhood characteristics. But the opportunity was neglected in these four studies (see Crocker, 1970; Smith, 1978; Schnare, 1976; Sonstelie and Portney, 1977). None of the four utilized more than two neighborhood characteristics. Only one used a measure of the age of the housing stock or degree of industrial or commercial development; and none investigated the effects of such variables as density, average lot size, or degree of physical deterioration.

5. CONCLUSIONS

I would like to conclude with two points. The first is that those researchers who are using the hedonic price technique in efforts to estimate the demand for air quality might benefit by giving greater attention to neighborhood characteristics as determinants of housing prices. This is a lesson that the students of the economics of neighborhood can teach the students of the economics of cleaner air.

The second point is that I think the hedonic price technique can be useful in analyzing the demand for neighborhood characteristics. It should be possible to estimate marginal implicit prices and marginal values at least. Solving the identification problem and estimating true demand functions may prove to be quite difficult, however, for some types of characteristics. In any case, those students of the economics of neighborhood might get some useful ideas by studying the problems in model specification and estimation that have been identified and discussed by those applying the technique to air quality. In this way there might be some valuable cross fertilization between these two closely related areas of study.

ACKNOWLEDGMENTS

This chapter is based on work done at Resources for the Future as part of a larger project on the theory and practice of measuring the benefits of pollution control. The author wishes to acknowledge helpful comments from and discussions with David Harrison, Jon Nelson, A. Mitchell Polinsky, Paul Portney, Daniel Rubinfeld, V. Kerry Smith, and Jon Sonstelie.

REFERENCES

Anderson, R. J., and Crocker, T. (1971). Air pollution and residential property values. *Urban Studies* **8,** 171–180.

Anderson, R. J., and Crocker, T. (1972). Air pollution and property values: A reply. *Review of Economics and Statistics* **54,** 470–473.

Berry, B., and Bednarz, R. S. (1975). A Hedonic model of prices and assessments for single family homes: Does the assessor follow the market or the market follow the assessor? *Land Economics* **51,** 21–40.

Bishop, J., and Cicchetti, C. (1975). Some institutional and conceptual thoughts on the measurement of indirect and intangible benefits and costs. In *Cost benefit analysis and water pollution policy,* Henry M. Peskin and Eugene P. Seskin (eds.). The Urban Institute, Washington, D.C.

Crocker, T. (1970). *Urban air pollution damage functions. Theory and measurement.* University of California, Riverside. Available through NTIS: PB 197–668.

Freeman, A. M., III. (1974). On estimating air pollution control benefits from land value studies. *Journal of Environmental Economics and Management* **1,** 74–83.

Freeman, A. M., III. (1979). *The benefits of environmental improvement: Theory and practice.* John Hopkins University Press for Resources for the Future, Inc., Baltimore.

Goodwin, S. A. (1977). Measuring the value of housing quality—A note. *Journal of Regional Science* **17**, 107–115.

Griliches, Z. (ed.). (1971). *Price indexes and quality change.* Harvard University Press, Cambridge, Massachusetts.

Harrison, D., Jr., and MacDonald, R. (1974). Willingness to pay in Boston and Los Angeles for a reduction in automobile-related pollutants. In National Academy of Sciences, *Air quality and automobile emission control,* Vol. IV: *The costs and benefits of automobile control.* National Academy of Sciences, Washington, D.C.

Harrison, D., Jr., and Rubinfeld, D. (1978). Hedonic housing prices and the demand for clean air. *Journal of Environmental Economics and Management* 5, 81–102.

Lind, R. C. (1973). Spatial equilibrium, the theory of rents, and the measurement of benefits from public programs. *Quarterly Journal of Economics* **87**, 188–207.

Neslon, J. P. (1978a). *Economic analysis of transportation noise abatement.* Ballinger, Cambridge.

Nelson, J. P. (1978b). Residential choice, hedonic prices, and the demand for urban air quality, *Journal of Urban Economics* **5**, 357–369.

Peckham, B. (1970). Air pollution and residential property values in Philadelphia. (Process).

Polinsky, A. M., and Rubinfeld, D. L. (1977). Property values and the benefits of environmental improvements: Theory and measurement. In *Public economics and the quality of life.* Lowdon Wingo and Alan Evans (eds.). Johns Hopkins Press, Baltimore.

Polinsky, A., and Shavell, S. (1975). The air pollution and property value debate. *Review of Economics and Statistics* **57**, 100–104.

Polinsky, A., and Shavell, S. (1976). Amenities and property values in a model of an urban area. *Journal of Public Economics* **5**, 199–229.

Ridker, R. G. (1967). *Economic costs of air pollution: Studies in measurement.* Praeger, New York.

Ridker, R. G., and Henning, J. A. (1967). The determinants of residential property values with special reference to air pollution. *Review of Economics and Statistics* **49**, 246–257.

Rosen, S. (1974). Hedonic prices and implicit markets: Product differentiation in pure competition. *Journal of Political Economy* **82**, 34–55.

Schnare, A. B. (1976). Racial and ethnic price differentials in an urban housing market. *Urban Studies* **13**, 107–120.

Schnare, A. B., and Struyk, R. J. (1976). Segmentation in urban housing markets. *Journal of Urban Economics* **3**, 146–166.

Smith, B. A. (1976). Measuring the value of urban amenities. *Journal of Urban Economics* **5**, 370–387.

Sonstelie, J. C., and Portney, P. R. (1977). Gross rent and a reinterpretation of the Tiebout hypothesis. (Process).

Spore, R. (1972). *Property value differentials as a measure of the economic costs of air pollution.* Pennsylvania State University, Center for Air Environment Studies.

Steele, W. (1972). The effect of air pollution on the value of single-family owner-occupied residential property in Charleston, South Carolina. Masters thesis, Clemson University.

Straszheim, M. (1974). Hedonic estimation of housing market prices: A further comment. *Review of Economics and Statistics* **56**, 404–406.

Wieand, K. F. (1973). Air pollution and property values: a study of the St. Louis area. *Journal of Regional Science* **13**, 91–95.

Zerbe, R., Jr. (1969). *The economics of air pollution: A cost–benefit approach.* Ontario Department of Public Health, Toronto.

__ 10 _____

The Disbenefits of Neighborhood and Environment to Urban Property

BRIAN J. L. BERRY
ROBERT S. BEDNARZ

1. CITY-CENTERED DISTANCE-DECAY RELATIONSHIPS: THE "CLASSICAL" MUTH–ALONSO MODEL

Traditional residential location theory, as formalized in the Muth–Alonso models, has focused on the role of distance from the city center in determining housing prices. The derivation begins by separating the market price of a house into two components: the price per unit of housing and the quantity of units purchased. The product of those two components is the total expenditure on housing by a family, and it can be derived using what are now traditional utility maximization procedures. Assume that a consumer's level of welfare depends upon the quantity of housing that he consumes H and the quantity of all other goods X:

$$U = U(H, X) \quad \text{where} \quad U_h, U_x > 0. \tag{1}$$

He also faces a budget constraint such that his total expenditure on housing $[P(k) \cdot H]$, where $P(k)$ is the price of a unit of housing, which is a function of the distance k from the central business district (CBD),

219

THE ECONOMICS OF NEIGHBORHOOD

plus his total expenditure on all other goods $[P_x X]$, plus his expenditure on travel (assumed for simplicity to depend only upon distance) $[T(k)]$, must equal his income (Y):

$$P_x X + P(k) \cdot H + T(k) - Y = 0 \qquad \text{where} \quad T_k > 0. \qquad (2)$$

This can be maximized by setting up the Lagrangian multipliers and taking the first derivatives:

$$(\partial L / \partial X) = U_x - \lambda Px = 0, \qquad (3a)$$

$$(\partial L / \partial H) = U_h - \lambda P(k) = 0, \qquad (3b)$$

$$(\partial L / \partial k) = -\lambda(H \cdot P_k + T_k) = 0, \qquad (3c)$$

$$(\partial L / \partial \lambda) = Y - [X + P(k) \cdot H + T(k)] = 0. \qquad (3d)$$

From the third utility maximization condition Eq. (3c) it is apparent that the marginal change in the cost of a given quantity of housing is given by

$$H \cdot P_k = -T_k. \qquad (4)$$

In order to determine the price at any given distance K_0 from the CBD of one unit of housing it is necessary to integrate Eq. (4) with respect to k,

$$\int_0^{K_0} H \cdot P_k \, dk = [A_0 - T_{K_0}]H, \qquad (5)$$

where T_{K_0} is the travel costs from distance K_0, and A_0 is the cost of the housing in the CBD $(k = 0)$. Defining the price of one unit of housing at the center of the city as equal to unity, then

$$H \cdot P_{K_0} = H(1 - T_{K_0}). \qquad (6a)$$

The way in which the price per unit of housing declines in response to distance depends upon the way in which travel costs increase. They might increase linearly, in which case the price of a unit of housing would decline linearly from the CBD and (6a) could be rewritten as

$$H \cdot P(k) = H(1 - \beta k) \qquad \text{where} \quad \beta > 0. \qquad (6b)$$

There is considerable evidence that the price per unit housing does not decline linearly but in some negative exponential fashion (implying that transportation costs increase less than proportionately). In this case Eq. (6a) would be rewritten (redefining A_0)

$$H \cdot P(k) = H \cdot e^{B'k} \qquad \text{where} \quad \beta' < 0. \qquad (6c)$$

Measuring H, a "unit of housing," poses a problem. There is no clear way of constructing a priori a weighting scheme that would determine exactly how many bathrooms were equivalent to one garage or to a bedroom, since separate prices of the components of a parcel of housing units (i.e., a complete residence) are not available. The number of housing units that any one house contains is a function of the number of separate components that it contains:

$$H = \Pi_i A_i^{\alpha_i}, \tag{7}$$

where A_i is the quantity of the ith component (bathroom, degree of modernization, age, etc.). This functional form has the intuitive appeal that it explains why the continual addition of a given component (e.g., the number of bedrooms) does not add a constant dollar value to the residence. The complete form of the model is then

$$\text{PRICE} = e^{\beta'k}[\Pi_i A^{\alpha_i}], \tag{8a}$$

where PRICE is the market price of the residence, or, in log form,

$$\log(\text{PRICE}) = \beta'k + \sum_i \alpha_i \log A_i + U, \tag{8b}$$

where U is a random disturbance term.

Having established the functional form in Eq. (8b), the next step is to determine the relevant attributes that enter into the definition of H. The potential list is enormous since it includes not only the physical properties of the building itself but also all possible "neighborhood amenities" and disamenities as well.

That the value of a housing unit depends on its characteristics and those of the neighborhood surrounding it, is easily grasped by thinking of the dwelling as an asset which satisfies certain needs of its occupants, such as shelter, privacy, and recreational space. It is the specific bundle of characteristics of the housing unit which determine what needs the dwelling can satisfy. It is obvious that some characteristics (benefits) will satisfy needs, and others (disbenefits) will hinder satisfaction. Furthermore, thinking of a housing unit in this way gives one a method of evaluating the relative importance of various characteristics initially. The task of choosing specific variables to explain the value of a dwelling is still formidable, however, and the choice varies greatly with the researcher both with respect to the types and numbers of variables chosen, as Table 1 reveals.

For example Evans (1973), interested in the influence of distance from CBD on property value, limited his independent variables to three: log of distance to CBD, log of floor space, and years of lease expired. By confining his sample to houses of one type located in neigh-

Table 1
Summary Table of Recent Work on Housing Value

Author	Date	Dependent Variable	Locational Variable(s)	Neighborhood Variables			Housing Variables	
				Racial–Ethnic	Neighborhood Characteristics	Environmental Pollution	Housing Characteristics	Housing Improvements
Ridker and Henning	1968	House price	Travel time to CBD Access to main highway	% nonwhite	Housing density School quality Socioeconomic group index Persons/dwelling unit Mean family income	Air pollution index	No. rooms Average house age	
Cubbin	1970	House price					Lot area Age House type	Garage area of: Reception rooms Kitchen Bedrooms Heating plant Modern kitchen
Kain and Quigley	1970	House price	Distance to CBD	% white	Median schooling Crime index		5 factors produced from 39 measurements: Age No. rooms Lot area	No. baths

Study	Year	Dependent variable	Accessibility	(Same variables as above plus the following)			Type of structure	
Lane	1970	Monthly rent	Distance to CBD					Heat, water, appliances, furniture; Included in rent; Hot water; Central heat; Owner occupied; Garage
Muth	1970	House price	Accessibility index	% black	No. manufacturing establishments; % housing built before 1940; % owner occupied housing units; % population over 20 yr; Income; Migration; Med-yrs. schooling; % workforce in white collar jobs; Population growth		Floor area; House type; No. floors	
Anderson and Crocker	1971	Housing expenditures/month	Distance to CBD	% nonwhite	Mean family income; % dilapidated Bldgs.; # Bldgs older than 20 years	SO: Levels Particulate level	No. Rooms	

(continued)

223

Table 1 (*continued*)

Author	Date	Dependent Variable	Locational Variable(s)	Neighborhood Variables			Housing Variables	
				Racial–Ethnic	Neighborhood Characteristics	Environmental Pollution	Housing Characteristics	Housing Improvements
Apps	1971	House price	Accessibility to employment Acessibility to schools				Floor area Storey height Age Condition Lot area Structure type	Garage
Massell and Stewart	1971	House price			Neighborhood quality index		Structure-size index	
Wabe	1971	Average house price	Rail travel time and cost to CBD		Social class Population density Distance to Green-Belt		Floor area Date of construction	Garage Central heating
Wilkinson	1971	Factor analysis	Distance to CBD		Socioeconomic index Residential density No. schools/ population		House type Age No. rooms Area	Attics Bedrooms Garage Garage space Bath Inside toilet
Evans	1973	Asking price	Distance to CBD				Floor area No. years of lease expired	

borhoods with similar environmental and socioeconomic characteristics, thereby holding those variables constant, he was able to account for 84% of the variance of the dependent variable. In another example, Kain and Quigley (1970a) took a different approach. They began by collapsing 39 neighborhood and housing characteristics to 5 factors using factor analysis. Two regression models were then constructed, one for owner occupied units and one for rental units. In the rental model, the 5 factors along with 23 other independent variables were regressed against monthly rent. In the owner occupied model, 9 more independent variables were added to the 5 factors. Many of the variables proved insignificant and R^2 were lower than that of Evans's model.

If a broader overview of past empirical work is attempted, it will be seen that most of the models seem to include at least a few variables from each of three general categories: locational measurements, housing characteristics, and neighborhood characteristics, within the last two categories, such features as neighborhood quality, environmental pollution, the type of improvements made to the property, etc., are frequently considered. Whether or not each subset is included seems quite random, however. Many studies neglect at least one of the three categories. For example, Apps (1971), Cubbin (1970), and Lane (1970) included no neighborhood characteristic variables in their regressions, while Massell and Stewart (1971) omitted locational variables. Muth (1970), attempting to determine the income elasticity of housing demand, formulated several models with housing value as the dependent variable but included no independent variables which measured housing characteristics.

Even when similar independent variables are included in several studies they often behave very differently. For example, Evans (1973) and Wilkinson (1971) both included the locational variable distance to CBD in their models while attempting to explain house price. In both cases the variable was significant, but in Evans' study its coefficient was negative while in Wilkinson's it was positive. To compound the situation further, Kain and Quigley (1970a) found distance to CBD insignificant at the 5% level.

2. MODELING STRATEGY IN THE CHICAGO CASE

It seems apparent that there has been confusion and a lack of theory in the variable selection process in most previous studies. Often, it appears as though the most important factor determining a variable list is simply the availability of data or a high level of significance of a variable's coefficient where larger models were run initially and only smaller "significant" models were published. Neither of these decision-making processes seems adequate.

The approach taken here is to include the "conventional" locational variable, distance to CBD [k], and to divide the bundle of housing characteristics (H) into two groups, one including properties of the house itself and another reflecting neighborhood factors. These two classes of variables are then further subdivided with a distinction being drawn in the first case between standard housing characteristics and the nature of housing improvements that have been made while the second is divided into neighborhood socioeconomic status and mobility characteristics, racial and ethnic characteristics of the residents, and environmental pollution.

The next step was to collect the variables for each of the subcategories that are listed in Table 2. Three sources served to supply these data. The housing characteristics and housing improvements variables were provided by the Society of Real Estate Appraisers' Market Data Center publication *Chicagoland Residential Sales Data* for a sample of 275 single-family homes in the City of Chicago in 1971. This publication consists of very detailed information concerning the type and condition of a sample of residential properties which sold in the Chicago area during the period 1970–1972. Besides the terms of the sale (price, mortgage, date, and type of financing), 27 characteristics of the building and land are recorded for each property.

The neighborhood characteristics and the racial and ethnic variables are census data. These figures pertain to the census tract in which the property is located.

Both the pollution variables and the distance measure are the result of Argonne National Laboratory's air quality display model. This pollution simulation program is capable of generating a daily sulfur dioxide and suspended particulates reading for every cell of a 1-kilometer square grid covering the City of Chicago. This grid also makes calculation of straight line distance from downtown Chicago relatively simple.

Finally, building and land assessments for the properties were obtained from the figures published by the Cook County Assessor's Office. Every property in a township is reassessed every four years (one fourth of Cook County being assessed each year) and the results published in a paper serving the appropriate township.

These variables were tested for their association with other variables and their contribution to the model itself. Once a tentative group

Table 2
List of Variables

Housing character- istics	Floor area	SQ FT	Floor area of the dwelling in square feet
	Age of dwelling	AGE	Age of the building in years
	Lot area	LOTAREA	Area of the property's lot in square feet
Housing improve- ments	Air conditioning	AC	Dummy variable for presence of central air conditioning
	Garage	GARAGE	Dummy indicating presence of a garage
	Improved attic	ATTIC	Dummy indicating an im- proved attic (containing rooms or a bath)
	Improved basement	BASEMENT	Dummy indicating basement with rooms or bath
	Number of baths	# BATHS	Number of bathrooms
Neighbor- hood character- istics	Median family income	MFI	Median family income of census tract in which property is located
	Multiple-family dwellings	APTS	Percentage multiple-family dwellings in the census tract
	Migration	MIGRTN	Percent of families in property's tract living in a different tract five years before
Racial and ethnic variables	% Blacks	BLACK	Percent black in census tract
	% Cubans/Mexicans	CUB-MEX	Percent Cuban and Mexican in census tract
	% Irish	IRISH	Percent Irish in census tract
Environ- mental pollution	Sulfur dioxide	SO_2	Average yearly sulfur dioxide intensity (micrograms per cubic meter)
	Particulates	PARTIC	Average yearly suspended particulates measurement (micrograms per cubic meter)
Accessibility	Distance to CBD	DIST.	Distance in kilometers from downtown Chicago

of variables was chosen, a choice concerning the order in which the groups of variables were to enter the model had to be made. The final decision was influenced by several considerations. First, in attempting to determine the relative importance of the various subgroups, it was helpful to consider the decision process of potential home seekers. It was felt that the basic characteristics of the structure (i.e., housing characteristics) were the first factor taken into account by people trying to make a choice among houses. Next, more specific details of the house (housing improvements) become important. Finally, the prospective buyer examines the neighborhood (neighborhood characteristics) and the type of people living in the area (racial and ethnic variables). The order in which the groups of variables were entered into the model was consistent with this interpretation as well as with statistical interpretation of the groups' relative importance.

Thus, housing characteristics and improvements were entered first because it was felt that the most important characteristics that determine the value of a housing unit are the properties of the house itself. The order in which the neighborhood variable groups were added to the model also reflected their relative importance: socioeconomic levels preceded racial characteristics and environmental pollution.

In the case of distance from CBD, interrelationships among the variables dictated that it be entered into the equation last. As can be seen from the simple correlation coefficients in Table 3, many of the

Table 3
Simple Correlation Coefficients among Model Variables

		Price	Price per Square Foot	Sulfur Dioxide	Partic-ulates	Distance from CBD
Housing character-istics	Floor area	.43	−.40	.11	.17	.05
	Age of dwelling	−.43	−.52	.14	.29	−.34
	Lot area	.37	.06	−.07	−.22	.31
Housing improve-ments	Air conditioning	.38	.32	−.13	−.15	.22
	Garage	.11	.02	−.01	−.07	.01
	Improved attic	.08	.13	−.01	−.10	.07
	Improved basement	.31	.20	−.15	−.09	.16
	Number of baths	.34	−.18	.03	.13	.05
Neighbor-hood character-istics	Median family income	.73	.61	−.21	−.37	.58
	Multiple-family dwellings	−.18	−.37	.14	.35	−.28
	Migration	.02	−.27	.03	.15	.03
Racial and ethnic variables	Blacks	−.40	−.57	.25	.50	−.40
	Cubans/Mexicans	−.19	−.22	.13	.24	−.34
	Irish	.29	.25	−.19	−.29	.29
Environ-mental pollution	Sulfur dioxide	−.18	−.28	1.00	.51	−.40
	Particulates	−.36	−.50	.51	1.00	−.74
Accessibility	Distance from CBD	.61	.58	−.40	−.74	1.00

characteristics of single-family dwellings are related to the unit's distance from the CBD. Entering distance last in the model allowed its effect on other variables to be determined after some idea of the importance and sign of the nondistance variables had already been acquired. The two pollution measurements were treated in substantially the same way since, in effect, they almost serve as proxies for the distance variable (simple correlation coefficients between the two and distance are $-.40$ and $-.74$). Because of the high correlation between the two pollution variables themselves $(.51)$, they were not entered together in any of the model runs. Similarly, the last run of the model was made with distance but neither of the pollution measurements.

3. RESULTS

Tables 4 and 5 present the results of the analyses, with the groups of independent variables regressed first on the selling price of the housing unit and second on the price per square foot of the unit. A series of nine regression models is presented in each case:

1. $P = f((1)$ housing characteristics)
2. $P = f((1) + (2)$ housing improvements)
3. $P = f((1) + (2) + (3)$ neighborhood characteristics)
4. $P = f((1) + (2) + (3) + (4)$ racial and ethnic variables)
5. $P = f((1) + (2) + (3) + (4) + (5a) SO_2)$
6. $P = f((1) + (2) + (3) + (4) + (5b)$ particulates)
7. $P = f((1) + (2) + (3) + (4) + (5a) + (6)$ distance)
8. $P = f((1) + (2) + (3) + (4) + (5b) + (6)$ distance)
9. $P = f((1) + (2) + (3) + (4) + (6).$

Table 6 shows the accumulative and incremental explanatory power of these successive regression models in the two cases. All of the groups of variables with the exception of environmental pollution always make a significant contribution to the explanatory power of the model. The results are in accordance with expectations.

Turning to the specific coefficients, the first model run, using selling price as the dependent variable yielded results which in general are not difficult to explain. The signs of the coefficients, for example, are those one would expect, at least for the first three groups of variables. However, the coefficients of each of the racial variables are negative. Some researchers in the past (see the summary in Kain, 1973) have estimated that holding housing quality and income levels constant (as is done in our model), blacks pay more for housing in the ghetto than

Table 4
Factors Influencing the Price of Single-Family Homes

					Model				
	1	2	3	4	5	6	7	8	9
R^2	.474	.568	.741	.772	.772	.773	.788	.790	.787
Constant	5.113	5.762	-2.641	-1.455	-1.455	-.381	-.410	-2.061	-.347
Housing characteristics Square feet	.457 (.058)	.318 (.069)	.247 (.057)	.323 (.055)	.323 (.055)	.330 (.056)	.338 (.054)	.336 (.054)	.344 (.054)
Age	-.252 (.023)	-.209 (.023)	-.135 (.020)	-.127 (.019)	-.127 (.019)	-.126 (.019)	-.122 (.018)	-.123 (.018)	-.123 (.018)
Lot area	.308 (.053)	.309 (.050)	.201 (.040)	.163 (.038)	.163 (.038)	.155 (.039)	.123 (.038)	.128 (.038)	.123 (.038)
Housing improvements Air conditioning		.211 (.047)	.082 (.039)	.070 (.037)	.070 (.037)	.070 (.037)	.079 (.036)	.080 (.036)	.078 (.036)
Attic		.178 (.051)	.155 (.040)	.149 (.038)	.149 (.038)	.144 (.039)	.122 (.037)	.126 (.037)	.124 (.037)
Basement		.116 (.037)	.087 (.029)	.085 (.027)	.085 (.027)	.084 (.027)	.078 (.027)	.074 (.026)	.074 (.027)
No. baths		.148 (.073)	.152 (.057)	.137 (.053)	.137 (.053)	.140 (.054)	.133 (.052)	.124 (.052)	.130 (.052)

	(1)	(2)	(3)	(4)	(5)	(6)	(7)	(8)
Garage	.068 (.038)	.065 (.030)	.062 (.029)	.062 (.029)	.062 (.029)	.070 (.028)	.073 (.028)	.071 (.028)
Neighborhood characteristics								
MFI		1.019 (.077)	.814 (.086)	.814 (.086)	.820 (.086)	.713 (.086)	.683 (.089)	.720 (.086)
Apartments		.044 (.022)	.027 (.022)	.027 (.022)	.036 (.023)	.060 (.022)	.055 (.023)	.061 (.022)
Migration		−.030 (.035)	.044 (.037)	.044 (.037)	.031 (.039)	−.033 (.040)	−.030 (.040)	−.034 (.040)
Racial and ethnic variables								
Black			−.031 (.006)	−.031 (.006)	−.028 (.006)	−.022 (.006)	−.025 (.006)	−.022 (.006)
Cuban–Mexican			−.026 (.007)	−.026 (.007)	−.023 (.007)	−.013 (.007)	−.014 (.007)	−.013 (.007)
Irish			−.016 (.010)	−.016 (.010)	−.016 (.010)	−.015 (.010)	−.015 (.010)	−.016 (.010)
Environmental pollution								
SO$_2$				−.002 (.074)		.033 (.032)		
Particulates					−.220 (.205)		.415 (.242)	
Accessibility								
Distance						.024 (.006)	.030 (.007)	.023 (.005)

231

Table 5
Determinants of the Price per Square Foot of Single-Family Homes

		Model								
		1	2	3	4	5	6	7	8	9
	R^2	.281	.391	.552	.629	.631	.635	.654	.654	.654
	Constant	2.750	2.371	-4.915	-2.524	-2.280	.107	-1.049	-1.686	-1.078
Housing characteristics	Age	-.267 (.026)	-.238 (.027)	-.164 (.026)	-.145 (.024)	-.145 (.024)	-.142 (.024)	-.139 (.023)	-.139 (.023)	-.138 (.023)
	Lot area	.125 (.056)	.151 (.055)	.044 (.049)	.012 (.046)	.010 (.046)	-.004 (.046)	-.032 (.045)	-.032 (.045)	-.032 (.045)
Housing improvements	Air conditioning		.210 (.055)	.077 (.050)	.060 (.046)	-.058 (.046)	.061 (.046)	.070 (.045)	.071 (.045)	.070 (.045)
	Attic		.157 (.060)	.122 (.052)	.116 (.048)	.116 (.048)	.105 (.048)	.087 (.047)	.087 (.047)	.086 (.047)
	Basement		.047 (.042)	.024 (.037)	.035 (.034)	.028 (.034)	.032 (.034)	.021 (.033)	.022 (.033)	.022 (.033)
	No. baths		-.296 (.066)	-.300 (.059)	-.249 (.054)	-.246 (.054)	-.232 (.054)	-.241 (.053)	-.246 (.053)	-.242 (.052)

	(1)	(2)	(3)	(4)	(5)	(6)	(7)	(8)
Garage	.075 (.045)	.067 (.039)	.054 (.036)	.065 (.036)	.054 (.036)	.065 (.035)	.066 (.035)	.065 (.035)
Neighborhood characteristics								
MFI		.913 (.099)	.589 (.105)	.596 (.105)	.609 (.105)	.483 (.106)	.465 (.109)	.480 (.105)
Apartments		.035 (.029)	.005 (.027)	.010 (.027)	.026 (.029)	.049 (.028)	.046 (.029)	.049 (.028)
Migration		-.107 (.045)	.017 (.046)	.009 (.046)	-.015 (.048)	-.081 (.050)	-.080 (.050)	-.081 (.050)
Racial and ethnic variables								
Black			-.048 (.007)	-.046 (.007)	-.041 (.008)	-.036 (.008)	-.037 (.008)	-.036 (.008)
Cuban–Mexican			-.032 (.009)	-.030 (.009)	-.026 (.009)	-.016 (.009)	-.016 (.009)	-.016 (.009)
Irish			-.017 (.013)	-.019 (.013)	-.019 (.013)	-.018 (.012)	-.017 (.012)	-.018 (.012)
Environmental pollution								
SO_2				-.056 (.040)		-.014 (.040)		
Particulates					-.532 (.253)		.146 (.304)	
Accessibility								
Distance						.028 (.007)	.031 (.008)	.029 (.007)

233

Table 6
Increases in Explanatory Power with the Addition of Variable Groups

	Price Model		Price per Square Foot Model	
Variable group added	R^2	F^a	R^2	F^a
Housing characteristics	.474	81.30	.281	53.17
Housing improvements	.568	11.54	.391	9.66
Neighborhood characteristics	.741	58.60	.552	31.60
Racial and ethnic variables	.772	11.89	.629	17.89

[a] F test of hypothesis that all coefficients in group equal zero.

nonblacks outside the ghetto. The results from this study show the opposite relationship between a neighborhood's blackness and housing prices, and reiterate the parameter for Spanish Americans and Irish Catholics in the city. Each of our racial variables measure the percentage of the housing unit's census tract population that is found in each subgroup. The negative relationship between price and the first two minorities in particular are emphasized by the small standard error and the relative stability of the coefficient. This difference between previous results and ours is the first needing explanation, and it can be done by looking at the relationships between housing starts, growth of demand, and filtering in a dual housing market.

The second sign which is different from that found by most other studies is the positive sign attached to distance from CBD. Although this result is unusual, it is not inexplicable. In fact, a modified form of the Muth–Alonso model is able to handle a positive price–distance relationship without difficulty. In this modified form, the price–distance gradient is shown to depend on two quantities. One of these is negative, the transport cost; one is positive, an amenity influence that increases with distance from the CBD. If the amenity increase outweighs the transport cost increase, a positive distance coefficient results.

Before we turn to these differences, however, several other features of the results presented in Tables 4 and 5 should be remarked upon. Of particular interest are changes in the size or significance of coefficient of APTS which is significant at the 5% level when it enters, suddenly becomes insignificant when the racial and ethnic variables enter the equation and then regains significance as distance enters. This large degree of interaction with other variables indicated by this sort of instability in a coefficient makes it difficult to determine the true relationship between the dependent and independent variables. It seems likely that in this case APTS initially was serving as a partial measure of the racial and ethnic variables, and, thus, when the latter entered the model the effect of APTS became small. Several other examples of this sort of behavior of coefficients can be found. The coefficients of AC, AGE, LOT AREA, and BASEMENT are all reduced when MFI and the other neighborhood characteristics enter the equation. Possible explanations for these changes of magnitude come to mind immediately. It is not hard to believe that air conditioning is highly associated with median family income and that the variable received undue importance in explaining price before the income variable entered. The slower depreciation rate indicated by the reduction in the size of the coefficient of AGE when MFI is added is not surprising either, since the more affluent should be able to maintain their homes more effectively. That LOT AREA is associated with affluence is what one would expect from the usual interpretation of the theory of land value which states that the wealthy should be expected to consume more land at a greater distance from the city center while the poor consume less at a shorter distance. Finally, in the case of BASEMENT it seems entirely possible that this measurement is a reflection of basement family rooms or dens which once again are probably correlated with income.

All of these variables, then, react in the same way when MFI enters the model: That part of their effect due to the underlying income component is reassigned to the actual income variable, MFI. In every case the size of the specific housing characteristic coefficient falls appreciably.

The same type of changes occur in the coefficients of LOT AREA and CUB-MEX when distance enters. The possible explanations for this behavior are similar also. It should be expected that the lot size depends on distance and that excluding distance from a model will inflate the coefficient of a lot size variable embodying a distance component. The population distribution of Cubans and Mexicans appears to be related to distance also (simple correlation coefficient of $-.34$). Once again, when the distance component of the variable is subtracted (by entering distance among the independent variables) the size of the coefficient of CUB-MEX decreases.

The results of the model with price per square foot as the dependent variable are quite similar to those described above. This should not be surprising since floor area was included as an independent variable in the first formulation. The coefficients of AGE and LOT AREA are reduced in size when MFI enters the equation just as in the first model. Likewise, the CUB-MEX coefficient decreases when distance is added. A few differences are worth noting, however. One of these is a highly significant negative coefficient attached to No. BATHS. This negative relation is probably caused by the high degree of correlation between the floor area and No. BATHS (.64). If dividing price by square feet of floor space is tantamount to dividing by No. BATHS, then the negative relationship is not hard to understand. Every time the value of the independent variable is increased, the size of the dependent variable decreases since, in fact, it is being divided by the former. The negative relationship is almost automatic as a result. Another difference is that the variable MIGRTN is significant (5%) when it enters but becomes insignificant when the racial and ethnic group are added. One hypothesis to explain this is that MIGRTN is serving as an indicator of neighborhoods undergoing racial turnover. Thus, in areas undergoing racial change, the values of MIGRTN will be high since many of the residents are newly arrived. These new arrivals will be minority group members. When the racial and ethnic variables enter and, are in a sense held constant, the importance of MIGRTN lessens and much of its influence is assumed by BLACK and CUB-MEX.

In both models all of the groups of variables added significantly to the explanatory power of the formulation except environmental pollution. The high correlation between distance and particulates ($-.74$) leads to great instability in the pollution measurement's coefficient. For example, in the price per square foot model, the coefficient of PARTIC changes from a significant negative to an insignificant positive parameter. Unfortunately, PARTIC is highly associated with many independent variables also. Perhaps the common underlying component of all of these variables is distance, and, if the dual nature of this component could somehow be extracted—the negative effect of transport costs and the positive relationship of neighborhood and environmental amenities to distance—the true nature of the relationship of several of the independent variables to the dependent would become apparent. It is to this question that we now turn.

4. CLASSICAL PROPERTY VALUE
   CONCEPTS RECONSIDERED

To reach our objective—a reasoned explanation for positive distance exponents for single-family housing prices in the central city—we should first reconsider the basics of property value theory, and then try to reformulate the Muth–Alonso model.

It was Sir Henry Maine who pointed out, over a century ago, that one of the essential ingredients in the emergence of modern urban–industrial society was a change in the concept of property ownership. Originally held in common by traditional social groups, property—particularly land and the capital invested on it—has been transformed into another exchangeable commodity with a price determined by competition among prospective users.

The value of property is not simply the value of the physical object, however; it is the value of a bundle of rights that property ownership conveys. Exchange of a piece of property involves the transfer of this set of rights from one individual to another. The rights derive their significance from the fact that they help a man form expectations which he can reasonably hold in his dealings with others—expectations that find expression in the laws, customs, and mores of society. An owner expects the community to protect his rights—which include rights to benefit or harm himself or others—and to permit him to act in those ways not prohibited in the specification of the rights.

The right to benefit or harm others and its complement, to be benefitted or harmed by others, is important because it involves *externalities*—the effects of each land user's activities on others—and their *internalization*—how the costs and gains are accounted for in property prices and land use. An individual property owner will try to maximize present value by assessing the future time streams of costs and benefits associated with alternative land uses, selecting that use which he believes will maximize the present value. In doing so, he will take into account the benefits conveyed to him by others and the costs imposed on him by others. Society does not, however, require the converse—that he receive rewards for the benefits he conveys to others and pay for the costs he imposes on them.

Hence, in any well-functioning competitive property market in which there are few constraints on the mobility of purchasers of property, the price of each piece of property should reflect the present value of the future stream of net benefits expected to flow over the useful life of the "highest and best" improvements, that is, those land uses that maximize returns, consistent with the societal definition of property rights. This generalization is, however, subject to the workings of time. Many capital investments cannot be changed overnight. A commitment to a particular land use may, therefore, be a commitment for several decades, and one which is fixed rather than mobile. Where major capital investments are involved it will only be in the *new* property market that one sees uses being established that, at any point in time are risk takers' estimates of the "highest and best." Elsewhere the toll that depreciation takes of fixed capital investments before their economically useful life has run out will be apparent.

As noted, the value of any site will be enhanced by benefits conveyed by others (both "windfalls" of particular actions, and in the longer term, *positive externalities* such as a "good neighborhood" and a "fine school district" or "excellent accessibility"). Likewise, they will be reduced by costs imposed by others (immediate "wipeouts," and longer term *negative externalities*, such as air pollution or the swath of noise associated with airport landing patterns). The private property market produces an "internalization" of many of these externalities in that the consumer bears the cost. Thus, a new highway will provide windfall profits to some landowners, while property owners along a bypassed route will suffer losses, and even what we have termed wipeouts. Subsequently, a new owner will be willing to pay more to occupy and use a site well endowed with positive externalities, while the price paid for properties which bear a heavy burden of negative externalities will be much lower.

One result is land uses that are patterned geographically because the purchase or rental of the physical commodity, land, conveys the exclusive right to occupy a particular *location* and to use a particular set of *site amenities*. One thus can distinguish between the *locational value* and the *amenity value* of the property. Both are relative values, in that they involve interdependencies and reflect externalities.

Locational value is determined by relative accessibility to the activity centers that serve as points of focus within any spatial organization, the lines and channels of movement to and from these centers, and the identifiable neighborhoods, communities, districts, and regions that are the essence of human territoriality. At any point in time these are a matter of inherited spatial organization, although over a span of time they will be affected by both public and private decisions. But since different uses have different needs for access to different things, the result is a mix of competing uses that varies from one location to another. As a result, both land use and land value vary systematically with relative location, a product of the desire to be as close as possible to certain things to benefit from their positive spillovers, and as far away as possible from others, to avoid the negative externalities.

Amenity value is in part a matter of the relative worth to prospective users of the physical attributes of the site, such as a waterfront location, and in part also a matter of the acquired social attributes of the site, such as neighborhood quality. Again, both land use and land value vary systematically with the relative worth of the amenities.

Those best able to pay will preempt the better-endowed sites and will relegate to those least able to compete the least desirable sites in the least desirable locations.

It is the interaction of amenity value and locational value that is of particular interest. Setting aside the fact that the classical formulations assume only a single center—the CBD—in an increasingly multi-centered pattern of urbanization in which access to peripheral locations seems as meaningful as access to the city center, there are still other interdependencies that are important. If, as Alonso maintains, the rich will preempt the periphery, putting expensive homes on large lots and relegating the poor to the city center, there are definite amenity value consequences: Status-derived amenities will increase with distance, while poverty- and crowding-related disamenities will decrease with distance. Thus, it was seen in Table 3 that income levels showed a strong positive relationship to distance from Chicago's CBD while particulate pollution showed a strong inverse relationship. We thus see the dilemma of intertwined positive and negative distance effects on amenity value that crosscut the conventional negative exponential CBD-related patterns of locational value. Clearly, a more general framework is required.

5. THE ROLE OF AMENITY VALUE IN POSITIVE DISTANCE EFFECTS: THE MUTH–ALONSO MODEL REFORMULATED

It is possible to reconstruct the classical Muth–Alonso type of model to achieve the desired result of simultaneously including distance-related locational and amenity values as housing value determinants. First, assume the consumer's welfare depends on the quantities of housing H, other goods X, and amenities A, he consumes:

$$U = U(H, X, A), \tag{9}$$

adding the budget constraint as before we can write

$$P_x X + P_h(k)H + T(k) - Y = 0, \tag{10}$$

where P_x is the price of other goods; $P(k)$ is the price of housing which is dependent on K, the distance from the CBD; $T(k)$ is the expenditure on travel; and Y is income.

Lagrangian maximization yields

$$(\partial U / \partial X) = -\lambda P_x = 0, \tag{11a}$$

$$(\partial U/\partial H) = -\lambda P_h = 0, \tag{11b}$$

$$\frac{\partial U}{\partial K} = \frac{\partial U}{\partial A}\frac{\partial A}{\partial K} - \lambda\left(H\frac{\partial P(K)}{\partial K} + \frac{\partial T(K)}{\partial K}\right) = 0. \tag{11c}$$

Let P_h be the price of a unit of housing. Then, in order to obtain an observable housing price, P_hH, we may multiply in (11c) by P_h/P_h and rewrite the equation as

$$-\frac{1}{\lambda}\frac{\partial U}{\partial K}\frac{\partial A}{\partial K} + \left(\frac{P_h}{P_h}\right)H\frac{\partial P(k)}{\partial k} = -\frac{\partial T(k)}{\partial k}, \tag{12}$$

thus

$$\frac{P_hH}{P_h}\frac{\partial P(k)}{\partial k} = -\frac{\partial T(k)}{\partial k} + \frac{1}{\lambda}\frac{\partial U}{\partial A}\frac{\partial A}{\partial k}. \tag{13}$$

In other words, the housing price–distance gradient now depends on two factors, one negative and one positive. The negative term is the familiar transport cost. The positive term involves the rate of change of amenities with respect to distance (along with the marginal utility of amenities and λ).

If constant prices are assumed, λ may be interpreted as the marginal utility of income since, in the general case, we can write

$$U(X_1, X_2, \ldots, X_n) \tag{14}$$

and

$$\sum_i P_iX_i = Y, \tag{15}$$

where the X_i are goods and P_i their prices. Then using the Lagrangian technique,

$$(\partial U/\partial Y) = \lambda \sum_{P_i} (\partial X_i/\partial Y). \tag{16}$$

From Eq. (15) we know that

$$dY = \sum_i P_i\, dX_i, \tag{17}$$

and, therefore,

$$\sum P_i(dX_i/dY) = 1. \tag{18}$$

finally, substituting into Eq. (16), we have

$$(dU/dY) = \lambda. \tag{19}$$

From (11a) and (11b) we know

$$(\partial U/\partial X)(1/\lambda) = -P_x \tag{20}$$

and

$$(\partial U/\partial H)(1/\lambda) = -P_h. \tag{21}$$

Following the analogy for amenities, write

$$(\partial U/\partial A)(1/\lambda) = -P_a, \tag{22}$$

where P_a is the amenity shadow price. Now Eq. (11c) can be rewritten as

$$-P_h H \frac{\partial P(k)}{P_h \partial k} = \frac{\partial T(k)}{\partial k} + P_a \frac{\partial A}{\partial K}. \tag{23}$$

In other words, change in housing prices is subject to two influences: the toll taken by transport costs and the positive effect of amenity values (argued earlier to increase with distance).

Now assume that the amount spent on housing, the transport cost gradient and change in amenities with respect to distance are invariant. Furthermore, let us say that $P(k)$ depends only on k. Then Eq. (23) may be rewritten as

$$-\frac{D[dP(k)/dk]}{P_h} = b + g, \tag{24}$$

where D is the amount spent on housing, b the transport cost gradient ($b < .0$), and g the rate of change of amenity with respect to distance (generally $g > .0$). Multiplying both sides of Eq. (24) by dk and integrating yields

$$-D \ln P_h + C = (b + g)K. \tag{25}$$

In exponential form, we can write

$$P_h^{-D} \exp^c = \exp[(b + g)k]. \tag{26}$$

Thus,

$$P_h = [\exp(b + g)(k/-D)][\exp(-C/-D)] \tag{27}$$

or

$$P_h = \alpha[\exp(bk/-D)][\exp(gk/-D)]. \tag{28}$$

This last equation is a form which can be estimated using standard statistical methods. It is not necessary to limit the amenity measurement to a single term. Additional exponential terms may be included with no difficulty.

The Chicago Data Reconsidered

If the foregoing is correct, then we can postulate the following: In the absence of amenity values, housing prices should decrease because of the toll taken by transport costs; however, with significant amenity values that increase with distance, housing prices will vary in a manner determined by the relative influence of the negative and positive components. If the distance exponent is positive, it should be greater in any model that does not hold constant amenity factors than in one that does, and the more comprehensive the accounting of the amenity component, the more likely will be the emergence of a negative distance factor.

This was tested in the Chicago case. For the stepwise models, the beta coefficients and F-levels for inclusion of the distance variable in the model were examined after regressing the dependent variables only on subset (1) housing characteristics, then after (1) + 2 housing improvements, etc. See Table 7. As more and more amenity factors were controlled, there was a progressive decrease in the beta coefficient for distance and in the F-level for including distance, indicating that distance was indeed serving as a surrogate for amenity variables positively related to distance from the city center. Or, to put it another way, as one proceeds into the central city there is a progressive increase in neighborhood and environmental disamenities whose toll on property values is far greater than the positive contribution to value of inner-city location.

Table 7
Variations in the Standardized Coefficient of Distance with the Addition of Variable Groups

Variable Group(s) in Equation	Beta	F^a
Price model		
(1) housing characteristics	.440	106.09
(1) + (2) housing improvements	.391	92.58
(1) + (2) + (3) neighborhood characteristics	.264	41.26
(1) + (2) + (3) + (4) racial and ethnic variables	.197	18.49
Price per square foot model		
(1)	.471	84.16
(1) + (2)	.433	78.25
(1) + (2) + (3)	.366	48.99
(1) + (2) + (3) + (4)	.253	19.04

[a] F is level to enter model as next independent variable.

6. DO BLACKS PAY MORE?

Kain (1973) argues that blacks consistently pay 10–13% more for homes than do majority whites, holding constant all relevant property characteristics, yet the parameters for blacks (and incidentally, for Chicago's Spanish-speaking minority too) belie this fact by their consistently significant negative signs. The explanation is to be found in the dynamics of Chicago's housing market. Most of the studies cited by Kain were undertaken using 1960 census data, thus reflecting the continuing impact on the poor of housing shortages that were only then being alleviated for the middle- and lower-middle class groups. Yet this situation changed dramatically during the 1960–1970 decade.

Between 1960 and 1970, 481,553 new housing units were built in metropolitan Chicago, permitting accelerated suburbanization of white families from the central city, rapid filtering of the housing stock, and improvement of housing conditions for most central city residents, additionally producing a surplus of abandoned housing in the city center. In 1970, 257,590 of the new units were occupied by white homeowners and 146,029 by white renters, another 13,849 by black homeowners and 27,153 by black renters, and 27,934 of the units were vacant. It was because the number of households in the metropolitan area in the decade increased by only 285,729—143,174 white homeowners and 25,797 white renters, 45,065 black homeowners, and 49,573 black renters, a ratio of 1.7 new housing units to each new family—that the massive chain of successive housing moves was initiated as families occupied homes vacated by the new suburban homeowners and renters, and so on down the chain of housing values (and, particularly, progressively inward from the suburbs to the core of the city). One consequence was that many families were enabled to improve their housing condition dramatically during the decade, while downward pressure was exerted on the prices of older housing units, and discriminatory pricing of identical units—black paying more than whites—was eliminated. Not only was there a dramatic improvement in the housing condition of Chicago's central-city minorities, as over 128,000 units were transferred from white to black occupancy, but 63,000 of the worst units in the city could be demolished at the time that tens of thousands of additional undesirable units were being abandoned. The Chicago region thus provides a classic example of filtering mechanisms at work, and as a result surpluses rather than deficits characterized Chicago's housing market in the 1960s, an important fact that serves as the backdrop against which the efficacy of federal housing programs must be judged and housing needs measured.

The evidence is provided in Tables 8–10. The massive growth of the suburban housing stock is shown in Table 8. In the decade, 352,057 new housing units were constructed, largely for whites. In the entire six-county metropolitan area, only 4188 out of 223,845 new homes were sold to blacks, and only 3712 out of 111,290 new apartments were rented to blacks. In addition, some 3208 blacks purchased homes previously owned by whites, and 2153 blacks moved into apartments previously rented by whites. In contrast to the net increase of 287,000 white families in suburban Chicago, only 13,261 new black families were able to obtain residences in suburbia, and many of these residences were in or contiguous to suburban "minighettos." The web of discrimination that limits geographical access to suburbia is responsible for one of the types of unmet housing need to which we will return later, inadequate access by minority residents with the capability to pay within reasonable proximity of the growing job centers of suburbia.

Contrast this picture with that of the central city shown in Tables 9 and 10. There was a net decline of 41,500 white homeowners and 76,900 white renters in the central city in the 1960–1970 decade as whites fled in fear of black neighbors to the "safety" of segregated suburbia, or left the Chicago region altogether. Net increases in the central city black population consisted of 37,669 new homeowners (more than doubling of black home ownership in the decade), and 43,708 new renters.

The complex dynamics of white-to-black filtering were as follows: Some 128,829 units were transferred from white to black occupacy, ownership and 20,267 in black rental of good-quality flats and apartments. In addition, 63,000 black families were able to move into better-quality housing from delapidated and other units that were demolished

Table 8
Changes in the Suburban Housing Stock, 1960–1970

	1960 Stock	New Construction 1960–1970	Withdrawn from Stock 1960–1970	Net Change in Stock 1960–1970	1970 Stock
Total housing units	812,652	352,057	83,980	+268,077	1,080,729
Occupied housing units	740,508	335,135	29,841	+305,294	1,045,802
Owner occupied	561,170	223,845	26,275	+197,570	758,740
White owners	555,480	219,657	34,998	+184,669	740,179
Black owners	8,690	4,188	(3,208)[a]	+ 7,396	16,086
Renter occupied	176,338	111,290	576	+110,714	287,052
White renters	167,964	107,578	4,859	+102,719	270,683
Black renters	8,374	3,712	(2,153)[a]	+ 5,865	14,239

[a] Net increase over new construction due to transfer of units from white to black occupancy.

Table 9

Changes in the Central City's Housing Stock, 1960–1970

	1960 Stock	New Construction 1960–1970	Withdrawn from Stock 1960–1970	Net Change in Stock 1960–1970	1970 Stock
Total housing units	1,214,598	129,496	134,988	− 5,492	1,209,106
Occupied housing units	1,157,409	118,484	138,039[a]	−19,555	1,137,854
Owner occupied	396,727	33,745	34,115[a]	− 370	396,357
White owners	360,117	24,084	65,609	−41,525	318,592
Black owners	36,610	9,661	(28,008)[b]	+37,669	74,279
Renter occupied	760,682	84,739	103,930[a]	−19,191	741,491
White renters	564,029	61,298	138,220	−76,922	487,107
Black renters	196,653	23,441	(20,267)[b]	+43,708	240,361

[a] These 138,039 units were demolished in the decade. Of the demolitions, 63,000 were in areas occupied by black residents in 1960, and 75,000 in white areas.

[b] Net increase over new construction due to transfer of units from white to black occupancy.

in the decade within the area of the 1960 ghetto, and finally, there was a net increase by 1960 of 17,554 units vacant in the black residential area of 1970, contributing to abandonment.

Put quite simply: There has been a vast increase in housing available in the metropolitan area, and a combination of accelerated filtering and rapid residential relocation has produced a substantial sag in demand in areas of traditional minority residence (i.e., those areas with the greatest minority proportions) as well as in other inner-city neighborhoods and communities (as evidenced by the consistent negative

Table 10

Dynamics of Chicago's Dual Housing Market

	White Market	Black Market
Occupied housing units in 1960	924,146	233,263
New construction 1960–1970	85,382	33,102
Demolitions 1960–1970	75,000	63,000
Housing stock in 1970 of 1960 market areas	934,528	203,365
Housing stock in 1970 of 1970 market areas	805,699	314,640
Transfers from white to black market 1960–1970	(−128,829)[a]	+111,275[a]

[a] Difference between these figures represents a net increase in vacancies in black residential areas of 17,554 unity by 1970, a growing surplus of property associated with abandonment.

sign associated with the Irish variable). Little wonder, then, that we find that, by 1971, blacks and other minorities were paying less than the white majority for housing systematically controlled in the models for quality, improvements, incomes, and other neighborhood factors.

REFERENCES

Anderson, R. J., Jr., and Crocker, T. D. (1971). Air pollution and residential property values. *Urban Studies* **8**(3), 171–180.

Apps, P. (1971). An approach to modelling residential demand. Unpublished paper.

Ball, M. J. (1973). Recent empirical work on the determinants of relative house prices. *Urban Studies* **10**(2), 213–233.

Cubbin, J. S. (1970). A hedonic approach to some aspects of the Coventry Housing Market. Warwick Economic Research Paper 14. Warwick University, England.

Evans, A. W. (1973). *The economics of residential location.* Macmillan, New York.

Garrison, W. L. (1959). *The benefits of rural roads to rural property.* Washington State Council for Highway Research, Seattle, Washington.

Harris, R. N. S., Tolley, G. S., and Harrell, C. (1968). The residence site choice. *Review of Economics and Statistics* **50**, 241–247.

Kain, J. F. (1973). What should America's housing policy be? Program on Regional and Urban Economics Discussion Paper 82.

Kain, J. F., and Quigley, J. M. (1970a). Evaluating the quality of the residential environment. *Environment and Planning* **2**, 23–32.

Kain, J. F., and Quigley, J. M. (1970b). Measuring the value of housing quality. *Journal of the American Statistical Association* **65**, 330, 512–519.

Lane, R. (1970). Some findings on residential location, house prices, and accessibility. Unpublished paper.

Massell, B. F., and Stewart, J. M. (1971). The determinants of residential property values. Stanford University, Program in Urban Studies Discussion Paper 6.

Muth, R. F. (1970). Permanent income, instrumental variables, and the income elasticity of housing demand. Washington University, Institute for Urban and Regional Studies Working Paper EDA 12.

Ridker, R., and Henning, J. (1968). The determination of residential property values with special reference to air pollution. *Review of Economics and Statistics* **49**(2), 246–257.

Vaughn, R. J. (1973). The impact of noise on property values—A preliminary report. Unpublished paper, University of Chicago.

Wabe, J. S. (1971). A study of house prices as a means of establishing the value of journey time, the rate of time preference and the valuation of some aspects of environment in the London metropolitan region. *Applied Economics* **11**, 247–256.

Wilkinson, R. K. (1971). The determinants of relative house prices. Unpublished paper.

11

A Computational Approach to the Study of Neighborhood Effects in General Equilibrium Urban Land Use Models

DONALD K. RICHTER

> *The other big deficiency in abstract models is that they lack some of the very features that make cities happen, and make them something slightly different from merely denser concentrations of population and capital: I have in mind the variety of production externalities, local public goods, cultural enclaves, and segregated ethnic and racial neighborhoods, whether voluntary or imposed. It is an open question how far economic theory can go in these directions without itself becoming something quite different*—SOLOW (1973, p. 3)

1. INTRODUCTION

The basic goal of this chapter is to communicate, in a nontechnical way, how general equilibrium computational techniques recently developed by mathematical economists may be useful in studying some of the neighborhood effects mentioned in the above quotation.

The basic framework used is a generalization of the standard long-run, spatial general equilibrium urban land use models usually associated with the names of Mills, Muth, and others. In our framework both commercial and residential land use is endogenously determined, and allowance is made for a wide variety of neighborhood effects. The notion of equilibrium involves standard elements (profit and utility maximization), with the notion extended to allow for neighborhood effects. For example, a household's choice of residential location may depend upon the location's racial composition, income level, air quality, and the like. In equilibrium, the actual mix of these various locational amenities and disamenities (which are endogenously de-

247

THE ECONOMICS OF NEIGHBORHOOD

termined) must be the same as the assumed mix upon which the location decision was based.

Even in the absence of neighborhood effects, general equilibrium urban land use models are analytically intractable unless drastic simplifying assumptions are made. Including endogenous neighborhood effects aggravates this difficulty, necessitating solution via numerical techniques. The computational technique of this chapter is based upon the "simplicial search" or "fixed point" algorithms which have been developed by mathematical economists and other researchers, in particular Scarf (1967, 1973), over the past decade. The technique's primary advantage over other numerical techniques is its flexibility, which allows one to study a wide range of neighborhood effects from a spatial general equilibrium viewpoint within the context of a single unifying computational framework.

Our primary concern in this chapter is the computational methodology, but we do not delve into the technical details of the inner workings of these fixed point algorithms. Instead we describe, in nontechnical terms, how a considerable range of urban spatial models involving neighborhood effects can be put into a form from which a numerical solution can be computed with a fixed point algorithm. We also indicate key economic assumptions which are sufficient to guarantee convergence of the algorithm to the desired solution.[1]

Examples of the types of comparative statics questions one could begin to investigate using the computational methodology of this chapter are what are the long-run effects on the income distribution and the spatial location of commercial activities and household residences of certain government policies, such as imposing pollution standards or effectively banning racial discrimination. (By computing equilibria in the absence of such policies, one could see how severe is the market failure caused by pollution and racial externalities.) How would a narrowing of the income differentials among households affect the spatial location of economic activity?

2. A SIMPLE MODEL

For expositional purposes we begin with the simplest possible model which is rich enough to illustrate our basic methodology.

---

[1] Readers interested in more technical and more general treatments of topics closely related to those discussed in this chapter are referred to Richter (1978a, c) and the references in those papers. Those papers also contain a substantial review of the literature on applications of fixed point algorithms to urban economics.

A fixed area of land is divided into a finite number of neighborhoods or localities, with land in each neighborhood treated as a single, homogeneous good. All neighborhoods can be used for residential or agricultural purposes, but only one neighborhood (call it neighborhood 1) is zoned commercially. (The amount of land in neighborhood 1 that is devoted to commercial use is endogenous. The zoning assumption is one way of recognizing the clustering of such activities while keeping the causes of such clustering exogenous to the model.)

There are two types of produced goods: a composite good produced by a nonincreasing returns to scale technology using capital, labor, and land from neighborhood 1 (reflecting our zoning assumption); and housing (for a particular neighborhood), produced with a nonincreasing returns to scale technology using capital and land (from the particular neighborhood). There is costless transport of the composite good and capital.

There are a large number of households which have identical tastes and initial endowments. Each household has one member who commutes to neighborhood 1. For simplicity we assume that this member has a fixed number of hours available for work and commuting and that the only transportation cost is time cost. Commuting times are exogenous. (It is assumed that neighborhoods are sufficiently small geographically so that a single number can serve as a good approximation to the commuting time from anywhere in a given neighborhood to neighborhood 1.) Each household purchases housing (in just one neighborhood) and the composite good to maximize a utility function subject to a budget constraint net of transportation cost. (In our context transportation cost takes the form of reduced labor income.)

We assume that the price of the composite good (p_c) and the rentals on agricultural land (p_f) and capital are exogenous. For specificity assume there are five neighborhoods. Then there are 11 endogenous prices: The price of land in neighborhood j (p_j); the price of housing in neighborhood j (p_{h_j}); and the wage (p_L). Define $p \equiv (p_1, \ldots, p_5, p_{h_1}, \ldots, p_{h_5}, p_L)$. Letting C denote the consumption of the composite good, H_j the consumption of housing in neighborhood j, and $I_j(p)$ the income (net of transportation cost) of a household which lives in neighborhood j, a typical budget constraint for a household living in neighborhood j is

$$p_c C + p_{h_j} H_j \leq I_j(p).$$

We define $I_j(p)$ to be the sum of exogenous income, profits distributed from the housing and composite goods industries to the household, the value of the initial endowments of land and housing of the household, and labor income. The income function is parameterized by j because transportation cost takes the form of reduced labor income.

We can summarize the utility maximizing behavior of each household with the indirect utility functions $V_j(p, I_j(p))$. $V_j(p, I_j(p))$ represents the maximum utility level obtainable by the household if it chooses to live in neighborhood j, given the vector of endogenous prices p and income $I_j(p)$. (The exogenous prices and other parameters are subsumed in the functional forms of V_j and I_j.) The index j allows both the budget constraint and the direct utility function to depend on j.

3. EXOGENOUS NEIGHBORHOOD EFFECTS

In this section we sketch the basic ideas underlying our computational technique when there is a collection of exogenous local amenities or disamenities associated with each neighborhood. Within any given neighborhood, the associated amenities or disamenities can directly affect both production activities that locate there and households that reside there. Using the model of Section 2, we assume these exogenous neighborhood effects are implicit in the income and indirect utility functions and the description of the production technology.

At an equilibrium price vector p^*, price-taking producers choose a feasible production plan which maximizes profits, each household chooses a neighborhood to live in by maximizing $V_j(p^*, I_j(p^*))$ over j, and the resulting excess demands for land, housing, and labor are zero (assuming free disposal in production).

In exploiting fixed-point techniques in finding such an equilibrium price vector, the key task is to define, for an arbitrary price vector p, a corresponding excess demand vector (or possibly a set of corresponding excess demand vectors) which embodies the notions of profit and utility maximization (including choice of neighborhood). Then the algorithm essentially consists of a systematic search over a set of price vectors for a vector which has a corresponding zero excess demand vector.

The derivation of a set of excess demand vectors corresponding to an arbitrary price vector p is illustrated in Fig. 1.

$$p \begin{cases} \longrightarrow s = (s_1, \ldots, s_5, s_{h_1}, \ldots, s_{h_5}, s_L) \text{ production plan} \\ \\ \begin{cases} v_j(p, I_j(p)) \\ j_\nu \text{ most preferred neighborhood} \\ y^\nu = (0, 0, 0, 0, 0, \ldots, H_{j_{\nu}}, \ldots, \tau_{j_\nu} - W) \text{ demands} \end{cases} \end{cases}$$

Figure 1

Given a vector of endogenous prices p (along with all of the exogenous parameters, including the local amenities and disamenities), we first find a vector s representing the endogenously priced components of a profit maximizing aggregate production plan, with negative coordinates denoting inputs and positive coordinates outputs. s_1 represents the total demand for land in neighborhood 1 in the production of the composite good, housing, and agricultural goods. s_j (for $j = 2, \ldots, 5$) represents the total demand for land in neighborhood j by the housing and agricultural industries. (Recall that the composite good industry cannot locate in these neighborhoods.) s_{h_j} (for $j = 1, \ldots, 5$) represents the output of housing in neighborhood j, and s_L denotes the demand for labor. These demands for inputs and supplies of outputs are created as follows.

If $p_j < p_f$ (the exogenous rental on agricultural land), then all of the available land in neighborhood j is assumed to be used in agriculture. Hence we set $s_j = -w_j$ (where w_j represents the total amount of land in neighborhood j which is available for commercial, residential, or agricultural use), $s_{h_j} = 0$, and (if $j = 1$) $s_L = 0$. (Labor is used as an input in the composite good industry only.)

If $p_j \geq p_f$, we calculate a profit maximizing output of housing, which becomes s_{h_j}, and an associated demand for land in neighborhood j by the housing industry. If $j = 1$, we also calculate a profit maximizing demand for labor by the composite good industry, which becomes s_L (measured negatively), and an associated demand for land by that industry. For $p_j > p_f$, the demand for land in neighborhood j for agricultural use is defined to be zero. For $p_j = p_f$, the demand for land in a neighborhood j for agricultural use is defined to be any number in the interval $[0, w_j]$. Summing these demands for land by the composite good, housing, and agricultural industries, and multiplying by -1, yields s_j.

In general there will not be a unique choice for s, either because the profit maximizing production plans corresponding to p in the housing and composite goods industries are not unique, or because of our convention with respect to the demand for land for agricultural use. Also note that the exogenous local amenities and disamenities may affect the determination of s.

Next we calculate the income $I_j(p)$ of a household which resides in neighborhood j. Some of the profits corresponding to the production plans just calculated in the housing and composite good industries may be included in $I_j(p)$.

The next task in Fig. 1 is to calculate a most preferred neighborhood j_v for an arbitrary household v. We do this by maximizing $V_j(p, I_j(p))$ (where the amenity levels in neighborhood j parameterize V_j

and possibly I_j) over j, and then calculate a demand vector y^v of endogenously priced goods which, together with the demands for any exogenously priced goods, yields this maximum utility level for the most preferred neighborhood chosen. This demand vector will have at most two nonzero coordinates—the demand for housing in neighborhood j_v (a household can live in only one neighborhood), and the last coordinate, representing the supply of labor. Letting W denote the total number of hours available to each household for work and commuting, and τ_j the round trip commuting time from neighborhood j to the commercial zone, $\tau_j - W$ represents the supply of labor, measured negatively. Note that the most preferred neighborhood j_v need not be unique. Thus even if the y^v corresponding to a particular j_v is unique, there may be more than one demand vector corresponding to p for household v because its most preferred neighborhood is not unique.

Let $w \equiv (w_1, \ldots, w_5, w_{h_1}, \ldots, w_{h_5}, w_L)$. As mentioned above, w_j (for $j = 1, \ldots, 5$) represents the amount of land in neighborhood j whose use is endogenously determined. (An exogenous fraction of the land in each neighborhood may be used for the transportation network and other purposes.) w_{h_j} denotes the amount of housing in neighborhood j which is initially available. w_L is by convention set equal to zero. The residents of the urban area do not necessarily own all of these initial supplies.

If there are r households, then associated with the vector p of endogenous prices is a set $E(p)$ of excess demands of the form $\Sigma_{v=1}^r y^v - s - w$, where s is part of a feasible aggregate production plan consistent with profit maximization as described above, and y^v ($v = 1, \ldots, r$) is a utility maximizing demand vector for some most preferred neighborhood j_v.[2] Thus implicit in the choice of r demand vectors is a partition of the households across neighborhoods. Even though the households have identical tastes and endowments, such a partition need not assign all the households to the same neighborhood if the most preferred neighborhood is nonunique. (In the partition underlying an equilibrium allocation, one would expect such a spreading out of the households into different neighborhoods.)

We will make one key assumption about the sets $E(p)$.

Assumption 1:   If the sum of the endogenous prices is sufficiently

---

[2] If the most preferred neighborhood for the households is nonunique or the utility maximizing demand vector corresponding to a most preferred neighborhood is nonunique, or the aggregate production plan is nonunique, then the set $E(p)$ will contain more than one vector.

large, the value of any excess demand vector corresponding to the price vector is negative.[3]

If the price of a good is large, one would expect excess demand for it to be negative, while if the price is small one would expect positive excess demand. Thus the assumption makes good economic sense, since the largest price weights are assigned to those goods whose excess demands can be expected to be negative, and the smallest weights to those goods whose excess demands are likely to be positive.

If the sets $E(p)$ satisfy this assumption and other mild regularity requirements which follow from assumptions (such as continuity of the utility functions) which are conventionally imposed on economic models, then a fixed point algorithm can be used to efficiently find a set $E(p^*)$ which contains zero. As noted above, p^* would be an equilibrium price vector for our model.

If the sets $E(p)$ each contain just a single element, then E is simply an excess demand *function*. However, if for some p, $E(p)$ contains more than one element, E becomes a set-valued function or *correspondence*. A fixed point algorithm is essentially a technique for finding the "zeros" of "well-behaved" correspondences. Thus our approach to the computation of an equilibrium solution to an urban land use model simply involves defining an excess demand correspondence which has all the optimization requirements of equilibrium built into it, seeing which assumptions have to be made in order to insure the correspondence is well behaved, and then letting a fixed point algorithm take over to find a zero of the correspondence.

This approach to computing urban land use equilibria is quite flexible, because well-behaved excess demand correspondences constructed in the manner described above are consistent with a broad range of specifications of the underlying technology and consumer behavior. For example, we could have begun our analysis of consumer behavior with the indirect utility functions $V_j(p, I_j(p))$, since all the information needed to determine the most preferred neighborhoods and demand vectors in Fig. 1 is embodied in them.[4] Because the neighborhood j is allowed to index the income and indirect utility functions, both the underlying direct utility functions and budget constraints can be parameterized by j. Thus we can allow, for example, for real costs

---

[3] More formally, there exists $d > 0$ such that for all $p \geqq 0$ whose coordinates sum to a number no less than d, $pe < 0$ for all $e \in E(p)$.

[4] Given an indirect utility function $V_j(p, I_j(p))$, where $p = (p_1, \ldots, p_m)$, the demand for good k as a function of p is given by the expression $(-\partial V_j/\partial p_k)/(\partial V_j/\partial I_j)$. (See Katzner, 1970, p. 60.)

of transportation (which corresponds to parameterizing the budget constraints by j), or for disutility from time spent commuting (which corresponds to parameterizing the direct utility functions by j). Moreover, each V_j is consistent with a broader range of consumer behavior than is specified in the simple model we have used. For example, introduction of a labor–leisure choice would still lead to indirect utility functions V_j with p and some income function $I_j(p)$ as arguments.

There is no problem with incorporating more than one type of household. We simply calculate most preferred neighborhoods and demand vectors as in Fig. 1 for each household type, and aggregate demand.

By extending the indexing on the income and indirect utility functions, we can incorporate into the analysis such features as alternative travel modes and multiple workplaces. By imposing appropriate constraints on the technology, costly transport of goods and phenomena such as minimum lot zoning can be included. Location of concentrations of production activities can be made endogenous to a much greater extent. Simple kinds of government tax and expenditure policies can be included. Instead of dealing with these extensions in this chapter,[5] we will continue to use our simple model and discuss in the next section how our procedure would change if the neighborhood effects are generated endogenously.

4. ENDOGENOUS NEIGHBORHOOD EFFECTS

We begin by examining a simple generalization of the model of the previous section. Suppose that some production activities generate pollution, with the pollution levels in the various neighborhoods depending upon the location of the polluting activities. (For example, production activities may pollute only the neighborhoods in which they locate, or nearby neighborhoods may be more adversely affected than neighborhoods farther from the source of production.)

Figure 2 illustrates the modifications we make to our procedure in the previous section.

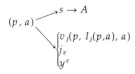

Figure 2

[5] Most of these extensions are discussed in Richter (1978a, c).

Instead of searching over a set of prices, we now search over price vectors p and vectors of neighborhood effects a. In this example the jth coordinate of a can be interpreted as the pollution level assumed to prevail in neighborhood j. Given (p, a), we calculate s as before. (The choice of production plans may be affected by the assumed pollution levels, which are treated parametrically by the various producers.) Given the spatial location of production activities implicit in the vector s, a vector A of actual pollution levels in the various neighborhoods is generated (which may differ from the assumed levels a upon which the production plans underlying s were based.)

Next we calculate most preferred neighborhoods and demand vectors as in Section 3, only now the V_j and I_j have as additional arguments the assumed pollution level vector a (or perhaps just the jth coordinate of a).

We then form a set of "augmented" excess demand vectors $(e, A - a)$ corresponding to (p, a). e is a vector of excess demands for the various endogenously priced goods, derived using the quantities illustrated in Fig. 2 exactly as we did in the previous section. The remaining coordinates consist of the implied or actual vector of neighborhood effects A minus the assumed vector of effects a.

Finding an equilibrium solution to such a model corresponds to finding a vector (p^*, a^*) which has an associated augmented excess demand vector which is 0. For then excess demands for all the endogenously priced goods would be zero, and the vector of neighborhood effects upon which these excess demands are based would in fact be the one which is actually generated in equilibrium.

In many cases a fixed point algorithm can be used to find a zero for this augmented excess demand correspondence. An assumption analogous to Assumption 1 of Section 3 again plays the key role in guaranteeing convergence.

Let us consider another example. Suppose there are two types of households—black and white. Suppose the racial composition of a neighborhood enters a household's direct utility function. The derivation of an appropriate augmented excess demand correspondence for this example is illustrated in Fig. 3.

The neighborhood effects vector a now summarizes the racial

Figure 3

composition of the various neighborhoods. (For example, the jth coordinate of a could denote the percentage of total households living in neighborhood j that are black.) Given (p, a), we calculate s as usual. Next, for households of type i ($i = 1, 2$), we calculate demand vectors and distribute these households among their most preferred neighborhoods. These demands and distribution are derived conditional on the assumed racial composition vector a. The resulting distribution of households implies an actual neighborhood racial composition vector A. As before we can associate with (p, a) a set of augmented excess demand vectors $(e, A - a)$. Again e represents the excess demand for endogenously priced goods, where now demands have been aggregated over the two household types. An equilibrium solution will correspond to a zero of this augmented excess demand correspondence, and again a fixed point algorithm can be used in many cases to find it.

The above examples should give the reader a feel for how endogenous neighborhood effects can be handled within our computational framework. Essentially excess demand vectors for endogenously priced goods, conditional on vectors of neighborhood effects, are derived with the optimization requirements of equilibrium embedded in them. Then these excess demand vectors are augmented to insure that, in equilibrium, the conditional decisions are made on the basis of correct expectations, that is, that the assumed and actual neighborhood effects are the same.

5. COMPUTATIONAL EXAMPLES

In this section computations are presented for the simple model of Section 2 (referred to as the base model or model B), and for simple extensions of that model which allow for pollution (model P) and traffic congestion (model C). The data underlying Muth's (1975) computations were used to generate some of the parameter values.

In the base model (see Section 2) there are five neighborhoods, with neighborhood 1 zoned commercially. The average (one-way) distance that a commuter must travel from neighborhood j to the commercial zone in neighborhood 1 is given in the first row of Table 1. The second row indicates the amount of land available in each neighborhood for residential, agricultural, or (in neighborhood 1) commercial use.

The housing and composite good technologies are described by constant elasticity of substitution production functions of the following form:

$$Q = A[\beta_1 x_1^{(\sigma-1)/\sigma} + \beta_2 x_2^{(\sigma-1)/\sigma} + \beta_3 x_3^{(\sigma-1)/\sigma}]^{h\sigma/(\sigma-1)},$$

Table 1
Geography

	Neighborhood				
	1	2	3	4	5
Distance[a] (miles)	1.5	2	3	4	5
Land (acres)	1507	2679	4019	5358	6698

[a] Since the size of the commercial zone in neighborhood 1 is endogenous, it is convenient to think of measuring these distances to an exogenous center of such a zone. For example, suppose neighborhood 1 is a circular area of land, with the commercial zone comprising a circular area of endogenous radius around the center of neighborhood 1. The commuting distance for a household residing in neighborhood 1 is assumed to be measured from the outer edge of this neighborhood. This will be a good approximation if the commercial zone turns out to occupy a large fraction of neighborhood 1.

where Q is output, σ the elasticity of substitution, h the degree of homogeneity, x_1 the input of capital, x_2 the input of labor, and x_3 the input of land. (For the composite good, x_3 represents land input from neighborhood 1, and for housing, x_3 represents land input from the neighborhood in which the housing is provided.) Values for the technology parameters are given in Table 2.

There are 189,000 identical households. The preferences of each household are summarized by the CES utility function

$$U = .75y_1^{.048} + .25y_2^{.048},$$

where y_1 is consumption of the composite good, and y_2 is consumption of housing in the neighborhood in which the household resides. This utility function implies an elasticity of substitution of 1.05. The coefficients of y_1 and y_2 correspond approximately to expenditure shares.

One member of each household is assumed to make 250 commuting work trips per year, with 8.76 hr available for work and commuting on each work day. Commuting times from the various neighborhoods to the commercial zone are generated from the commuting distances of Table 1 under the assumption of an average velocity of 21.3 mi/hr. We also assume money costs of 1.8¢ per commuter per mile.

Table 2
Technology Parameters

Good	β_1	β_2	β_3	σ	h	A
Composite	.1	7.5	.16	2	.5	100
Housing[a]	2.42	0	.025	.75	1	1

[a] β_1 and β_3 for housing are derived conditional on the elasticity of substitution, using Muth's methodology and data (1975, p. 314).

Table 3
Other Parameters

Agricultural land rent	$100/yr/acre
Capital rental	$108/yr
Composite good price	$10000

Income for each household consists of labor income plus an exogenous income of $600 per year.

The remaining parameters for model B are given in Table 3.

In model P the composite good industry pollutes the air, with the amount of pollution increasing with output. The amount of pollution in each neighborhood is a function of the distance of the neighborhood from the commercial zone, where the industry must locate. The amount of pollution in a given neighborhood enters the utility function of the households living in that neighborhood. These ideas are included in a very simple manner in model P by assuming the utility for a household residing in neighborhood j is given by the function

$$U_j = (1 - \alpha_j Q)[.75y_1^{.048} + .25y_2^{.048}],$$

where Q is the output of the composite good industry. The values of α_j used in model P are shown in Table 4.

The declining nature of the coefficients captures the notion that pollution affects the more distant neighborhoods less severely. The only difference between model P and model B is that, in the latter model, all the α coefficients equal zero.

In model C we introduce transportation congestion by treating travel time cost in a given neighborhood as a function of the number of commuters who must travel through that neighborhood in their daily work trips. More specifically we define the time t_j (in hours) it takes a commuter to travel one mile in neighborhood j by the following equation:

$$t_j \equiv .047 + \gamma \max\left(\frac{\#_j}{G_j} - 50, 0\right),$$

Table 4
Pollution Coefficients—Model P

α_1	α_2	α_3	α_4	α_5
3×10^{-7}	1.5×10^{-7}	$.7 \times 10^{-7}$	$.4 \times 10^{-7}$	$.2 \times 10^{-7}$

where $\#_j$ is the number of commuters who travel through neighborhood j,[6] and G_j is the number of acres of land in neighborhood j which are devoted to the transportation network. Model B corresponds to the case in which $\gamma = 0$, with the first term implying the average uncongested velocity of 21.3 mi/hr in each neighborhood. In model C, $\gamma = 1.75 \times 10^{-3}$ and the G_j were chosen to be 60% of the corresponding entries in the second row of Table 1. (G_j represents acreage in addition to these entries.) Aside from the specification of γ, models B and C are equivalent.

Table 5 presents some of the results of the numerical computations for models B, P, and C.

The equilibrium solutions presented in Table 5 are approximate in the sense that excess demands may not be exactly zero. In each of the solutions presented, the absolute value of excess demand for land in any neighborhood was less than .5% of the total equilibrium supply or demand for land in the neighborhood. The largest absolute value of excess demand for labor was less than .009% of total equilibrium supply or demand. Excess demand for housing in all the solutions was exactly zero.

A note of caution is in order. In general, models of the type described in this chapter do not satisfy known analytic sufficient conditions which insure the uniqueness of an equilibrium solution. However, one can check on the possibility of multiple equilibria by initiating search for an equilibrium price vector at different locations in the set of candidate equilibrium vectors, and seeing whether the same equilibrium solution is found.[7]

The computer programming involved in making operational the applications described in this chapter is not difficult. Essentially all one must do is write a computer subroutine which computes an excess demand vector corresponding to any given candidate (augmented) price vector. Such a subroutine can then be plugged into a standard canned fixed-point program. The canned program passes the subroutine a candidate price vector, and the subroutine returns a corresponding excess demand vector. On the basis of this excess demand vector, the canned program then chooses the next candidate price vector for the

---

[6] We assume that all commuters living in neighborhood j must pass through neighborhoods 1, . . . , $j - 1$ (but do not pass through neighborhoods $j + 1$, . . . , 5). $\#_j$ is defined to equal the total number of households in neighborhoods $j + 1$, . . . , 5, plus one-half the number residing in neighborhood j.

[7] Of course, even if the same equilibrium solution is found, this procedure does not constitute a proof of uniqueness.

Table 5

Equilibrium Solutions

	Model	Neighborhood 1	2	3	4	5
Population density[a]	B	33.85	26.12	14.42	6.89	—[b]
	P	—[c]	13.38	15.11	10.21	5.70
	C	41.98	27.46	11.73	4.81	—
Land rent[d]	B	2876	2037	925	346	100
	P	2061	856	988	583	267
	C	3628	2064	666	203	100
Housing price[e]	B	2038	1992	1904	1819	—
	P	—	1896	1910	1861	1800
	C	2071	1994	1873	1781	—
Capital/land in housing[f]	B	364	281	155	74	—
	P	—	147	163	110	61
	C	433	284	121	50	—
Housing per household	B	.61	.62	.64	.67	—
	P	—	.66	.65	.66	.67
	C	.58	.60	.63	.65	—
Velocity[g]	C	3.6	12.8	21.3	21.3	21.3
Size of commercial zone[h]	B	.70				
	P	1				
	C	.57				
Wage[i]	B	2.00				
	P	2.00				
	C	2.09				

[a] Number of households per acre of land that is used for residential purposes in the neighborhood.

[b] All land in neighborhood 5 whose use is endogenously determined was used in agriculture. The same result held in model C. In models B and C, only land in neighborhood 5 was used in agriculture. In model P, no land in any neighborhood was used in agriculture.

[c] All land available for residential, commercial, or agricultural purposes was used commercially.

[d] Dollars/year/acre.

[e] Dollars/year.

[f] Units of structure/acre.

[g] Mi/hr. In models B and P, the velocity was 21.3 in all neighborhoods.

[h] The fraction of the land in neighborhood 1 whose use is endoganously determined which was used commercially.

[i] Dollars/hr.

subroutine to examine. This process continues until an equilibrium price vector is found. The flexibility of the algorithm stems from the feature that the only program which may need modification for different applications is the computer subroutine which calculates the excess demands. And generally speaking, each excess demand computer subroutine can be parameterized to handle a wide variety of applications,[8] including, with reference to our particular examples, pollution taxes and congestion tolls.

REFERENCES

Katzner, D. W. (1970). *Static demand theory*. MacMillan, New York.

King, A. T. (1977). Computing general equilibrium prices for spatial economies. *Review of Economics and Statistics* **59**, 340–350.

MacKinnon, J. (1974). Urban general equilibrium models and simplicial search algorithms. *Journal of Urban Economics* **1**, 161–183.

MacKinnon, J. (1975). An algorithm for the generalized transportation problem. *Regional Science and Urban Economics* **5**, 445–464.

Mills, E. S., and MacKinnon, J. (1973). Notes on the new urban economics. *The Bell Journal of Economics and Management Science* **4**, 593–601.

Muth, R. (1975). Numerical solution of urban residential land use models. *Journal of Urban Economics* **2**, 307–332.

Polinksy, A. M., and Shavell, S. (1976). Amenities and property values in a model of an urban area. *Journal of Public Economics* **5**, 119–129.

Richter, D. K. (1978a). A computational approach to resource allocation in spatial urban models. Discussion Paper No. 88, Department of Economics, Boston College.

Richter, D. K. (1978b). Existence and computation of a Tiebout general equilibrium. *Econometrica* **46**, 779–805.

Richter, D. K. (1978c). The computation of urban land use equilibria. *Journal of Economic Theory* **19**, 1–27.

Scarf, H. (1967). On the computation of equilibrium prices. In *Ten economic studies in the tradition of Irving Fisher*, W. Fellner *et al.* (eds.). Wiley, New York.

Scarf, H., with the collaboration of T. Hansen. (1973). *The computation of economic equilibria*. Yale University Press, New Haven.

Solow, R. (1975). On equilibrium models of urban location. In *Essays in modern economics*, J. M. Parkin (ed.). Longmans, London.

[8] The canned fixed-point program used for the computations described in Table 5 was developed at the Computer Research Center of the National Bureau of Economic Research. An equilibrium solution for model B was found in about 4 sec of computation time on an IBM370-168 computer. Search was initiated from the center of the candidate price vector set, and 526 excess demand vectors were calculated before the equilibrium was found.

_12

Local Public Goods and the Market for Neighborhoods

BRYAN ELLICKSON

1. INTRODUCTION

The notion of a market for neighborhoods can mean different things to different people. The phrase may be used, for example, simply to indicate that consumers shop for neighborhoods as well as houses. When an economist says that a market exists, however, he usually means that the market is competitive. To claim that a market is competitive implies in turn that it is efficient, that a prima facie case exists against intervention in the market and that the proper role of government is to confine its actions to the redistribution of income.

To assert that the market for neighborhoods is competitive represents, therefore, a very strong claim. The main purpose of this chapter is to establish conditions under which such a competitive market could exist and, assuming that these conditions are satisfied, to investigate the properties that such markets would exhibit.

Establishing conditions under which a competitive market for neighborhoods could exist is not a trivial task. The existence of neighborhoods implies the existence of externalities, commonly thought to be a source of market failure. Residence in a neighborhood can also be viewed as consumption of a public good, and public goods are another potential source of market failure. There is little basis in conventional

THE ECONOMICS OF NEIGHBORHOOD

economic theory to justify the belief that competitive behavior is possible under such conditions.

In this chapter we view the development of a competitive theory of the market for neighborhoods as essentially equivalent to the formulation of a theory of competitive equilibrium in an economy with local public goods. Over the past two decades, economists have made considerable progress in justifying the notion of a competitive market for local public goods. But this theory has not been given a solid theoretical foundation. In a recent paper on this subject (Ellickson, 1979) I have provided the necessary foundations, an effort that has required a substantial rethinking of the entire theory of public goods.

This chapter represents an application of my theory of local public goods to the market for neighborhoods. Application of the theory is not, however, immediate. In developing my theory of local public goods, I abstracted from any explicit consideration of the housing market. But to discuss the market for neighborhoods, it is impossible to separate the choice of a house from the choice of a neighborhood. Therefore, I begin this chapter by presenting in Section 2 a theory of residential choice in which housing is characterized by an arbitrary number of attributes. The resulting theory is shown to be empirically testable, and I end this section with a summary of some empirical evidence that, from the point of view of consumers, neighborhoods matter.

In Section 3, I present an overview of my theory of local public goods and its application to the market for neighborhoods. Sections 4 and 5 treat two specific examples of the theory designed to highlight certain aspects of particular relevance to neighborhoods.

At this juncture I want to comment on the style in which this chapter is written. I have made a strenuous effort to avoid introducing mathematical technicalities wherever possible. Thus, in particular, my discussion of residential choice in Section 2 and local public goods in Section 3 represents a paraphrase of the formal theory. I refer the reader interested in technical details to my other papers on the subject (Ellickson, 1977b, 1978, 1979). In those instances where a mathematical statement seemed essential, I have followed the mathematics with a verbal summary of the main results.

2. RESIDENTIAL CHOICE

My main purpose in this chapter is to consider the workings of a market for neighborhoods. A necessary first step is the development of a model of residential choice: How does a consumer choose a place to live?

Over the last decade and a half, economists have made considerable progress in answering this question. Against this background, it is easy to overlook the intrinsic difficulty that the problem poses for economic analysis. Economics works best when dealing with commodities that are homogeneous and perfectly divisible. The housing options open to a consumer in a particular metropolitan area, however, are (a) differentiated (because of location if nothing else); and (b) indivisible (a consumer either chooses to reside in a particular house or he does not). The housing market should, therefore, be very difficult to model. Nevertheless, we now have quite successful models of such markets. How has this been accomplished?

2.1. The New Urban Economics

Consider the following stylized version of the standard model of urban residential location. Suppose that when a consumer chooses a house, all that he cares about is accessibility to the central business district z_1 and lot size z_2. Letting x denote the vector of commodities consumed other than housing, we assume that the consumer's utility function is given by

$$U(x, z_1, z_2). \tag{1}$$

Assume that the consumer faces a budget constraint

$$p_x x + r(z_1)z_2 = y, \tag{2}$$

where p_x is the vector of prices for the commodities included in x, $r(z_1)$ is the price of a unit of land as a function of accessibility, and y is the consumer's income. Maximizing Eq. (1) subject to Eq. (2) yields the demand side of the standard model of Alonso (1964) and Muth (1969), where $r(z_1)$ is assumed given. By introducing more explicit assumptions into the analysis regarding the form of consumer utility functions, the supply of land and the distribution of income, it is possible to derive explicitly the price function $r(z_1)$ which will sustain equilibrium.[1]

In this way we obtain a coherent model of equilibrium for an urban housing market. There can be no reasonable quarrel with the value of such efforts: They have been instrumental in giving direction and substance to urban economics as a field. But in some respects these models

---

[1] See Mills and MacKinnon (1973) for a useful review of the "new urban economics" as this class of model is called.

are not very satisfactory. The main thrust of the new urban economics has been toward the specific rather than the general, toward explicit computation of solutions for particular models rather than analytic characterization of solutions for general models. As a result we have no general proof that competitive equilibria will exist for urban residential housing markets and no proof that, if such equilibria exist, they will be Pareto optimal. Of greater concern for our present purpose, we have no practical way of characterizing housing market equilibrium if housing involves more than two characteristics: explicit computation is simply not feasible.

2.2. A General Model of Residential Choice

How then are we to develop a model of housing market equilibrium flexible enough to admit multiple characteristics so that, in particular, neighborhood characteristics can be allowed to influence housing choice? Suppose we return to our initial characterization of housing markets as involving a collection of differentiated indivisible commodities. When Alonso and Muth developed their model, economic theory provided little guidance on how to proceed: Markets with indivisible commodities were uncharted terrain while product differentiation seemed to lead, if anywhere, in the direction of monopolistic rather than perfect competition. The situation is far different today. We now have general existence theorems for competitive equilibrim with indivisible commodities (Broome, 1972; Mas-Colell, 1977), and we know that product differentiation (with or without indivisibilities) can, under appropriate circumstances, be consistent with perfect competition (Mas-Colell, 1975; Hart, 1977). It seems reasonable to suppose that urban economics could profit from these new developments and, as we shall see, that is indeed the case.

What do these recent developments in economic theory imply about how to model the urban housing market? The introduction of housing characteristics does have a role to play: The assumption that houses with similar attributes will be treated as close substitutes by consumers provides an ingredient essential to justification of the price-taking hypothesis underlying competitive analysis.[2] However, it is not necessary to assume that one of the characteristics functions as a divisible commodity.[3] This assumption is adopted in the new urban

[2] To be more precise, Mas-Colell (1975) uses this condition on preferences to obtain equivalence between the set of competitive allocations and the core of the economy, justifying the competitive hypothesis in the manner of Edgeworth (1881).

[3] Lot size z_2 played this role in the stylized version of the new urban economics presented above; in some variations, "housing services" assumes the same role.

economics because it facilitiates explicit computation, the only way to establish that equilibrium exists in such models. But in the more general setting, existence can be demonstrated nonconstructively, freeing us to be more flexible in the models that we employ.

Thus, we are now free to assume that consumer utility depends on an arbitrary number s of housing characteristics so that the utility function for the nth consumer is

$$U_n(x_n, z_n), \tag{3}$$

where x_n is an r-dimensional vector of private divisible goods other than housing and z_n is an s-dimensional vector of housing characteristics. We assume that z_n belongs to some set K of potential housing characteristics, where K is a compact metric space. Prices of the non-housing commodities are given by an r-dimensional price vector p_x. Housing prices are described by a function $h: K \rightarrow R$, traditionally called a *hedonic price function*. If K is infinite, then the assumptions imposed on preferences (that houses with similar attributes are close substitutes) imply that the function h is continuous; if K is finite, then this "function" simply associates to each house of type z a price $h(z)$. In competitive equilibrium the consumer then maximizes Eq. (3) subject to the budget constraint

$$p_x x_n + h(z_n) = p_x \bar{x}_n \equiv y_n, \tag{4}$$

where $\bar{x}_n$ is the consumer's initial endowment[4] and y_n is the consumer's income.

The formulation of residential choice we have presented is sufficiently general to meet our needs, but as it stands it is not very easy to use. In particular, there is no way to use this constrained maximum to derive a demand function for houses, the technique that economists normally use to convert the results of utility maximization to usable form. True the maximization of Eq. (3) subject to Eq. (4) yields a solution (x_n^*, z_n^*), but how can we describe the dependence of this solution on the underlying parameters in a useful way? If we cannot estimate demand functions, then what can we estimate to gain some insight into the nature of consumer behavior?

One approach, common to several recent empirical studies of the housing market, is to estimate the hedonic price function h. Such estimates do provide a useful check on whether relevant characteristics have been left out of the model. However, it is clear within the present setting that hedonic price functions convey little information about

---

[4] Houses are produced, so none are initially owned. To keep matters as simple as possible, we will assume that, apart from housing production, we are dealing with an exchange economy.

consumer behavior: They are simply vehicles for describing equilibrium housing prices, and equilibrium prices result from the interplay of demand and supply.[5] Because the shape of the hedonic function depends on supply as well as demand, characteristics can be relevant to residential choice even if their introduction into the hedonic price function yields a coefficient not significantly different from zero.[6] Clearly some other approach is needed if our model of residential choice is to yield testable implications about consumer behavior.

The problem we face is a reflection of the indivisibility of the housing commodities: What we want to explain is not the quantity but the type of housing that will be chosen. We need a way of viewing the decision process that focuses on this essential aspect of residential choice. The solution we propose involves the revival of one of the earliest devices employed in the theory of residential location, Alonso's *bid price function*.

2.3. Reformulation of the Model in Terms of Bid Price

Suppose we consider again the maximization of Eq. (3) subject to Eq. (4) where we now hold constant the choice of a house. z_n is fixed and the consumer is required to spend $h(z_n)$ on housing. His income net of housing expenses is $y_n - h(z_n)$, and he maximizes $U_n(x_n, z_n)$ subject to the constraint $p_x x_n = y_n - h(z_n)$. Assume that the utility function is strictly quasi-concave in x_n. We may then describe the solution to this constrained maximization problem in terms of an *indirect utility function* with all of the usual properties[7]:

$$\phi_n(p_x, z_n, y_n - h(z_n)). \tag{5}$$

The function ϕ_n gives the maximum utility the consumer can achieve given the price vector p_x, his income y_n, and the type of house z_n he has been assigned. The consumer then chooses the type of house that maximizes utility, that is, the vector of characteristics z_n^* which solves the problem

$$\max_{z_n \in K} \phi_n(p_x, z_n, y_n - h(z_n)). \tag{6}$$

To translate this solution into the language of bid price functions,

---

[5] For a forceful statement of this position, see Rosen (1974).

[6] This observation will be justified in Section 5.

[7] Indirect utility functions have been employed in related contexts by Ellickson (1971), Solow (1973), and Polinsky and Shavell (1976).

we then consider a level curve for the indirect utility function, substituting bid price V_n for the hedonic price $h(z_n)$:

$$\phi_n(p_x, z_n, y_n - V_n) = u_n, \tag{7}$$

where u_n represents some particular level of utility. For a given price vector p_x, income y_n and the utility level u_n, Eq. (7) defines an implicit relation between housing characteristics z_n and housing price V_n. Assuming consumers are not satiated, the indirect utility function will be a (strictly) monotonic increasing function of income net of housing cost, and therefore strictly decreasing as a function of housing cost. Hence, we can solve Eq. (7) to obtain the *bid price function*:

$$V_n = \psi_n(p_x, z_n, y_n, u_n). \tag{8}$$

Constrained maximization of Eq. (3) subject to Eq. (4) is equivalent to the maximization given by Eq. (6). The maximization represented by Eq. (6) is in turn equivalent to selecting a house that places the consumer on the bid price function corresponding to the highest achievable level of utility, illustrated in Figs. 1a and 1b as the point of tangency of the hedonic price function h and the bid price function ψ. Figure 1a portrays the tangency condition for a characteristic consumers regard as desirable (e.g., lot or structure size, neighborhood quality) while Fig. 1b presents the corresponding tangency for an undesirable characteristic (e.g., level of pollution, age of the structure).

For the reader impatient with mathematical detail, we summarize where we have come so far. Houses are indivisible commodities, which means that the conventional tools of consumer demand analysis are of limited relevance. Consumers in a competitive market maximize utility

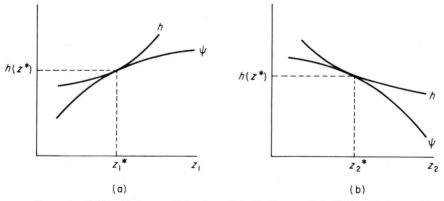

Figure 1. (*a*) *Equilibrium condition for a desirable characteristic.* (*b*) *Equilibrium condition for an undesirable characteristic.*

subject to a budget constraint, but the solution to this problem of constrained maximization cannot usefully be described in terms of demand functions. However, the solution can be described through the use of bid price analysis, where the hedonic function (representing the options offered to the consumer by the market) replaces the budget constraint and the family of bid price functions (one for each level of utility) replace the indifference curves of conventional theory. A consumer chooses the point on the hedonic price function which places him on his lowest bid price function (corresponding to the highest level of utility) just as, in the standard theory, a consumer chooses the point on the budget plane which puts him on his highest indifference contour.

At this juncture it is important to introduce a caveat. Figures 1a and 1b implicitly assume the existence of a continuous variety of housing types, but even if the set K of characteristics is finite all of the analysis presented so far goes through unscathed. The consumer's choice of a house no longer involves the tangency of two curves, but the consumer still ends up selecting the point on the hedonic function which places him on the lowest bid price function.

A primary virtue of the bid price analysis is the ease with which it accommodates the traditional hypotheses about housing markets that have been advanced in the urban economics literature. Much of urban economics consists of a variety of propositions asserting that the housing market sorts households of various types into different regions of the housing characteristics space. For example, high-income households are assumed to choose newer housing, larger lots and bigger houses, higher quality neighborhoods, better schools, and less polluted locations than their low-income counterparts. Since in equilibrium the hedonic price function will be an envelope of individual consumers' bid price functions, these hypotheses are equivalent to the assertion that the slope of a bid price function with respect to any of these characteristics is an increasing function of income.

There is a danger, however, in treating characteristics one at a time as is done in much of the literature. It is easy to imagine, for example, that a high-income household may choose an old house if it is located in a high-quality neighborhood. The usual assertions about the slope of bid price functions make sense only ceteris paribus; for example, holding other housing characteristics fixed, it does seem reasonable to suppose that high-income households are willing to pay more for a reduction in the age of a house than are low-income households. Thus, it is important to view this bid price analysis in a multidimensional setting.

2.4. Empirical Implementation of the Model

I have made the case that bid price analysis provides a useful way to describe consumer behavior in a competitive housing market. However, I have not yet resolved the question of how this approach can be given empirical content. One approach that has been attempted on a number of occasions is to estimate directly the bid price functions for various types of consumer. A major difficulty with this procedure, which I do not think can be eliminated in a satisfactory manner, is that market data provide information only on actual and not on bid price. There is another way to proceed, however, that seems to give quite satisfactory results. Since I have discussed this technique and the empirical results elsewhere (Ellickson, 1977b, 1978), I will present here only a few of the main conclusions.

Suppose we have classified consumers into types indexed by a set T (for concreteness, suppose households are classified by income, race, and family size). Let N index the set of consumers in the market and N_t the households of type t. The bid prices for a house with characteristics z by consumers of type t are then given by

$$V_{tn} = \psi_{tn}(p_x, z_n, y_n, u_n), \qquad n \in N_t. \tag{9}$$

To translate this model into a form suitable for econometric estimation we replace Eq. (9) by a *stochastic bid price function* of the form

$$V_{tn} = \tilde{\psi}_t(z_n) + \varepsilon_{tn}, \qquad n \in N_t, \tag{10}$$

where $\tilde{\psi}_t(z)$ is interpreted as the bid price function of a representative consumer of type t and ε_{tn} is a random disturbance term reflecting differences in tastes and income among consumers of the given type. In determining the probability that a given house will be occupied by a consumer of type t, the relevant variables are the maximum bids from consumers of each type:

$$V_t^* = \max_{n \in N_t} V_{tn} = \tilde{\psi}_t(z) + \varepsilon_{t'}^*, \qquad t \in T, \tag{11}$$

where $\varepsilon_t^* = \max_{n \in N_t} \varepsilon_{tn}$. The probability that a house with characteristics z will be occupied by a consumer of type t is given by

$$p(t|z) = \text{prob}\{\tilde{\psi}_t(z) + \varepsilon_t^* > \tilde{\psi}_{t'}(z) + \varepsilon_{t'}^*; t' \neq t; t, t' \in T\}. \tag{12}$$

Readers familiar with McFadden's (1974) approach to qualitative choice will recognize this formulation. There are two crucial differences between his approach and mine. First, we are dealing here with conditional probabilities $p(t|z)$ rather than $p(z|t)$. Second, the fact that the random variables ε_t^* will have a type 1 extreme value distribution is an implication of the bid price model; unlike the McFadden model, this property is not an ad hoc assumption imposed simply to obtain a convenient estimator (see Ellickson (1978)).

If the disturbance terms ε_t^* are independently and identically distributed with the type 1 extreme value distribution (which McFadden calls the Weibull distribution), then Eq. (12) takes the form

$$p(t|z) = \frac{\exp[\tilde{\psi}_t(z)]}{\Sigma_{t' \in T} \exp[\tilde{\psi}_{t'}(z)]}.$$ (13)

Assuming that the bid price functions are linear in the parameters, we obtain

$$p(t|z) = \frac{\exp(\alpha_t z)}{\Sigma_{t' \in T} \exp(\alpha_{t'} z)},$$ (14)

a conditional logit model identical in form with McFadden's except that $p(t|z)$ replaces $p(z|t)$ as the dependent variable and bid price functions replace the utility functions for the representative consumer. The parameters of this model can be estimated through maximum likelihood in exactly the same way that McFadden estimates his model where the parameters are now interpreted as the coefficients of the nonstochastic part of the bid price function for each type of household.

In the paper cited above (Ellickson, 1977b), I estimated this model using data drawn from a sample survey of 28,000 households in the San Francisco Bay area conducted by the Bay Area Transportation Study Commission (BATSC) in 1965. Lack of space precludes a detailed recapitulation of the results obtained. Suffice it to say that the model performs extremely well. Higher-income households exhibit a (statistically significant) stronger preference relative to low-income households for more accessible locations,[8] newer housing, larger lots, more rooms, a better neighborhood (measured by median census tract income in 1960) and higher housing quality (measured by the residual from a hedonic regression). Furthermore, whites exhibit a stronger preference than blacks for housing located in census tracts that are predominately white and in attendance areas of elementary schools whose students are predominantly white.

To summarize what has been accomplished thus far, we have a model of residential choice sufficiently flexible to accommodate a variety of housing characteristics including those that pertain to the neigh-

[8] Precisely the result one expects since the model separates out the effect of savings in commuting time obtained by residing near the central business district (CBD) and the savings in housing costs obtained by living in less accessible locations.

borhood in which a house is situated. We have demonstrated that the model is empirically testable, and we have found that it performs extremely well. The traditional hypotheses regarding the effect of accessibility, age of the house, number of rooms, lot size, and housing quality are supported by the data. What is more significant for our present purpose, neighborhood characteristics (median tract income, percentage black in the census tract and in the elementary schools) have a strong impact on consumer behavior.

Thus, we now have one necessary ingredient for a theory of competitive equilibrium in a housing market with neighborhoods: a model of residential choice by consumers who act as price takers. But this alone does not justify the conclusion that such an equilibrium can exist. We have not demonstrated the existence of a price vector p_x and a hedonic price function h that will support a competitive equilibrium. To answer that question we must venture outside the demand side to explore the more fundamental question: How are the various types of houses supplied in the housing market and, in particular, is it possible to have a competitive supply of neighborhoods? It is to this question that we now turn.

3. THE COMPETITIVE SUPPLY OF LOCAL PUBLIC GOODS

In the analysis presented in Section 2 we have skirted around the issue of existence of competitive equilibrium. We noted the recent progress that has been made in establishing existence of competitive equilibrium for economics with indivisible (Broome, 1972; Mas-Colell, 1977) and differentiated (Mas-Colell, 1975) commodities. But while this work holds the key to solving our problem, the connection is not immediate. All of these models are confined to the case of a pure exchange economy.

3.1. Local Public Goods and Indivisible Private Goods

My basic claim is that if we introduce production (subject to initial increasing returns to scale) into the models of competitive equilibrium with *indivisible commodities* developed by Broome (1972) and Mas-Colell (1977) we obtain as well a model of competitive equilibrium with *local public goods*. To put the matter differently, the notion of a local public good is not a logically distinct concept in economics—it is simply a special case of an indivisible private commodity. A formal justification for this claim is presented elsewhere (Ellickson, 1979). My aim here is to give a heuristic argument in favor of this point of view which I hope will convince the reader that the approach makes sense.

To keep matters simple, ignore for now the interpretation of neighborhood characteristics as local public goods. Consider an economy in which consumers must choose among several alternative public goods, each provided by a different "firm": Elementary schools can serve as a concrete illustration. The conjecture that a competitive equilibrium could exist for such an economy is due to Tiebout (1956), and over the years the Tiebout model has attracted considerable attention. However, despite its intuitive appeal, there is no satisfactory existence proof for Tiebout equilibrium.

The key to developing a formal theory of competitive equilibrium with local public goods is to recognize that the choice of a particular public good by a consumer involves an indivisibility: the consumer either chooses to consume the public good or he does not. This is a simple and intuitively obvious observation, but its implications are profound. What it means is that if we refer to the quality z of a public good, we must be careful to recognize that this quality is just a label for a type of public good. Consumers do not buy public goods by the pound, they choose among alternative public goods. To use the terminology we employed in the Section 2, the quality of a public good is simply a characteristic and, as in the model of residential choice, we want to avoid treating characteristics as though they were divisible commodities.

Once we have adopted this point of view, there is no longer any particular advantage to assuming that alternative public good types can be described by a *scalar* quality index z. There is no difficulty, for example, in allowing z to be some finite dimensional *vector* of characteristics as in Section 2. In fact, if the set K of alternative types of public good that could be produced is finite, it is not necessary to introduce characteristics into the analysis at all. If the set K is infinite the introduction of characteristics may be decisive in establishing existence of a competitive equilibrium, but this I have not proved.[9] However, if K is finite, then the use of characteristics is unnecessary in proving existence, and in the paper cited above (Ellickson, 1979) I make no mention of them at all.

In this paper I have introduced characteristics for two reasons: (*a*) to clarify the connection between the traditional theory of public goods

[9] The conjecture is based upon the work of Mas-Colell on differentiated commodities.

and that presented here; and (b) to establish a bridge between the treatment of public goods and the theory of residential location outlined in the preceding section. However, in this paper I assume that K is finite, and in that case the introduction of characteristics is inessential. They should be regarded as simply a mnemonic device, a convenient way to label the alternative types of public good that could be provided by the economy.

If we consider schools, for example, the components of z could represent pupil–teacher ratios, racial composition, dummy variable indexes for teaching style (Montessori, military, etc.) and so on. The preferences of the nth consumer can then, just as in Section 2, be described by a utility function of the form $U_n(x_n, z_n)$. Note that for consumers choosing the same public good, the characteristic vector z enters all utility functions just as in the traditional theory of public goods.

3.2. The Production of Local Public Goods

Up to this point I have said nothing about how public goods are produced. It is here that the alternative theory of public goods I have been describing begins to exhibit its decisive advantage over the traditional theory.

In the standard literature there are two notions of scale that one has to contend with, scale with respect to "output" z and scale with respect to the number of consumers provided the public good. For pure public goods only the former type of scale is relevant since the public good is available to everyone, but for local public goods it seems necessary to consider scale of the latter type as well. However, when viewed from our perspective, it makes little sense to talk about scale with respect to z (which we call the *quality* or the *type*, not the output, of the public good). Even if z is a scalar, what does it mean to double quality? Once we realize that z may be a collection of dummy variables, the whole notion of scale with respect to z becomes nonsensical. Fortunately, it turns out that scale with respect to quality is irrelevant to the issue of whether a competitive equilibrium exists. All that matters is scale with respect to the number of consumers provided with the public good.

Consider now the production of a public good of type z, say a school described by a particular set of characteristics. We assume that no one owns the public good initially, but that it is produced using inputs of private commodities. To facilitate the use of a diagram, suppose that only one type of input (x) is used to produce the public good. Figure 2 illustrates a typical production set where, bowing to the usual conventions in general equilibrium theory, we represent inputs as neg-

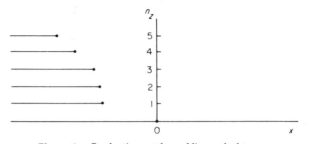

Figure 2. *Production set for public good of type z.*

ative numbers and outputs as positive. The horizontal lines represent the combinations of inputs and outputs that are feasible for the firm producing the public good of type z. Note in particular that output is measured in terms of the number n_z of consumers provided the public good. Contrary to the usual practice in public good theory, we do not refer to z as output but rather as the type (or occasionally the quality) of the public good.

Figure 2 illustrates an assumption that is basic to the proof of existence of a competitive equilibrium: After a certain scale is reached, production of the public good exhibits constant returns to scale (when restricted to integer outputs).[10] We will refer to the minimum scale $\bar{n}_z$ after which one has constant returns as the *optimal size of the jurisdiction;* in Fig. 2, $\bar{n}_z = 3$.

3.3. Competitive Equilibrium with Local Public Goods

We are now ready to state the following:

Tiebout's conjecture: If the optimal size of jurisdictions is small relative to the size of the economy for each type of local public good and the usual assumptions are imposed on consumer preferences, then a competitive equilibrium exists for for the economy.

Unfortunately, Tiebout's conjecture is false. It is not difficult to exhibit an economy satisfying the conditions of his theorem for which there exists no competitive equilibrium. But his result is nearly true in a sense that can be made quite precise.

The reason why Tiebout's conjecture fails is the presence of nonconvexity, holes in the production sets of firms and the consumption

---

[10] Diminishing returns to scale can also be incorporated into the model without much difficulty.

sets[11] of consumers that preclude the use of the standard procedures for proving existence of equilibrium. In the present instance, these non-convexities arise as a consequence of the indivisibilities and the increasing returns that have been introduced into the model. In the last few years, techniques have been developed to handle this type of situation.[12] The basic idea is to construct an artificial version of the original economy by filling in the gaps using as little filler as possible. The artificial economy so constructed satisfies the convexity assumptions needed to establish existence of a competitive equilibrium. The final step is to demonstrate that the resulting equilibrium can nearly be attained by the original economy provided that the nonconvexities are "small" relative to the size of the economy.

While the mathematic tools needed to prove the result are rather sophisticated, the conclusion should be intuitively obvious to most economists. The key idea is the treatment of local public goods as indivisible private goods. Once that step is accepted, the rest follows directly. The approximation result is not much different from that needed to justify almost any application of competitive equilibrium analysis: most commodities come in discrete units, and U-shaped cost curves are accepted by most economists as the norm; approximation theorems of the sort I have been discussing are, therefore, basic to essentially all of economics.

Returning to the context of local public goods, we may loosely summarize the main result as follows:

Tiebout's theorem: If the optimal size of firms producing public goods is small relative to the size of the economy and the usual assumptions are imposed on consumer preferences, then an approximate competitive equilibrium exists for the economy. If the firms are producing public goods in the region where economies to scale are exhausted, the equilibrium can be regarded as exact.

3.4. A Competitive Market for Neighborhoods

With this theory of competitive equilibrium with local public goods as background, we are now ready to discuss the notion of a com-

---

[11] For the reader unfamiliar with this bit of terminology, a consumption set is the set of all commodity bundles that a consumer is physically able to consume in the absence of a budget constraint; in the standard model, it is often assumed to be the entire nonnegative orthant.

[12] The basic idea was first conceived by Farrell (1959) and Rothenberg (1960) and given a precise formulation by Starr (1969). Arrow and Hahn (1971) extended Starr's results to economies with production. A number of papers have elaborated on the idea in recent years.

petitive market for neighborhoods. In treating neighborhood attributes as local public goods, it is convenient to distinguish between two types of neighborhood characteristics:

Type A designates a neighborhood characteristic that is independent of the characteristics of the houses or the consumers that are located in the neighborhood.

Type B denotes neighborhood characteristics defined in terms of the people or the types of houses in the neighborhood.

I believe that most examples of neighborhood characteristics are of type B. It is useful to begin with type A, however, because this sort of characteristic fits more directly into our theoretical framework. An example would be neighborhood schools if consumers cared only about characteristics such as pupil/teacher ratios or availability of a football field and not about the racial or socioeconomic composition of the student body.

What would a competitive market for neighborhood characteristics of type A look like if it existed? The outcome would essentially be that described by McGuire (1974) in his refinement of the Tiebout model: Consumers in a particular jurisdiction would all pay the same amount to receive the public good (equal tuition per child in the case of schools since it is children who "use" the schools); and the jurisdictions would be stratified, grouping together households who have the same tastes regarding public goods.

How likely is it that a competitive equilibrium of this sort could exist? In the case of schools, I suspect that scale economies are exhausted quite quickly, probably upon reaching the size of a typical elementary public or private school. Were school services provided privately it seems quite probable that the market for schools would be quite competitive. However, most elementary and secondary schooling in the United States is not provided privately but by relatively large public school districts, and the taxes used to pay for these schools presumably exhibit some degree of progressivity. Consumers without children who desire to contribute nothing to the public schools seldom if ever have that option. It is not difficult to see the reasons for these deviations from a competitive solution: Existing political jurisdictions can prevent entry into the business of providing alternative schools (including no schools), and such barriers to entry can frustrate the operation of a competitive process. It is not hard to construct examples where such behavior on the part of existing jurisdictions is perfectly rational.[13] I will return briefly to this issue in the concluding section.

---

[13] See Ellickson (1977a).

Neighborhood characteristics of type B are more interesting from a theoretical point of view, and I think that there is ample reason to assume they constitute an empirically significant phenomenon. Returning to the case of schools, the heated resistance to busing provides evidence of a sort, though of course we could accept the testimony of parents who say they simply do not like to have their children ride buses. Large lot zoning, segregation of land uses, and the like provide evidence of a different sort. I will admit to a strong preference for two-acre zoning, a woodsy environment, and an absence of motor homes. But I am not going to delve into empirical issues here. The main question I want to address is whether such neighborhood characteristics could be supplied through a competitive process.

In a sense the answer is quite straightforward: In a competitive equilibrium, firms produce entire neighborhoods. It seems plausible to assume that economies to scale are exhausted relatively quickly, perhaps at about the size of a typical housing tract designed by a developer. If consumers are sensitive to the average housing quality, minimum lot size or ethnic composition of neighborhoods, then the competitive model implies that developers will cater to these tastes. It is tempting to point to the behavior of developers (and, more dramatically, the designers of "new towns") as evidence of this competitive behavior. But what makes type B characteristics interesting and worth a separate discussion is that usually we do not observe neighborhoods being produced by single firms. More typically the characteristics of a neighborhood are determined by the actions of many different landlords and homeowners, each presumably acting in his own best interests.

The absence of single firms producing neighborhoods does not necessarily imply that a competitive market for neighborhoods will fail to exist. The landlords and homeowners in a neighborhood may behave as though their actions were guided by a single firm. The widespread reliance on housing codes, zoning ordinances, and restrictive covenants as devices to restrict the behavior of individual economic agents can be taken as evidence of the coordination of decision making needed to sustain competitive allocations. It is even possible to argue that competition among neighborhoods will tend to encourage the development of such institutions: neighborhoods that fail to engage in this cooperative behavior will fail to "survive"; consumers will move out of neighborhoods in which noncooperative behavior leads to undermaintenance. Following Alchian's (1950) lead, we can argue that this Darwinian struggle results in the competitive solution.

Nevertheless it seems clear that in raising this issue, the question whether the market for neighborhoods will induce economic agents to act cooperatively, we have reached the core of the problem of justifying the competitive theory of neighborhoods. I believe that it is this issue, rather than that of whether scale economies are exhausted, that is responsible for most of the divergence in opinion among economists on what would constitute an optimal housing policy. I suspect that most economists would be willing to grant that increasing returns to scale is not a significant barrier to the realization of a competitive equilibrium for neighborhoods, but they would differ on the question of whether the requisite coordination of actions would be forthcoming in the presence of fragmented ownership of housing parcels. At the level of generality of the theory presented in this section it is difficult to get a handle on this problem. Therefore, in the following two sections we turn to much more specific models intended to bring the issue of coordination into sharper focus.

4. COOPERATION, COMPETITION AND THE SUPPLY OF NEIGHBORHOODS

In the preceding section, I argued that neighborhood characteristics of type B raise the most interesting questions regarding the existence of a competitive market for neighborhoods. Neighborhood characteristics of type B are characteristics defined either in terms of the type of housing or in terms of the types of consumer located in the neighborhood. In this section we will be concerned with characteristics of the first kind, characteristics which depend on the type of housing in the neighborhood. In Section 5, we will treat characteristics of the second kind.

4.1. Competitive Equilibrium and Neighborhoods: An Example

The model I will present is the simplest model I have been able to construct capable of illustrating the phenomenon we are interested in, cooperation among distinct economic agents to produce a neighborhood. We will assume there is only one housing characteristic consumers care about, the average "quality" of housing in the neighborhood in which they reside. Let N index the set of consumers in the urban area and $J \subset N$ the subset who live in the jth neighborhood. Let z_n denote the amount of housing purchased by the nth household, where z_n is produced subject to constant returns to scale using az_n units of the divisible private good x, where a is a positive constant. The average housing quality in neighborhood j is then defined as

$$\bar{z}_j = \frac{1}{|J|} \sum_{n \in J} z_n,$$

where $|J|$ equals the number of consumers residing in neighborhood j.

All consumers have the same utility function,

$$U_n = x_n \bar{z},$$

where x_n is the amount of the private good consumed by the nth consumer and $\bar{z}$ is the average quality of housing in the neighborhood where consumer n lives. The nth consumer is assumed to have an initial endowment $\bar{x}_n$ of the divisible commodity.

We have assumed that the production of *housing* exhibits constant returns to scale. However, the production of *neighborhood quality* is subject to increasing returns at least over an initial range where the neighborhood is small: a single house certainly does not constitute a neighborhood. Recall that for a given type (quality) of neighborhood $\bar{z}$ we measure output in terms of the number of consumers residing in the neighborhood. We will assume that there exists some minimum size $\bar{n}$ of neighborhood after which scale economies are exhausted. After that point the neighborhood can be expanded at constant returns to scale.

If we follow the procedure described in Section 3 to construct an artificial (convexified) version of this economy, and let the price of the divisible commodity x serve as numeraire with $p_x = 1$, then the marginal (= average) cost of supplying an additional unit of the neighborhood of type $\bar{z}$ is equal to $a\bar{z}$; that is, we are adding one consumer to the neighborhood, and in order to maintain neighborhood quality at $\bar{z}$ the consumer added must be supplied a house of quality $z_n = \bar{z}$. Using the terminology of Section 2, this result implies that the hedonic price function faced by consumers is given by $h(\bar{z}) = a\bar{z}$. The nth consumer then maximizes $U_n = x_n \bar{z}$ subject to the budget constraint $p_x x_n + h(\bar{z}) = p_x \bar{x}_n$, or making the substitutions $p_x = 1$ and $h(\bar{z}) = a\bar{z}$, $x_n + a\bar{z} = \bar{x}_n$. It is an easy exercise to show that the consumer will choose

$$(x_n^*, z_n^*) = (\bar{x}_n/2, \bar{x}_n/2a).$$

Thus, in the artifically constructed economy a consumer with initial endowment $\bar{x}_n$ will choose to live in a neighborhood of quality $\bar{x}_n/2a$, paying a price $h(\bar{x}_n/2a) = \bar{x}_n/2$. In the original economy before convexification it may not be possible to achieve this allocation for all consumers. We must have enough consumers of each type (i.e., with the same initial endowment and hence choosing the same neighborhood type) to enable consumers of the same type to form at least one neighborhood of size greater than or equal to $\bar{n}$. If this condition is satisfied, we will then have a competitive equilibrium for this economy and, in particular, a competitive market for neighborhoods. Neighborhoods will be stratified with all consumers in the neighborhood having the same initial endowment.[14] All houses in a neighborhood will be identical in quality with neighborhood quality equal, by definition, to the quality of a typical house.

The example presented above is not intended to be realistic, but rather to provide a vehicle for studying the properties of a competitive market for neighborhoods. At the end of Section 3, I remarked that coordination of the actions of individual homeowners and landlords is perhaps the central issue in justifying the claim that a competitive market for neighborhoods can exist. It is this issue that we now wish to explore.

4.2. Noncooperative Behavior and the Quality of Neighborhoods

Considering a competitive equilibrium for the economy described above, we fix our attention on some particular neighborhood. Using the properties we have established for the competitive equilibrium, we know that this neighborhood will be populated by a group of consumers with identical endowments $\bar{x}_n = b$ and that each consumer has purchased a house of quality $b/2a$. Neighborhood quality is then also equal to $b/2a$.

Will consumers living in this neighborhood, each acting in his own best interests, agree to maintain this pattern of behavior? Our competitive analysis suggests that they will, but there is an alternative model of consumer behavior that implies they will not: the prisoner's dilemma analysis of neighborhood blight first formulated by Davis and Whinston (1961) and elaborated by Schall (1976).

To illustrate the Davis–Whinston approach to this problem, suppose that there are n_0 consumers in the neighborhood we have selected. Assume that no consumer has the option to leave and no additional consumer can enter. Each consumer has an endowment of b units of the divisible good x, and the problem is to determine how much of this endowment each consumer will spend on housing. The average amount of housing produced in the neighborhood now takes the form of a pure

---

[14] Recall that in this example utility functions are the same for all consumers.

public good in the sense of Samuelson (1954) (because we have assumed consumers cannot enter or leave the neighborhood). Therefore,
we can determine the amount of housing that must be produced in the
neighborhood to achieve a Pareto optimum by equating the sum of
marginal rates of substitution to the marginal rate of transformation:

$$\sum_{n=1}^{no} \text{MRS}_n = \text{MRT}. \tag{15}$$

Because of the assumed form of the utility functions,

$$\text{MRS}_n = \left(\frac{\partial U_n}{\partial \bar{z}}\right) \bigg/ \left(\frac{\partial U_n}{\partial x_n}\right) = x_n/\bar{z} \qquad (n = 1, \ldots, n_0).$$

We have assumed that to produce z_n units of housing services, consumer n must use az_n units of x as input. So the neighborhood faces the
production constraint

$$\sum_{n=1}^{no} x_n + a \sum_{n=1}^{no} z_n = n_0 b,$$

or letting $x = \sum_{n=1}^{no} x_n$ and $\bar{z} = (1/n_0)\sum_{n=1}^{no} z_n$,

$$x + an_0\bar{z} = n_0 b.$$

The production possibility frontier for this neighborhood is then given
by

$$F(x, \bar{z}) = x + an_0\bar{z} - n_0 b = 0, \tag{16}$$

and therefore $\text{MRT} = (\partial F/\partial \bar{z})/(\partial F/\partial x) = an_0$; substituting into (15), we
obtain $(1/\bar{z})\sum_{n=1}^{no} x_n = an_0$ or $x = an_0\bar{z}$. Substituting this into (16) yields

$$\bar{z} = b/2a. \tag{17}$$

Thus, a cooperative solution leads to precisely the neighborhood quality produced by the competitive process. Given the symmetry among
consumers, it is natural to assume that each will contribute equally to
the provision of the aggregate quantity of housing services, and that is
precisely the competitive allocation.

The basic claim of Davis and Whinston is that consumers will not
act in this cooperative manner. Consider some particular consumer living in this neighborhood. Given the housing consumption of the other
consumers in the neighborhood, consumer n will maximize $x_n\bar{z}$ subject
to the constraint $x_n + az_n = b$, where as before $\bar{z} = (1/n_0)\sum_{n=1}^{no} z_n$. The
constrained maximum is then determined by the first-order condition
$x_n = an_0\bar{z}$ and the budget constraint. Substituting the former into the

latter yields the *reaction functions* for each of the n consumers (in implicit form):

$$an_0\bar{z} + az_n = b \qquad (n = 1, \ldots, n_0). \tag{18}$$

Because of the symmetry among consumers, it is clear that the solution to this system of equations will have all consumers choosing the same level of z_n, so we have $az_n(1 + n_0) = b$ or

$$z_n = b/a(1 + n_0) \tag{19}$$

as the *noncooperative solution*. The quality of the neighborhood is then also equal to $b/a(1 + n_0)$.

Comparing the cooperative (competitive) solutions given by Eq. (17) and the noncooperative solution given by Eq. (19), we see that if $n_0 > 1$ (i.e., more than one consumer resides in the neighborhood) then noncooperative behavior leads to neighborhood quality that is less than optimal, precisely the "blight" phenomenon of the Davis–Whinston model.

How is blight avoided in the competitive theory of neighborhoods? In his perceptive critique of the Davis–Whinston analysis, Rothenberg (1967) observes that their model reaches too far: It implies that all neighborhoods and not just slum neighborhoods will be subject to blight, an implication which Rothenberg finds unacceptable on intuitive grounds. Thus, he concludes that homeowners in high-quality neighborhoods must be finding some way to cooperate, either through explicit mechanisms such as zoning ordinances and housing codes or through less visible forms of social pressure. Our competitive model suggests that another mechanism may be at work, ignored by Davis–Whinston and Rothenberg alike. If a neighborhood is subject to blight, consumers may simply move to a better neighborhood, one in which the optimal quality is maintained either through the actions of a single firm or because zoning, housing codes, and social pressure are effective in that neighborhood. Because the noncooperative solution is not Pareto optimal, such moves will make consumers better off.

I do not think that on a priori grounds we can conclude that the competitive model is correct and noncompetitive models are wrong. It is true that the failure to allow consumers to move is a severe weakness in the Davis–Whinston analysis. But Hurwicz (1974) has demonstrated that essentially all competitive models are vulnerable to strategic maneuvers of the sort that Davis and Whinston emphasize. Given the current state of the art, economists' belief in the relevance of the price-taking hypothesis to actual market behavior has to be regarded as primarily a matter of faith, and this chapter is no exception.

I conclude this section with a brief comment on matters of terminology. It is common in the literature to see arguments of the Davis–Whinston sort referred to as "supply models" and competitive models as "demand models." This represents an abuse of language. All competitive equilibrium models have a supply side. What sets competitive analysis apart is its reliance on the price-taking hypothesis. The proper distinction is between models that are competitive and those that are not. In this light, Schall's (1976) designation of noncooperative solutions of the sort we have been discussing as "competitive" seems particularly inappropriate.

5. THE COMPETITIVE SUPPLY OF NEIGHBORS

In the preceding section we presented an example of one form that neighborhood characteristics can take, attributes described in terms of the housing in the neighborhood. In this section we will provide an example of the other form, characteristics defined in terms of the people who live in the neighborhood. Income, occupation, and ethnicity could each serve as an example. I will focus on race.

We will assume that there exist two types of consumer: blacks and whites. Suppose that all consumers have utility functions of the form

$$U_n = \begin{cases} x_n z_n(1 + w), & 0 \le w \le t_i \\ x_n z_n(1 + t_i), & t_i \le w \le 1, \end{cases}$$

where w is the proportion of whites in the neighborhood, and t_i is a "tolerance" parameter equal to t_B for blacks and t_w for whites. We will assume $0 \le t_B \le t_w \le 1$. As in Section 4, z_n represents housing consumption and x_n the consumption of a nonhousing divisible commodity by consumer n. We will assume again that consumer n can be provided z_n using az_n units of the nonhousing commodity as input. All consumers have an identical initial endowment $\bar{x}_n = b$.

While housing is produced under conditions of constant returns, we assume that the production of neighborhoods exhibits increasing returns when neighborhoods are small (e.g., a single consumer does not constitute a neighborhood). But we also assume that after neighborhoods reach some critical minimum size, they can be expanded subject to constant returns to scale while maintaining the same racial composition (neighborhood type).

With these assumptions we can again apply the technique described in Section 3 to find a competitive equilibrium. If we construct the artificial (convexified) economy corresponding to the one previously described, and let the nonhousing commodity serve as numeraire with $p_x = 1$, then we obtain the hedonic price function $h(z, w) = az$. Since both blacks and whites prefer living in a white neighborhood, it appears that all consumers will reside in all-white neighborhoods. Clearly this is impossible for blacks, and it is here that we discover why neighborhood characteristics that depend on the attributes of ones neighbors are of independent analytic interest.

At this stage it is convenient to distinguish between two cases: Case I in which firms are unable to charge different prices to blacks and whites living in the same neighborhood (presumably because it is against the law), and Case II in which such "price discrimination" is possible.

We begin with Case I. If $t_w = 1$ (so that whites have no tolerance for living with blacks) and there are enough whites and blacks to form segregated neighborhoods that exhaust the economics of neighborhood formation, then competition results in complete segregation. It is easy to see why this must be so. To turn a nonnegative profit, a firm producing an integrated neighborhood must charge each consumer a price $p_z \geq a$ for each unit of housing. But in that case another firm offering an all-white neighborhood and charging a price $p_z = a$ will attract all of the white consumers, and the integrated neighborhood will "tip" to all black.

Note that in this competitive equilibrium, the price of housing is the same ($= a$) in the black and in the white neighborhoods. Thus, contrary to the conclusion of the popular Bailey (1959) model, whites do not have to pay for their prejudice. And this is true despite the fact that in this equilibrium blacks would be willing to pay more than whites are paying in order to live in the white neighborhoods.

This indictment of the Bailey model is not confined to the special case we have been considering. Even if we relax the assumption that blacks and whites have identical endowments, it is easy to construct examples in which we get complete segregation even though blacks would be willing to pay more than whites actually pay to live in white neighborhoods and even though the price of housing in black and white neighborhoods is identical. The fatal flaw in the Bailey model is its neglect of the supply side of the market.[15]

An objection could be raised to the preceding analysis that we have relied heavily on the notion that single firms produce neighborhoods. The response is identical to that of Section 4: A "survival of the fittest" argument implies that consumers in white neighborhoods will act as

---

[15] Arrow (1971) has made the same point in much the same way in the context of segregated labor markets.

though their actions were guided by a single firm. The restriction against black entry can be enforced through restrictive covenants, the actions of real estate brokers, or simply by making life miserable for blacks who have the temerity to buy into the neighborhood. Thus, we reach the conclusion, implicit in the "cooperative behavior" of Section 4, that *competition implies collusion.*

The notion that competition and discrimination can go hand in hand should come as a rather unpleasant surprise. We tend to think of competition as good and discrimination as bad, so their conjunction is dissonant. To gain some perspective, it is worthwhile considering a related example involving discrimination that seems less objectionable than that based on race. Schelling (1969) tells a story about an ice cream parlor that tipped when it became a teenage hangout, no longer frequented by its former clientele. Since the teenagers evidently were unwilling to spend much money, the place eventually went out of business. Obviously the firm was not a profit maximizer. If it were, the owner would have hung up a sign saying "No Loitering," perhaps selectively enforcing this discriminatory rule against the younger customers while allowing regular customers to remain. He then would have been acting competitively, as do the firms producing racially segregated neighborhoods in our model, and he would be able to stay in business.

It is worth noting at this point the implications of the model developed in this section for the theory of residential choice presented in Section 2. I remarked in Section 2 that hedonic price functions do not necessarily convey much information because these functions result from the interplay of supply and demand. This remark is graphically illustrated by the results of this section: It is possible to get complete stratification with respect to racial composition even though whites pay no premium for living in all-white neighborhoods.[16]

If $t_w < 1$, then the implications for blacks are not quite so bleak. If, as seems reasonable, we assume that the number of blacks exceeds that which could be accommodated by integrated neighborhoods with percentage black less than $1 - t_w$ in each neighborhood, then it is easy to show that competitive equilibrium will involve the existence of two sorts of neighborhoods: one set that is integrated with precisely the fraction $1 - t_w$ black and a residual category of completely black neighborhoods. When blacks enter a metropolitan area they will then be channeled to black neighborhoods with entry to white neighborhoods governed by the tolerance of whites for living among blacks.

Up to this point we have assumed that firms are unable to charge

[16] Much the same objection can be raised to Oates' (1969) test of the Tiebout model. See Hamilton (1976).

different prices to blacks and whites living in the same neighborhood. It is worth noting that such price discrimination (Case II) is quite consistent with a competitive model. Firms producing integrated neighborhoods can be regarded as producing a joint product, a neighborhood with a fraction w of white slots and $1 - w$ black slots. It is easy to show that an integrated neighborhood may be viable provided that (a) whites are offered housing at a discount relative to housing in all-white neighborhoods and (b) blacks are charged a premium for the "privilege" of living in an integrated neighborhood. What accounts for this rather bizarre phenomenon is the presence of a hidden input: Only whites are able to contribute to the whiteness of a neighborhood.[17]

In concluding this section I feel that it is necessary to issue a warning that would be unnecessary were the topic less encumbered with emotional content: The demonstration that an allocation is Pareto optimal does not mean that it is socially acceptable. In the present instance I have indicated that a competitive allocation may involve complete segregation. A competitive allocation is Pareto optimal so that it is not possible to make some consumers better off without making others worse off. But that does not mean that we have to accept such an allocation as being in any sense just, and there is nothing inconsistent about espousing open housing legislation to frustrate this competitive process.

It is also important to recognize that the approach I have adopted is not the only possible model of segregation even within a competitive context. Following the usual tradition in economics I have treated preferences as fixed, but it can be argued that explaining why consumers care about the racial composition of their neighborhood is really the central issue. For example, an aversion on the part of whites to living among blacks may reflect an incorrect judgment of the consequences so that preferences will be altered by integration. Different models of segregation can have dramatically different policy implications, and therefore any exercise of this sort must be treated with care.

6. CONCLUSION

In this chapter I have sketched the outlines of a competitive theory of neighborhoods. In some respects the theory seems to be relatively complete, but it is clear that important issues remain to be resolved. For

[17] It is somewhat questionable whether one should call this behavior "price discrimination" since firms are simply producing joint products.

example, some means need to be developed to give the supply side of these models empirical content comparable to the methods available for the demand side (as presented in Section 2). Without a supply side we have no way to account for the options that actually are made available to consumers, options which the demand analysis takes as given.

If we are to apply the theory of local public goods to neighborhoods with any degree of confidence, we also need a better way to define neighborhoods. In the examples presented in Sections 4 and 5, I was necessarily rather hazy in justifying the assumptions about returns to scale in the production of neighborhoods required for the theory. At this level of abstraction, it does not seem possible to be more specific. The reason, I believe, for this inherent ambiguity is that a proper notion of neighborhood (more precisely, those aspects of neighborhood involving what I have called characteristics of type B) must be defined spatially.

The most promising approach to a better definition of neighborhood seems to be that of Schelling (1969) who essentially defines neighborhoods in terms of the characteristics of adjacent neighbors; more generally we would include characteristics of adjacent houses as well. If we consider his simplest model of consumers strung out along a line, then from the point of view of any consumer the relevant "neighborhood" is defined in terms of the consumers within, for example, two places to the left or right of his position. Approaching the problem in this way builds in a natural notion of initial increasing returns (neighborhoods always include five people) and a justification for eventual constant returns (a particular sequence of blacks and whites can be repeated indefinitely). Racial composition of these neighborhoods in the Schelling model functions much as it does in the model presented in this chapter: It can be viewed as a form of local public good. But there the similarlity ends. Schelling has no prices or competitive markets in his model, and it seems very dificult to capture his notion of neighborhood within the confines of more standard economic analysis. Nevertheless, I suspect that it is possible and that the resulting theory would be far richer than the one I have presented.

To the theorist the construction of competitive models is an end in itself. For the policymaker, on the other hand, abstract analysis may seem pretty useless. I think that conclusion is unwarranted. Perhaps the most important lesson to be drawn from work such as this is an appreciation of just how subtle the competitive process can be. Based on experience with a few models, it is often assumed that externalities wreck havoc with the invisible hand, that collusion and competition are antithetical and that a neighborhood going downhill is evidence of suboptimality. The models we have presented imply that all of these phenomena can be consistent with an efficient competitive process.

Of course, the fact that competitive equilibrium is consistent with such phenomena does not prove that the world is competitive. I am certain that the same facts could be explained by alternative noncompetitive models. The discipline of constructing a competitive model can contribute to the evaluation of noncompetitive models: We have seen, for example, that the Bailey model of segregation and the Davis–Whinston model of blight do not stand up under such scrutiny. But the development of more logically consistent noncompetitive models may be the most useful by-product of competitive analysis.

Economists have not made much progress in going beyond competitive analysis. Recent work by Lancaster (1975), Spence (1976), and Dixit–Stiglitz (1977) represents one approach that can be applied to the market for neighborhoods. One advantage of my interpretation of local public goods as indivisible private goods is that such efforts to develop a theory of product differentiation extend immediately to this new context.

I will admit to a vague sense that the approach taken in the recent literature on product differentiation is not very satisfactory. More germane to the subject of this chapter, I do not believe that it points to the basic source of suboptimality in the market for neighborhoods. It seems evident that a much more serious problem arises because of the barriers to entry erected by existing political jurisdictions. In our competitive analysis we tacitly assumed that any group of consumers wishing to form a neighborhood could do so, subject to the constraints imposed by the market. But high-income consumers cannot form a neighborhood in the central city without buying into the problems of the central city as well, subjecting themselves to taxes intended to help the poor, sharing schools of poor quality, and incurring the risk of busing. Low-income consumers are unable to form lower-quality neighborhoods in affluent suburbs because the residents of the suburb want to avoid the erosion of their tax base and the possibility of contributing more to income redistribution.[18] I find it hard to believe that this is a portrait of a fully competitive process.

ACKNOWLEDGMENT

I would like to thank Joseph Ostroy for his helpful comments.

[18] For a more explicit treatment of some of these issues, see Ellickson (1977a).

REFERENCES

Alchian, A. A. (1950). Uncertainty, evolution and economic theory. *Journal of Political Economy* **58**, 211–221.

Alonso, W. (1964). *Location and land use.* Harvard University Press, Cambridge, Massachusetts.

Arrow, K. J. (1971). *Some models of racial discrimination in the labor market.* The Rand Corporation, RM-6253-RC.

Arrow, K. J., and Hahn, F. H. (1971). *General competitive analysis.* Holden-Day, San Francisco.

Bailey, M. J. (1959). Note on the economics of residential zoning and urban renewal. *Land Economics* **35**, 288–292.

Broome, J. (1972). Approximate equilibrium in economics with indivisible commodities. *Journal of Economic Theory* **5**, 224–249.

Davis, O. A., and Whinston, A. B. (1961). The economics of urban renewal. *Law and Contemporary Problems* **26**, 105–117.

Dixit, A. K., and Stiglitz, J. E. (1977). Monopolistic competition and optimal product diversity. *American Economic Review* **67**, 297–308.

Edgeworth, F. Y. (1881). *Mathematical psychics.* P. Kegan, London.

Ellickson, B. (1971). Jurisdictional fragmentation and residential choice. *American Economic Review* **61**, 334–339.

Ellickson, B. (1977a). The politics and economics of decentralization. *Journal of Urban Economics* **4**, 135–149.

Ellickson, B., with B. Fishman and P. A. Morrison. (1977b). *Economic analysis of urban housing markets: A new approach.* The Rand Corporation, R-2024-NSF.

Ellickson, B. (1978). An alternative test of the hedonic theory of housing markets, working paper, University of California, Los Angeles.

Ellickson, B. (1979). Competitive equilibrium with local public goods. *Journal of Economic Theory* (in press).

Farrell, M. J. (1959). The convexity assumption in the theory of competitive markets. *Journal of Political Economy* **67**, 377–391.

Hamilton, B. W. (1976). The effects of property taxes and local public spending on property values: A theoretical comment. *Journal of Political Economy* **84**, 647–650.

Hart, O. D. (1977). Monopolistic competition in a large economy with differentiated commodities. Working paper, Churchill College, Cambridge.

Hurwicz, L. (1974). The design of mechanisms for resource allocation. In *Frontiers of quantitative economics*, Vol. II, M. D. Intriligator and D. A. Kendrick (eds.). American Elsevier, New York.

Lancaster, K. (1975). Socially optimal product differentiation. *American Economic Review* **65**, 567–585.

Mas-Colell, A. (1975). A model of equilibrium with differentiated commodities. *Journal of Mathematical Economics* **2**, 263–295.

Mas-Colell, A. (1977). Indivisible commodities and general equilibrium theory. *Journal of Economic Theory* **16**, 443–456.

McFadden, D. (1974). Conditional logit analysis of qualitative choice behavior. In *Frontiers in econometrics*, Paul Zarembka (ed.). Academic Press, New York.

McGuire, M. (1974). Group segregation and optimal jurisdictions. *Journal of Political Economy* **82**, 112–132.

Mills, E. S., and MacKinnon, J. (1973). Notes on the new urban economics. *Bell Journal of Economics and Management Science* **4**, 593–601.

Muth, R. F. (1969). *Cities and housing*. University of Chicago Press, Chicago.

Oates, W. E. (1969). The effects of property taxes and local public spending on property values: An empirical study of tax capitalization and the Tiebout hypothesis. *Journal of Political Economy* **77**, 957–970.

Polinsky, A. M., and Shavell, S. (1976). Amenities and property values in a model of an urban area. *Journal of Public Economics* **5**, 119–129.

Rosen, S. (1974). Hedonic prices and implicit markets: Product differentiation in pure competition. *Journal of Political Economy* **82**, 34–55.

Rothenberg, J. (1960). Non-convexity, aggregation, and Pareto optimality. *Journal of Political Economy* **68**, 435–478.

Rothenberg, J. (1967). *Economic evaluation of urban renewal*. The Brookings Institution, Washington, D.C.

Samuelson, P. A. (1954). The pure theory of public expenditures. *Review of Economics and Statistics* **36**, 387–389.

Schall, L. D. (1976). Urban renewal policy and economic efficiency. *American Economic Review* **66**, 612–628.

Schelling, T. C. (1969). *Models of segregation*. The Rand Corporation, RM-6014-RC.

Solow, R. M. (1973). On equilibrium models of urban location. In *Essays in modern economics*, M. Parkin (ed.). Longmans, Green, London.

Spence, A. M. (1976). Product selection, fixed costs, and monopolistic competition. *Review of Économoic Studies* **43**, 217–235.

Starr, R. (1969). Quasi-equilibria in markets with non-convex preferences. *Econometrica* **37**, 25–38.

Tiebout, C. (1956). A pure theory of local expenditures. *Journal of Political Economy* **64**, 416–424.

Index